Developing Multicultural Leadership using Knowledge Dynamics and Cultural Intelligence

A fascinating book on the role played by cultural intelligence and knowledge dynamics in developing multicultural leadership. The book is supported by complex research performed by Dr Dan Paiuc and a wealth of literature. It is the first book to reveal the importance of cultural intelligence and knowledge dynamics in the contemporary global multicultural business environment.

—*Professor Emeritus Constantin Brătianu,* **UNESCO Department for Business Administration, Bucharest University of Economic Studies, Romania. President of the International Association for Knowledge Management, University of Padua, Italy**

Leadership in a multicultural environment is a critical job of managers in today's global organizations. Dan Paiuc's research and insights shed light on the topic and will be a benefit to both managers and fellow researchers.

—*David Rogers,* **Columbia Business School. Author, The Digital Transformation Roadmap**

The retail world has multiple examples of large, seemingly competent companies, dominant in their own markets, who fail when entering new markets and countries. It is often the subtle, not recognized, cultural differences that result in failed enterprises. There is much to learn regarding diverse cultural environments.

—*Jim Inglis,* **Author, Breakthrough retailing – how a bleeding orange culture can change everything. President, Inglis Retailing. Past Executive Vice President, The Home Depot**

In today's fast-paced and interconnected world, multicultural leadership has become a necessity. This book, based on a comprehensive study, delves into the impact of cultural intelligence and knowledge dynamics on multicultural leadership. It not only offers valuable insights for practitioners in the discipline but also contributes to academic research and guides organizations in identifying the competencies required for effective multicultural leadership. A must-read for those seeking to navigate diverse cultural contexts and drive business performance.

—*Irina Leca,* **CEO & Co-Founder, Nooka Space**

Developing Multicultural Leadership using Knowledge Dynamics and Cultural Intelligence

BY

DAN PAIUC

United Kingdom – North America – Japan – India – Malaysia – China

Emerald Publishing Limited
Emerald Publishing, Floor 5, Northspring, 21-23 Wellington Street, Leeds LS1 4DL

First edition 2024

British Library Cataloguing in Publication Data
A catalogue record for this book is available from the British Library

ISBN: 978-1-83549-433-2 (Print)
ISBN: 978-1-83549-432-5 (Online)
ISBN: 978-1-83549-434-9 (Epub)

INVESTOR IN PEOPLE

Disclaimer

In this publication, the author articulates his viewpoint and presents ideas based on his doctoral research. Its purpose is to offer guidance about the topics addressed. This publication is intended to serve as a sole basis for further academic studies and also for enhancing and optimising the decision-making of practitioners within multicultural contexts. The author disclaims any responsibility for liability or risks which is incurred as a direct or indirect consequence of the use of any of the content of this book.

Contents

List of Acronyms and Abbreviations

AMOS	Analysis of Moment Structures
CB-SEM	Covariance-Based Structural Equation Modeling
CEO	Chief Executive Officer
CQ	Cultural Intelligence
d.i.y	Do It Yourself
DV	Dependent Variable
E-commerce	Electronic Commerce
GDPR	General Data Protection Regulation
IF	Individual Factors
IV	Independent Variable
KD	Knowledge Dynamics
ML	Multicultural Leadership
OC	Organizational Context
PLS-SEM	Partial Least Squares-Structural Equation Modeling
SEM	Structural Equation Modeling
SmartPLS	Software Tools for (PLS-SEM)
SPSS	Statistical Package for the Social Science
VOSViewer	Visualization of Similarities Software

About the Author

Dan Paiuc is a PhD graduate researcher in Management at the National University of Political Studies and Public Administration, Romania, a C-level practitioner within the international retail scene, a keynote speaker, and a humanitarian.

Preface

Background

The importance of effectively working in diverse cultural contexts is becoming increasingly evident, especially in today's interconnected global society. In addition, 90% of the most influential business executives from 68 nations have identified multicultural leadership as the top priority for the senior management teams of the 21st century. In front of a workforce more multicultural than ever before, with people from various ethnic, racial, and cultural environments, leaders need to navigate cultural and societal differences and build on them. Since the World Health Organization declared the COVID-19 pandemic on March 11, 2020, the work-from-anywhere phenomenon has conquered the globe and propelled multicultural leadership to become the new standard in today's fast-paced and polycentric world. Taking this into account, a considerable amount of emphasis was placed on the factors that impact and influence multicultural leadership in an effort to explain the interconnections that would maximize results and promote a healthier company's culture and growth.

Purpose

This book aims to investigate the impact and effects of cultural intelligence and knowledge dynamics on multicultural leadership in an organizational context. It seeks to contribute to a greater comprehension of the factors influencing multicultural leadership and driving business performance. Ultimately, this research could be valuable in helping organizations identify the competencies and characteristics required for effective multicultural leadership and providing guidance on cultivating and leveraging these qualities. Furthermore, aside from providing support to practitioners within the multicultural leadership *arena*, this study's primary objective is to share significant insights with other cross-disciplinary researchers and students. This book can inform and build future topic-related research and educational endeavors by disseminating the findings and contributing to the body of knowledge on multicultural leadership.

Methods

After a systemic and bibliometric literature review, the methodology was based on mixed-methods research. In the first phase, during our qualitative analysis, we approached 15 multicultural leaders as subjects of study and conducted semi-structured interviews. Through this, we better understood how cultural intelligence and knowledge dynamics affect and impact multicultural leadership. We conducted a thematic content analysis in conjunction with a cross-case and network analysis to ascertain the similarities and differences between the cases. A quantitative analysis based on 396 validated questionnaires with global amplitude has been carried out in order to provide more robust evidence not only on the influence of cultural intelligence, knowledge dynamics, and organizational context on multinational leadership but also in regards the possible influence of knowledge dynamics and organizational context on cultural intelligence.

As a constructive result of the presented analysis, four of the five main hypothesized relationships fit and validate the proposed model.

Conclusions

According to the study's findings, cultural intelligence, knowledge dynamics, and organizational context are the main vectors of multinational leadership with demonstrated impacting roles. Also, the influence of knowledge dynamics on cultural intelligence was investigated and proven, while our research did not positively showcase the direct connection between organizational context and cultural intelligence. The results of this study make significant contributions to both the academic community and the business world. In terms of academic research, being the first study to examine how organizational context, knowledge dynamics, and cultural intelligence affect multicultural leadership paved the way for subsequent studies related to the enhancements of global management. From the business perspective, our book provides multicultural leadership with new levers to maximize revenues and accelerate growth while building on an agile company's culture.

Acknowledgments

I would like to express my heartfelt gratitude to my professor, coordinator, and mentor, Dr Constantin Brătianu, for his guidance, expertise, and continuous support throughout my PhD journey and last academic years. His insightful feedback, encouragement, fairness, kindness, and generosity have been invaluable and significantly shaped this book. The enduring legacy of his influence on my present and future self is a steadfast reality.

I also extend my thanks to my wife Ira, my sons Alexandru and Ian, and my parents Magda and Florentin – for their unwavering support and love throughout this process. Their encouragement, endless belief, and sacrifice have helped me finalize the book you're reading.

Finally, I would like to acknowledge all those who have contributed in various ways to my book, including my professors, colleagues, associates, students, and friends. I am grateful for their constructive exchanges, criticism, and thoughtful comments, which have helped refine my work.

Thank you all for your invaluable support.

Dan Paiuc

Chapter 1

Introduction

The 21st century has witnessed an upsurge in multiculturalism and diversity in various sectors of the global workforce, including leadership (Paiuc, 2021b). Effective multicultural leadership (ML) has become crucial in promoting organizational success in today's borderless business environment. ML is a complex process that involves the facilitation of knowledge dynamics (KD) and cross-cultural communication and collaboration (Engelsberger et al., 2022). Moreover, developing cultural intelligence (CQ) is imperative in agilely framing the KD flows and in promoting effective engagement and intercultural competencies (Earley & Ang, 2003). This book aims to investigate the relationship between the development of ML, KD, and CQ within an organizational context (OC).

1.1 Existing Background

One potential explanation for the high failure rate (70%) of international business ventures during the early 2000s pertains to discrepancies in cultural norms and values, as re-posited by Paiuc (2021a). Looking at more recent events, it is evident that some significant retailers with international aspirations have yet to learn from their past experiences. For example, in 2014, Kingfisher, a British-originated company, sold its 39 B&Q stores and permanently withdrew from China (Rankin, 2014), while the American flagship retailer Home Depot closed its last seven out of 12 Chinese outlets by 2012. In addition, Target, a Minneapolis-based company, shut down all its 133 Canadian stores in 2015, just 2 years after the launch, resulting in a total net loss of $2 billion. Other notable examples include the British retailer Tesco, which made a similar mistake in the United States in 2013, resulting in writing down the value of its global operations by $3.5 billion (Davey & Holton, 2013). Likewise, Walmart, considered the world's largest generalist brick-and-mortar retailer, failed to make any significant headway in the German market back in 2015, where it eventually closed all 85 stores in response to poor sales performance. Furthermore, coming closer to Eastern Europe; Baumax, Praktiker, and Obi, three DIY and home improvement retailers with German roots, failed to compete in the Romanian DIY market, so they had to

Developing Multicultural Leadership using Knowledge Dynamics and Cultural Intelligence, 1–4
Copyright © 2024 Dan Paiuc
Published under exclusive licence by Emerald Publishing Limited
doi:10.1108/978-1-83549-432-520241002

exit it in around 2015. They needed to understand and integrate the local speci-
ficities with their exported business model and have missed their new customers'
cultural expectations (Cornell, 2015).

KD play an important role in the success of companies and their overall
impact on the world. For instance, a study by Aamir et al. (2021) found that
knowledge sharing and team collaboration led to better corporate performance
and productivity. Another study by Cardoni et al. (2020) found that companies
that actively invested in knowledge management techniques had higher profitability and a competitive advantage over their peers. In terms of the impact of
KD on the larger world, a study by Cohendet et al. (2021) found that companies
that prioritize knowledge creation and dissemination tend to contribute more to
the global innovation ecosystem. Overall, these studies demonstrate the critical
role that KD play in a company's success and its impact on the business world. By
promoting knowledge sharing, collaboration, and investing in knowledge management techniques, companies can accelerate innovation and remain competitive
in the global marketplace.

According to recent statistics, diverse leadership and inclusion practices
significantly impact organizational performance and results globally (Cox &
Blake, 2021). For instance, a study by McKinsey & Company revealed that
companies in the top quartile for racial and ethnic diversity in their leadership are
36% more likely to have above average financial returns (Hunt et al., 2015).
Additionally, research conducted by Harvard Business Review found that diverse
leadership teams are better equipped to handle complex business challenges and
are more innovative and creative (Hunt et al., 2015). A 2021 study by the Centre
for Creative Leadership also found that organizations with diverse and inclusive
leadership had a 77% increase in organizational agility and adaptability, a 67%
increase in innovation, and a 46% increase in employee engagement (Centre for
Creative Leadership, 2021). One example of a company that has successfully
implemented ML practices is Accenture. In 2021, the company reported that its
global executive leadership team was 34.2% female, 35.5% ethnically diverse, and
23.2% racially diverse (Accenture, 2021). This diversity has contributed to
Accenture's financial success, including a 4.3% increase in revenue in 2020
(Accenture, 2021). Building also on ML, the tech giant Intel reported that in 2020,
40% of its employees and 25% of its executive leadership team were women, and
44% of its US workforce were people of color (Intel, 2020). According to its
public reports, Intel's emphasis on diversity and inclusion has helped the company
maintain its position as a top performer in the tech industry. Another study by
Ferreira et al. (2020) investigated the dynamic capabilities and mediating effects
of innovation on the competitive advantage and firm's performance and the
moderating role of organizational learning capability. They found that companies
with more culturally diverse leadership teams outperformed their less diverse
counterparts in terms of profitability, revenue growth, and shareholder value.
From the analysis below, ML and diversity in executive teams significantly
impact organizational performance and have been shown to enhance financial
returns and employee engagement.

One up-to-date study conducted in 2021, Seidu et al. (2021) found that organizational culture, with its involvement and consistency dimensions, is one of the key determinants of successful cross-cultural leadership and can significantly affect employee performance. However, adaptability as an organizational culture dimension had no statistically significant relation with performance.

On an international and globalized scale, strong organizational culture that values diversity, equity, and inclusion improves company performance and increases employee satisfaction (Lindholm, 2022). For example, Ikea, the global furniture company with a presence in over 50 countries, centers diversity and multiculturalism as their main pillar of its organizational culture. Their focus includes creating a diverse and inclusive workplace, providing development opportunities for employees from different backgrounds, and supporting community partners that promote diversity and inclusion (Ikea Group, 2021). In terms of outcomes, research shows that Ikea's strong commitment to diversity and inclusion has resulted in increased customer satisfaction, higher employee retention rates, and improved business performance (Ikea Group, 2021). In conclusion, these analyses and statistics highlight the importance of OC in shaping the success of ML and overall company outcomes. Embracing diversity and promoting a multicultural organizational culture can improve employee performance and better financial results.

1.2 Research Problem and Purpose

The need for more research in linking CQ and KD to ML and bottom-line results is a topic of critical importance in today's globalized business environment.

On a different basis and individual correlation assessments: Stoermer et al. (2021) found that CQ positively relates to knowledge sharing behavior, while Muñoz-Pascual et al. (2019) identified that ML is deeply related to innovation performance and bottom-line results.

Also, Cortes and Herrmann's (2020) research, based on a sample of 194 executives and CEOs from 97 Ecuadorian companies, discovered that organizational structure plays a significant role in shaping transformational leadership behavior and influencing employee work attitudes. From the same perspective, Sudargini et al. (2023) explored the relationship between organizational culture and servant leadership and found that a culture of trust, accountability, and transparency can also contribute to ML development within an organization.

Our research target is to analyze the development of ML based on KD and CQ – we have split the analyses around the below research questions that will be presented at an extent level during the methodology chapter. The primary research question at this stage is:

- What is the influence and impact of KD, CQ, and OC on multinational leadership?

Therefore, the secondary research question, based on the proposed model, presented within the methodology chapter is:

- What is the impact of KD and OC on CQ?

1.3 Structure of the Book

The research is split into six main chapters. The first chapter is introductive, positioning our research within its context and underlining the study's reasonings. The second chapter presents an in-depth literature review, followed by a bibliometric work that underlines both the main researched patterns as well as the existing study gaps. The third chapter of the book focuses on the research methodology used, including details on the research objectives and hypothesis, methods and approaches employed, as well as information on the samples and the studied target groups – all based on the research model. Chapters 4 and 5 expose the results of qualitative and quantitative studies. Chapter 6 reflects our general conclusions and shares recommendations for new research-related directions.

Chapter 2

Theoretical Background

2.1 Introduction to Systemic Literature Review

This chapter is structured in three parts. While in the first one, we present the systematic literature review approach and methodology, in the second, we propose the literature review for our four main variables, aim for interconnections and underline the research gaps. In the last and third part, we execute a bibliometric study that points toward our possible first answers to our research hypothesis – from the literature review perspective.

To examine the existing literature on the subjects of cultural intelligence (CQ), knowledge dynamics (KD), organizational context (OC), and multicultural leadership (ML), we used different methodological steps. First, we have defined the research variables and the research model. In the second step, we search for specific variables in books and journal papers since 2018 in well-known academic databases (such as Scopus, Web of Science, JSTOR, SpringerLink, Google Scholar, Business Source Complete, ProQuest, ScienceDirect, Taylor and Francis, Emerald Insight, and Wiley Online Library) by using relevant keywords and expressions. From this, the published articles (between 2018 and 2023) on the subsequent variables and the most complete versions of the studies were included in the literature review. After having analyzed at first hand all the recent literature reviews (last 6 years), as a third step, we have extended and enhanced the study within the last 30 years in order to capture all the relevant and classic theories that have built the variables and their possible interconnections.

This study greatly expands on the relatively reduced amount of combined linked shreds of evidence on ML, KD, CQ, and OC. Cross-cultural management studies have recently focused on identifying the factors that facilitate expatriates' adaptation to foreign environments as multinational enterprises (MNEs) and the ones that impact performance and maximize efficiency by levering multicultural backgrounds (Zhong et al., 2021). As a significant component, CQ has received much attention, especially in the last 5 years (Aminullah et al., 2022; Chen et al., 2022).

Developing Multicultural Leadership using Knowledge Dynamics and Cultural Intelligence, 5–23
Copyright © 2024 Dan Paiuc
Published under exclusive licence by Emerald Publishing Limited
doi:10.1108/978-1-83549-432-520241004

2.2 CQ Literature Review and Identified Gaps

Confucius summarized the essential principle that all people are the same and that only their behaviors vary 500 years before anthropologists, sociologists, and historians began their long-term quest to define culture. Within the current framework and through a simplification of the existing theories, culture comprises a multitude of acquired behaviors and conduct practices, irrespective of the extent to which individuals engage in them deliberately, as indicated by Kemmelmeier and Kusano (2018).

Indeed, the Dutch researcher Geert Hofstede's studies on cultural dimensions have significantly impacted the field of sociology and cross-cultural communication (Peterson, 2018). Hofstede's work (Hofstede, 2010), which aimed to develop a framework to analyze cultural differences that could be applied to various societies and contexts, was rooted in surveying one hundred thousand IBM employees from 40 countries between 1967 and 1973. As a result, he identified six cultural dimensions: power distance, individualism/collectivism, masculinity/femininity, uncertainty avoidance, long-term/short-term orientation, and indulgence/restraint. Power distance refers to the degree to which people accept and expect an unequal distribution of power in society, while individualism/collectivism refers to the degree to which people prioritize individual achievement or group harmony. Masculinity/femininity refers to the proportion to which a culture values competitiveness and assertion or nurturing and cooperation. Uncertainty avoidance refers to the degree to which people feel threatened by ambiguity and uncertainty, while long-term/short-term orientation refers to what extent a culture values immediate versus future-oriented thinking. Finally, indulgence/restraint expresses the level to which a culture values free gratification of basic and natural human desires. Hofstede's study was groundbreaking because it showed that cultural differences could be measured and quantified and is considered the growing field of CQ (Livermore, 2009).

As part of the workforce's globalization perspective, CQ or cultural quotient was introduced to the public as a potential emergent concept at the beginning of the 21st century. In 2003, researchers Ang and Early published a book for Stanford University Press in which they defined for the first time CQ as the ability to perceive, relate to, and work efficiently in culturally diverse contexts (Earley & Ang, 2003). Initially envisioned by Ang and Early as a combination of three factors: motivational, behavioral, and mental, CQ, through the work of Ang et al. (2006) and relying on Sternberg's intelligence framework (Sternberg & Detterman, 1986), was reconstructed on its actual four main pillars: behavioral CQ, cognitive CQ, metacognitive CQ, and motivational CQ. Based on these four elements, the CQ scale developed by Dr. Christopher Earley and Dr. Soon Ang as a self-report questionnaire that allows individuals to measure their own CQ level was utilized during our quantitative research. *Behavioral* CQ pertains to one's nonverbal and verbal ability to display culturally appropriate behavior and effectively communicate with individuals from different cultural backgrounds (Ang & Van Dyne, 2015). It stands for the capacity to respond effectively in a variety of cultural contexts and accomplish established goals. *Cognitive* CQ refers to an individual's understanding and knowledge of different cultures (Christensen et al., 2019; Czerwionka et al., 2015). *Metacognitive* CQ involves the ability to recognize one's own cultural biases and adapt to accommodate other cultures (Ang & Van Dyne, 2008), while last but not least, *motivational* CQ describes a person's ability to focus their energy and attention on learning about cultural differences. It comprises the level of commitment made to adjusting to and comprehending cross-cultural dynamics (Jangsiriwattana, 2021; Jannesari et al., 2022).

CQ is a critical factor in successful cross-cultural communication (Charoensukmongkol, 2020). Modern intelligence theories (Ramalu & Subramaniam, 2019; Shearer, 2020), rooted in the pioneering work of Earley and Ang, barely repositioned CQ, which describes a person's innate ability to adapt and function well in contexts that are unfamiliar and diverse in terms of culture (Österlind & Henoch, 2021). Presbitero (2020) contended that when people interact with individuals from different cultural backgrounds, the commonly observed aptitudes such as cognitive intelligence, emotional intelligence, and social intelligence that influence cognition and social behaviors in culturally homogeneous settings may not always be relevant.

Additionally, recent discoveries have shown that CQ influences humans' cognitive capacities (Vlajčić et al., 2019). Being a relatively new idea, the study of CQ in corporate contexts is still in its infancy (Taras, 2020). However, there is growing empirical proof that CQ is important in management and organizational studies. Decision-making (E Souza et al., 2021), leadership (Rickley & Stackhouse, 2022), expatriate assignments, and negotiation (Grosz et al., 2023) are just a few of the contexts in which CQ has started to be studied. Following the claim made by Men and Yue (2019) that although employees demonstrated strong interpersonal skills within their own culture, those skills will not necessarily be translated to the same level of effectiveness when navigating interpersonal dynamics in unfamiliar cultural contexts, the study of CQ attracted more attention in organizational settings (Du et al., 2022). In other words, interpersonal skills acquired inside one's own culture might not be the same as those needed for effective adaptation to other cultures (Chen, 2019; Zhou et al., 2022).

In the study on senior expatriate managers' leadership styles, Charoensukmongkol (2021) discovered that metacognitive and motivational CQ play important roles in boosting leaders' effectiveness. According to (Yuan et al., 2023), these elements support their capacity to set a positive example, integrate their behavior with cultural norms, promote teamwork, and establish trust. In one more study on expatriates, Cavazotte et al. (2021) discovered a link between behavioral CQ and job performance, particularly in terms of contextual and assignment-specific performance. The ability of multicultural leaders to successfully modify their verbal and nonverbal communication methods, enabling them to fulfill the expectations of others, is credited with this link.

Fu and Charoensukmongkol (2021) found that the benefits of CQ on cultural adjustment and cultural effectiveness were moderated by multicultural leaders' prior international work and travel experiences. According to their study results, the degree to which CQ influences a leader's capacity to acclimatize to new countries and demonstrate cultural effectiveness can vary depending on prior overseas experiences.

Furthermore, Yang (2021) showed how even a brief study-abroad experience could improve CQ. He exposed that studying abroad can attenuate the link between CQ and cultural sensitivity and effectiveness, underscoring the value of exposure to other cultures in promoting personal cultural sensitivity and effectiveness.

Ott and Iskhakova (2019) investigated how foreign experience affected CQ. They discovered that non-work-related overseas experiences had a more substantial impact on leaders' CQ than experiences linked to their jobs. This shows that exposure to nonwork-related international encounters might significantly influence expatriate CQ development. Building on this, Iskhakova and Ott (2020) found that having international experience improved all aspects of CQ. This conclusion highlighted the overall beneficial impact of international experience on the various components of CQ. While numerous studies are exploring the general relationship between international experience and CQ, there needs to be more research specifically investigating how international experience affects CQ in specific domains, such as KD and bottom-line financial results.

Iskhakova et al. (2022) stated that global managers with international experience had the opportunity to interact with different cultures, deepening their cultural knowledge in this way. This exposure to diverse cultural environments allows them to develop cross-cultural cognitive skills. Gabel-Shemueli et al. (2019) proposed that CQ was recognized as a valuable personal resource that aids individuals in effectively regulating themselves and adapting to culturally diverse organizational settings. Within the Conservation of Resources (COR) theory framework, proposed by Dr Stevan Hobfoll (Dudek et al., 2007), personal resources also refer to positive self-evaluations linked to resilience and individuals' perceived ability to exert control and influence in their environment. Individuals with higher CQ may exhibit greater motivation and eagerness to develop personal and work-related resources, facilitating their intercultural business tasks and interactions while also mitigating work-related stress (Jabeen et al., 2022).

Furthermore, people with high levels of CQ have the cognitive skills necessary to successfully plan for and handle any stress that can result from dealing with different cultures. They can handle such circumstances more deftly due to their increased knowledge and grasp of the cultural milieu. CQ is also essential in preventing the depletion of other resources important for cross-cultural encounters (Presbitero, 2020). People with high cognitive abilities consistently display a wide variety of verbal and nonverbal behaviors, which reduces the possibility of resource loss during cross-cultural contact (Puzzo et al., 2023).

High CQ helped to meet employees' needs and promote higher engagement in culturally diverse situations, according to a prior study (Rüth & Netzer, 2020). For example, those with high CQ are more able to deal with the obstacles posed by diversity, such as communication barriers, problems with teamwork, and negotiation difficulties (Paiuc, 2021a). Their improved CQ makes overcoming these obstacles easier, promoting a healthy and fruitful work atmosphere in multicultural contexts (Richter et al., 2021). High CQ also gives workers a stronger sense of autonomy since they believe they have more influence and control over their surroundings. Through better monitoring, analysis, and behavior adaptation, people with higher CQ feel more in control of their interactions and outcomes (Stahl & Maznevski, 2021). Moreover, Stahl and Maznevski (2021) also said that those with high CQ could overcome unfavorable reactions and misconceptions resulting from social categorization processes, which can help satisfy the need for relatedness. People with high CQ can promote stronger interactions and lessen potential prejudices by improving their grasp of the cultural backgrounds of other team members. This encourages a feeling of relatedness and connection, resulting in a more welcoming and inclusive workplace (Afsar et al., 2021; Bratianu & Paiuc, 2023b).

Drawing from the notion that prior international experience enhances leaders' ability to adapt to different cultures, several studies have explored the influence of such experiences on cross-cultural adaptation dynamics. Cheung et al. (2021) discovered that individuals who had experienced work, knowledge, or educational engagements abroad rather than leisure travel developed higher levels of CQ. By enabling employees to understand, appreciate, and collaborate effectively with individuals from diverse cultural backgrounds, CQ fosters cross-cultural collaboration and idea exchange and creates a dynamic knowledge environment.

Employees' sense of integration and acceptance inside the company was also aided by CQ, which made it easier to understand cultural differences. CQ assisted people in bridging divides and fostering relationships among one another (Stoermer et al., 2021). From this perspective, CQ contributes to a more inclusive, collaborative, and globally oriented approach to KD in organizations (Paiuc, 2021a; Stoermer et al., 2021).

According to Whiting (2020), the top 10 abilities required for professional accomplishment in 2025 fall into four categories: working with people (which is based on CQ and ML), problem-solving, self-management, as one of the characteristics of knowmads, (Bratianu et al., 2021), and technology use and development.

In the studied literature, we have identified a literature gap on CQ due to a need for more specific investigations on the impact of international experience on CQ in many domains, such as KD and the company's financial results. While existing studies have examined the overall relationship between foreign experience and CQ, more analysis needs to be conducted on how international experience affects CQ in these specific circumstances. From the same perspective, relatively few studies have analyzed the possible impact of KD on CQ (Liu et al., 2022). Researchers can also contribute to a more thorough knowledge of the role of CQ in organizational contexts and improve individuals' effectiveness in culturally varied workplaces by filling these gaps.

2.3 KD Literature Review and Identified Gaps

One could assert that the notion of "knowledge" is imbued with a multifaceted and intricate semantic landscape, which has elicited diverse and nuanced interpretations throughout the course of history.

Aristotle classified in his works, more than 2000 years ago, knowledge as a hierarchy of three distinct levels – theoretical (episteme), practical (phronesis), and productive (techne) (Aristotle, 2020). Theoretical knowledge is focused on understanding what, why, and how things exist in the world. It is derived from rational contemplation and the discovery of empirical evidence through natural sciences such as physics, biology, and metaphysics philosophy. It is done to comprehend nature, reality, and existence in general (Marquez, 2022). Practical knowledge deals with the application of theory toward action or decision-making. It is obtained through experience, skill, and personal growth. It involves recognizing what is within your power to control, identifying the end goal or objective, and then developing and implementing a plan to achieve that goal. Productive knowledge, conversely, is centered on creativity, craftsmanship, and technology. It is the know-how of producing artifacts or works that serve a practical or esthetic purpose. This knowledge covers crafting, design, engineering, music, art, and other creative fields. According to Aristotle, these three types of knowledge – theoretical, practical, and productive – are all distinct yet interrelated. He believed their successful integration leads to profound wisdom and fulfillment of human potential. Following Tsoukas and Cummings (1997), Aristotle considered that both craft knowledge (techne) and practical wisdom (phronesis) are forms of practical knowledge, as opposed to theoretical scientific knowledge (episteme). The distinction between techne and phronesis is action and production (Tsoukas & Cummings, 1997). On the other hand, for Plato, knowledge was a result of thinking, specifically rational thought. He saw knowledge as a result of disciplined thought and philosophical inquiry rather than simple observation or experience (Plato, 2021).

An analysis by Puzzo et al. (2023) focused on cultural knowledge, a precursor to CQ, and emphasized the significance of foreign investors being mindful of cultural traditions and practices. This awareness is crucial for establishing productive relationships with local partners and enhancing KD's success. Given that CQ is a higher order cognitive function compared to cultural awareness, it is reasonable to assume that CQ also facilitates KD. Kadam and Kareem Abdul (2022) supported this claim by demonstrating that trust and openness to diversity, which are inherent in the CQ concept, promote knowledge development. Furthermore, they also discovered that knowledge concealment was one of the potential hurdles to positive individual and organizational performance.

KD in businesses has received extensive attention in the fields of organizational studies and knowledge management (KM) (Manesh et al., 2020). One prominent model in this area is the SECI model (Avdimiotis et al., 2022), which illustrates a spiral knowledge creation and transfer process. This model underscores the significance of social interactions, conversations, and collective learning in driving KD. It emphasizes the importance of socialization, externalization, combination, and internalization within organizations for facilitating effective KD. These activities are crucial for the efficient development, exchange, and utilization of knowledge within the OC (Adesina & Ocholla, 2019; Canonico et al., 2020).

Bratianu and Bejinaru (2019) established the KD thermodynamic approach to support the notion of KD, which employs thermodynamic concepts in studying knowledge inside organizations. It regards knowledge as a dynamic resource that flows, changes, and dispels within organizational systems like energy does in thermodynamics. This paradigm addresses issues such as knowledge formation, conversion, transmission, storage, and dissipation, revealing how knowledge behaves and impacts organizational processes. This approach provides a unique perspective on managing knowledge for greater organizational performance, innovation, and competitive advantage.

Additionally, the literature emphasized how crucial KD were in fostering innovation within organizations. The value of knowledge integration, sharing, and the generation of new knowledge through interactions between people or communities of practice was repeatedly stressed by academics (Schneider et al., 2019). According to Sima et al. (2020), successful KD support creativity by facilitating the synthesis of existing information and the emergence of novel ideas. They also promoted an atmosphere at work that respected and encouraged innovation. Li et al. (2021) also stated that companies could use their intellectual capital by promoting effective knowledge flow and transformation to produce new solutions and advance ongoing development.

According to Galetto et al. (2023), communities of practice, a concept popularized by Etienne Wenger, highlighted the importance of social networks within organizations for fostering knowledge sharing and collaborative learning. Communities of practice have been recognized in the literature for their contribution to KD by giving people a forum to exchange ideas, work together to solve problems, and co-create common knowledge. These organizations fostered a sense of belonging while promoting internal information sharing and developing a body of knowledge.

The literature also acknowledged the significance of organizational culture in determining KD. The prevailing culture inside a company significantly impacted how knowledge was viewed, valued, and distributed. Effective KD often results from a culture that values transparency, cooperation, and trust (Farzaneh et al., 2021). Conversely, a culture that discourages knowledge sharing or places more importance on individuals hoarding knowledge could impede the flow of knowledge and hinder the organization's ability to leverage its intellectual capital (Pereira & Mohiya, 2021). Therefore, developing a supportive organizational culture that promotes and rewards information sharing was essential to cultivate a company with solid KD (Farzaneh et al., 2021).

Pandey et al. (2021) discovered that KD processes were significantly influenced by a culture that valued learning, welcomed experimentation, and promoted information sharing. They also illustrated that businesses with a strong learning culture were more likely to support knowledge production, application, and dissemination throughout the entire organization. Furthermore, the organization's values, norms, and leadership practices were key in creating a climate that fostered and supported KD.

Davidavičienė et al. (2020) identified that the advancement of technology and KM systems significantly impacted KD within organizations. The literature also investigated how information and communication technologies (ICTs) supported the creation of virtual communities, facilitated knowledge exchange, and enhanced teamwork (Lo & Tian, 2020). Another crucial aspect in fostering KD within organizations was the effective integration and implementation of KM systems. According to Fayyaz et al. (2021), by utilizing ICTs and putting in place strong KM systems, businesses improved the flow of information, encouraged collaboration, and enabled the establishment of online communities where information was generated and shared. They also illustrated that regardless of location or affiliation, employees accessed knowledge resources, contributed to them, and used them thanks to the platforms and tools provided by these technological breakthroughs. Meanwhile, the literature stressed the significance of judicious technology and KM system adoption and utilization to enhance KD within organizations (Chowdhury et al., 2022).

The body of research (Deepu & Ravi, 2021) on KD in organizations covered a wide range of angles and subjects. For example, knowledge creation, innovation, communities of practice, organizational culture, and the function of technology and KM systems were all topics that were covered. By examining topics including information transfer methods, organizational learning procedures, and the effects of contextual factors on KD, ongoing studies attempted to further our understanding of KD (Zhang et al., 2020).

So, the research also emphasized the importance of KM in various applications, including its function in optimizing sustainability-related techniques to efficiently manage this complex notion (Martins et al., 2019). As KM matured as a strategic strategy, organizations were able to recognize the critical competencies required to foster a culture of innovative thinking and learning capable of translating sustainability concepts into practical applications. Organizations needed to design relevant measures associated with sustainability goals (Al Shraah et al., 2021). Recent studies stated that organizations underwent a revolutionary shift by incorporating KM within the context of sustainability, where social and environmental responsibility became as important as economic viability. Given the difficulties associated with complying with sustainability criteria, KM served as a basis for adopting sustainable development practices. As a result, organizations increasingly relied on their knowledge-generating resources and leadership style. Within the sustainability framework, KM was viewed as a new developmental paradigm aimed at improving compliance with economic, environmental, and social sustainability principles (Abaker et al., 2019; Ahmad et al., 2021; Kadam & Kareem Abdul, 2022).

Moreover, within an organization, KD facilitate by ML. That plays a crucial role in supporting knowledge generation, application, sharing, and submission in many cultural contexts (Iskhakova et al., 2022).

A lack of detailed exploration characterizes the literature gap in the context of KD approach inside organizations. While several areas, such as the SECI model, organizational culture, technology, and KM systems, and the significance of communities of practice, have been investigated, more detailed research is still required. There is a particular gap in understanding how KD influences innovation, creativity, and organizational effectiveness. More research is needed to delve deeper into the mechanisms and elements that drive effective knowledge production, transfer, and utilization processes, as well as the impact of KD on CQ and on sustainable development and organizational goals accomplishment.

2.4 ML Literature Review and Identified Gaps

Most studies on ML emphasize the importance of CQ in successfully managing diverse teams (Berraies, 2019). Berraies stated that multicultural leaders with high CQ levels could comprehend and adapt to many cultural circumstances. They can communicate, navigate cultural quirks, and promote inclusive team dynamics. According to research, these leaders are more adept at managing diversity and capitalizing on cultural differences to improve team output and organizational results (Batsa et al., 2020).

Cultural differences are pivotal in leadership effectiveness, as diverse cultural environments necessitate distinct managerial behaviors (Schein, 1997). Furthering this analysis, Ang et al. (2011) demonstrated that CQ is both predictive and determinative of leadership potential. Effective leadership in multinational and multicultural environments can be achieved, according to Goleman (1996), by employing three primary leadership drivers: vision (by rallying people toward change), service (by creating emotional ties), and leading others to excellence (by developing and growing people for future roles and responsibilities).

Iskhakova and Ott (2020) stated that multicultural and inclusive leadership are closely related. Inclusive leaders foster an atmosphere where people from various cultural origins are integrated, valued, and respected. According to the literature, multicultural leaders that practice inclusive leadership behaviors help their team members to feel trusted, comfortable, and like they belong (Berraies, 2019). These leaders foster an inclusive environment by encouraging other viewpoints, knowledge sharing, and cooperation. This all-inclusive strategy significantly affects the organization's KD (Lovin et al., 2021).

Stahl and Maznevski (2021) argued that conflict management was a key aspect of ML. They also suggest that cultural differences occasionally lead to mis-understandings and conflicts among diverse teams. That is why the ability to manage disputes while keeping cognizant of cultural differences was found to be a trait of effective multicultural leaders (Stahl & Maznevski, 2021), as they were skilled at negotiating and resolving conflicts brought on by cultural differences (Chen, 2019). By proactively addressing difficulties (Pretorius et al., 2019), encouraging open communication (Fayyaz et al., 2021), and supporting under-standing (Du et al., 2022), learning (Ahmad et al., 2021), and the development of creative solutions (Akanmu et al., 2021), multicultural leaders were able to establish an environment, backed by emotional intelligence, that supported KD (Barron & Hurley, 2011).

Additionally, many organizations are encouraged and provided with resources for developing ML competencies, according to the research of Li et al. (2021). Training programs and development activities were found to be effective in improving leaders' CQ, intercultural communication abilities, and inclusive leadership traits (Cavazotte et al., 2021). Businesses prioritizing and investing in ML development were more likely to benefit from a range of viewpoints and experiences, which positively impacted internal KD (Canonico et al., 2020).

The research also emphasized the importance of organizational support, inclusive leadership techniques, conflict management abilities, and CQ in the context of effective ML (Fermín et al., 2020). These skills allowed multicultural leaders to successfully traverse cultural barriers, create inclusive teams, resolve disputes, and advance KD inside their organizations (Bach-Mortensen & Montgomery, 2018). One more study also emphasized the significance of these elements in empowering leaders to capitalize on diversity (Abaker et al., 2019), encourage teamwork (Iskhakova & Ott, 2020), and facilitate the sharing of information (Fayyaz et al., 2021; Martins et al., 2019) and ideas (Richter et al., 2021) in multicultural contexts (Lovin et al., 2021).

The ongoing processes of globalization, the circular economy, and the digital revolution are gradually forming a global identity that aims to mold individuals' CQ and even KD processes (Liu et al., 2021). Jose (2023) identified that the rise of globalization as a distinguishing feature of the 21st century prompted managers to investigate cutting-edge ML strategies. Previous research emphasized the importance of these strategies for ensuring economic prosperity and promoting corporate growth.

The need for managers to have specific leadership abilities to manage cultural diversity in the workplace effectively was well noted in earlier writings (Cooke et al., 2020). According to Akdere et al. (2021), practising ML requires a deep immersion in diverse cultures to understand their unique values and contextual nuances. The key was negotiating the opportunities and navigating the difficulties that came in a world that was becoming more interconnected.

According to Burgess et al. (2022), managers need to create ML strategies to support cultural diversity in the workplace. These tactics attempted to emphasize the value of multicultural abilities and encouraged staff to actively develop them because they directly impacted career advancement and performance reviews (Nocker & Sena, 2019). Meanwhile, comprehensive multicultural training programs have been implemented by leaders to encourage teamwork and understanding among coworkers (Habibi Soola et al., 2022). Additionally, Nocker and Sena (2019) said that the leaders' responsibility was to improve and modify current curricula to support this effort. By exposing managers to various cultures, geographical regions, short-term initiatives, and medium-term professional role rotations, these programs improved their ability to handle cultural diversity. This all-encompassing strategy was included in the new talent management process (Ahmad et al., 2021).

Mishra et al. (2020) also stressed the importance of incorporating multicultural perspectives into company strategies and decision-making. To ensure the appropriate and efficient delivery of messages, leaders had to be able to engage and interact with a variety of audiences across multiple cultures (Mishra et al., 2020). First and foremost, leaders must show tolerance and respect for all cultures, carefully considering societal norms to prevent misunderstandings or mistakes (Smith & Ruiz, 2020). Second, they ought to have made an effort to learn more about other cultures, considering things like history and language learning (Khalilzadeh & Khodi, 2021). Thirdly, since time was crucial in building relationships with high-context cultures, leaders should have fostered flexibility and refrained from hurrying the process. Finally, using universal humor, speaking plainly, and avoiding jargon, all helped to promote good cross-cultural communication (Kamales & Knorr, 2019).

By reviewing and referencing earlier material, it became clear that ML's abilities were essential for successfully navigating cultural diversity at work (Shliakhovchuk, 2019) and incorporating multicultural insights into decision-making processes (Guan et al., 2020; Kamales & Knorr, 2019).

Additionally, the recent literature emphasized that ML promotes inclusivity (Vassallo, 2021), uses other viewpoints, and creates productive teams (Batsa et al., 2020). It fosters social cohesiveness, increases global competitiveness (Rüth & Netzer, 2020), supports CQ development (Afsar et al., 2021), and encourages inclusiveness. Multicultural leaders foster innovative cultures, close cultural gaps, and advance equality by appreciating varied perspectives and accepting cultural differences (Feitosa et al., 2022). In a linked and interconnected world, ML is essential for creating understanding, encouraging creativity, and igniting good change (Maker, 2022).

On the basis of the studied literature, there is a need for additional research into the precise ways in which ML practises, and behaviors influence organizational growth. There is also a requirement for effective techniques, training programs, and interventions to improve ML competencies, particularly regarding developing KD. More study is needed to close this gap and better understand how KD and CQ impact ML in various organizational settings.

Meanwhile, future research must address the scarcity of comprehensive investigation and analysis of the intricate mechanisms and strategies that contribute to the effectiveness of KD within diverse teams, delving into ML. While the importance of CQ and OC has been mentioned in the context of ML, there needs to be a more in-depth examination of how these vectors directly impact knowledge generation, sharing, and utilization.

2.5 OC Literature Review and Identified Gaps

Creating an inclusive organizational environment is recognized as a unique approach to facilitating work group functioning (Randel et al., 2018) and emphasized by Roberson and Perry (2022). The concept of diversity within the organizational environment is the lead role in determining an inclusive environment within any organization (Roberson & Perry, 2022). Additionally, the thematic analysis by Roberson and Perry (2022) underlined the significance of fostering environments where team members can freely share and enhance each other's ideas, and leaders prioritize creating opportunities for leveraging member contributions in decision-making, even when those contributions deviate from established team standard norms. Such environments are vital to enhancing autonomy and innovation by accepting diversity and strengthening the company culture. Drawing from research indicates that leaders who exhibit openness and respect toward new ideas and feedback create a supportive climate (Qi et al., 2019) and suggest that such an environment encourages employees to feel at ease in experimenting and expressing alternative perspectives. Thus, an inclusive organizational environment leads to innovation among employees or team members of the workplace. Not only an inclusive environment but also digital transformation is said to enhance adaptability in an OC (Sun et al., 2023), as leaders must adapt their strategies accordingly. Hanelt et al. (2021) discovered four dimensions of digital transformation within organizations: technology impact, systemic shift, compartmentalized adaptation, and holistic coevolution. Somehow, traditional frameworks on organizational adaptability only provide limited coverage of the nature of digital transformation.

OCs represented by community culture, diversity, and inclusion are reported to be strong factors in enhancing workers' CQ (Bratianu & Paiuc, 2022). Likewise, entrepreneurship as a characteristic of organizational leadership is reported to be associated with CQ and institutional success (Caputo et al., 2018; Sharma, 2019) examined the moderating role of CQ on the relationship between exposure to cultural diversity and community and conflict management styles. They also confirmed the strong relationship between a multicultural environment and CQ within the organization. Furthermore, they provided empirical evidence of how significant CQ is in enhancing productivity and performance in varied international settings by effectively handling diversity (Caputo et al., 2018). CQ is a fundamental skill for multinational leadership and global management and a key driver of inclusive leadership. Specifically, it plays a crucial role in promoting inclusive leadership practices (Paiuc, 2021a). Individuals with high CQ notably accept cultural differences and are less prone to making erroneous and shallow judgments during cross-cultural interactions (Afsar et al., 2021). People with increased level of CQ can effectively balance and integrate the knowledge and perspectives of diverse team members (Ratasuk & Charoensukmongkol, 2020). Highly culturally intelligent individuals, as noted in the research by Afsar et al. (2021), have a tendency to reduce differences between various cultural groups and promote a sense of familiarity and acceptance in their relationships. This inclination is likely to enhance their sense of belonging, which is crucial to their perceived inclusion within a work group. Perceived inclusion encompasses knowledge sharing and active involvement in decision-making processes, as Barak (2017) described. It has been linked to engagement in learning behaviors such as dialogue and collaboration, as noted by Zhu et al. (2019). Through knowledge sharing and dialogue, individuals have the opportunity to acquire and contemplate culturally diverse knowledge, thereby enhancing their cognitive and meta-cognitive CQ.

Collaboration and decision-making participation enable individuals to practice their newly acquired knowledge, thereby enhancing their behavioral CQ (Grapin & Pereiras, 2019). Engaging in dialogue and collaboration within culturally diverse contexts encourages individuals to learn about and appreciate cultural differences, thereby fostering motivational CQ. By actively prioritizing inclusion and the development of CQ at all levels of the organization, it becomes possible to attain a more multicultural approach to organizational development, as highlighted by Grapin and Pereiras (2019).

The knowledge dynamic depends on the OC (Ashok et al., 2021; Engelsberger et al., 2022). Organizational culture and KM practices are interlinked, as reported by Ashok et al. (2021) in their single-case study findings from a public sector organization. A multicultural environment and diversity in a workplace can have effects on KD in both directions. It can be devastating in case of low communication and connectivity among team members or a source of knowledge sharing when inclusion, innovation, and openness are ensured in the organizational environment (Engelsberger et al., 2022). Empirical evidence gathered by Raza and Awang (2020) claimed that a multicultural environment could positively affect knowledge sharing behavior if employees' CQ is high. Similarly, the leader's emotional knowledge is highlighted by Goleman (2000, 2021) in his book *Leadership: the power of emotional intelligence*, which stipulates that when a leader understands his employee's emotions and speaks while disseminating motivational expressions, it not only increases the employee's job performance but is also a key to organizational success. The empirical investigation of the relationship between spiritual knowledge, CQ, and leadership effectiveness lacked findings in recent literature. However, it is important to highlight that the few existing field-related studies indicated a positive and significant influence of CQ and spiritual knowledge on global leadership effectiveness, specifically in terms of decision-making, performance, and commitment (Osman-Gani & Hassan, 2018). Thus, CQ needs to be studied in the context of its effect on employees' and leaders' knowledge and performance, as well as on their professional behavior. Somehow, the vice versa could not be found in the literature on how KD can influence CQ.

In conclusion, the literature extensively covers the OC, aiming to support its significance for CQ and leadership success through empirical and secondary evidence. Nevertheless, there needs to be more exploration of the impact of organizational elements such as flexibility, transparency, agility, and change on CQ. Recent studies on organizations have failed to make substantial progress in establishing a more meaningful connection between a more digital OC and KD. Similarly, the existing literature needs to include more depth and more complex research on the relationship between KD and the subcategories of CQ. Consequently, in this study model, KD is considered the independent variable, comprising sub-factors such as rational knowledge, emotional knowledge, and spiritual knowledge.

2.6 Bibliometric Analysis of the Key Connections CQ-KD-OC-ML

The information in Table 1 was retrieved on June 4, 2023, from the Scopus database, the world's largest abstract and citation database for peer-reviewed research literature. The retrieval method consisted of an advanced search function, and the retrieval interval was standard from the platform's early days of

Table 1. Main Concepts Searched Results on Scopus.

Variable	Searched Expressions in Scopus	Returned Results	
		All Fields	Title, Abstract, Keywords
CQ	"cultural intelligence"	9,150 (*1)	1,168 ✔
KD	"knowledge dynamics"	3,721 ✔	418
ML	"multicultural leadership" OR "multinational leadership" OR "multinational management" OR "multicultural management"	1904 ✔	177
ML	"multicultural leadership" OR "multinational leadership"	250 (*2)	45
OC	"organizational context"	49,557 (*3)	8,963 ✔

Source: Author's own results.

inception until the beginning of June 2023. The default values provided by Scopus were used and deployed on the remaining retrieval parameters.

Scopus records comprising extensive data (*citation, bibliographical, abstract and keywords*, and *additional information*) were exported under CSV files.

While the aim was to build on *all fields* data in the case of CQ (*1) and OC (*3), the upload of the CSV files into Vosviewer was not possible due to the "out of memory" of the system, so we had to restrain to *title, abstract, keywords* results. For ML, as the initial search (*2) returned only 250 answers, we had enlarged the research area with additional "multicultural management" or "multinational management" in order to obtain 1904 results.

We have driven our bibliometric analysis using VOSviewer version 1.6.19 (Visualization of Similarities), leveraging the about mentioned number of items per each main variable, with a focus on the co-occurrence analysis, having all keywords as unit of measurement and a full counting methodology – as presented in Table 2.

Table 2. Main Variables' Keywords Meeting the Threshold in Vosviewer.

Variable	Number of Items	Keywords	Minimum Number of Occurrences of a Keyword	Keywords Meeting the Threshold
CQ	1,168 ✔	3,590	5	239
KD	3,721 ✔	12,872	5	943
ML	1904 ✔	4,406	5	225
OC	8,963 ✔	25,151	5	2,490

Source: Author's own research.

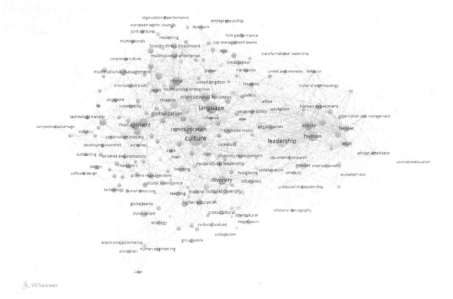

Fig. 1.   ML and MD Bibliometric Map – 1904 Item – All Fields
Selection. *Source:* Author's own research.

Fig. 1 represents the bibliometric map of ML with main underlined drivers: "culture" (total link strength 201), "language" (113), "globalization" (99), "decision making" (97), and "diversity" (95).

From the map and Table 3, we can conclude that CQ, represented by 25 keywords from 8 clusters, is a main driver of ML with a cumulated link strength of almost 25% from the total of 3,671. KD counts for 203 cumulated link strength (5.5%), while OC ranks 153 (4.2%) (Table 3).

Fig. 2 shows a zooming area of the same map, this time in density visualization mode in order to underline the CQ and KD direct connections to ML:

Further, we will double test the connection and links starting from CQ, KD, and OC (Fig. 3).

For CQ, from a total link strength of 13,249, ML (represented by leadership and management variations) accounts for the score of 435 (3.3%). If to this we will add "performance" attributes as a sign of effective leadership, the total score will rise to 647 (4.9%), demonstrating the bivalent connections of the two concepts.

KD is present in CQ map with a total link strength of 245 (1.85%), while OC represents 1.63% with 216 total link strength.

We are performing the same approach for KD – with a total link strength of 49,347, in which ML represents the main vector with a share of 10.7% and cumulated links strength of 5,291; OC – 2.2% (1,075) and CQ – 0.4% (192), as represented in Fig. 4.

Table 3. ML – Main Drivers as per the Bibliometric Analyze.

Drivers	CQ - driven by " culture"		KD - driven by "knowledge", "information"		OC - driven by "organization", "context"	
Total link strength	909	24,80%	203	5,50%	153	4,20%
Items	25 items (8 clusters):					
	Cluster 1 - 2 items		Cluster 1 - 2 items		Cluster 3 - 1 item	
	cultural difference		knowledge management		organizational performance	
	cultural dimensions		knowledge transfer		Cluster 5 - 2 items	
	Cluster 2 - 2 items		Cluster 1 - 3 items		organizational performance	
	cultural distance		information management		organization and management	
	intercultural communication		information systems		Cluster 6 - 1 item	
	Cluster 3 - 3 items		information use		organizational framework	
	corporate culture		Cluster 3 - 1 item		Cluster 6 - 1 item	
	multicultural leadership		information technology		context	
	multicultural teams		Cluster 2 - 1 item			
	Cluster 4 - 7 items		social capital			
	cultural differences					
	cultural diversity					
	cultural values					
	multicultural management					
	multiculturalism					
	national culture					
	national cultures					
	Cluster 5 - 3 items					
	cultural anthropology					
	cultural competence					
	organizational culture					
	Cluster 6 - 6 items					
	cross-culture					
	cultural intelligence					
	culture					
	intercultural					
	intercultural competence					
	organizational culture					
	Cluster 7 - 1 item					
	cross-cultural management					
	Cluster 8 - 1 item					
	multicultural					

Source: Author's own research.

Our last analyses and double check start this time from OC, which has a total link strength of 359,339. CQ, with a cumulated link strength of 8,963, represents 2.5% and KD – 2.3% (8,295). ML is by far the main connection of OC, with a share of 9.8% and a cumulated link strength of 35,348 (Fig. 5).

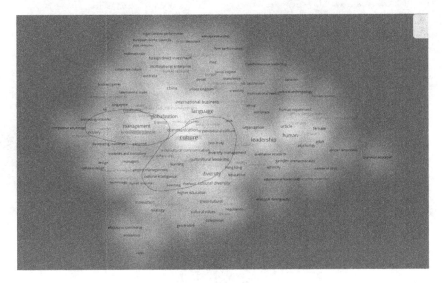

Fig. 2.   ML and MD Density Map – 1904 Items – All Fields Selection
With Circled Vectors. *Source:* Author's own research.

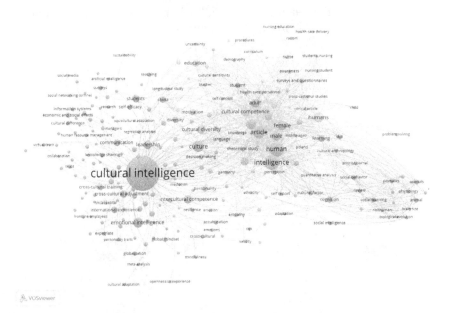

Fig. 3.   CQ Bibliometric Map – 1,168 Items – Title-Abstract-
Keywords Selection. *Source:* Author's own research.

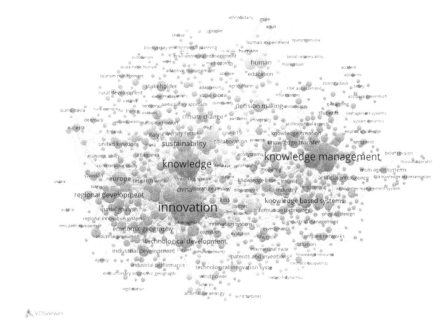

Fig. 4.   KD Bibliometric Map – 3,721 Items – All Fields Selection.
Source: Author's own research.

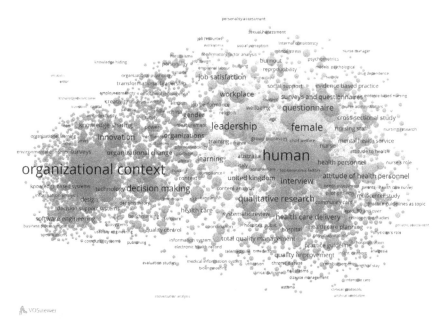

Fig. 5.   Organizational Context Map – 8,963 Items – Title-Abstract-
Keywords Selection – Minimum Number of Occurrences of Keyword 5 –
25,151 Results – 2,490 Met the Threshold. *Source:* Author's own research.

In this bibliometric section, we have analyzed the various relationship and connections between our main studied variables, and we can conclude at this stage that all four are related with main strong connections: CQ-ML (4.9%) with reciprocating ML-CQ (25%), KD-ML (10.7%), and OC-ML (9.8%). This reinforces our conceptual model and demonstrates the direct influence of CQ, KD, and OC on ML.

Chapter 3

Methodology

3.1 Research Methodology and Approach

While the literature review was discussed and analyzed in the previous chapter, and the research gaps were identified, this chapter focuses on formulating the research question and hypotheses. It provides a detailed description of the research methodology used to test these hypotheses, build the samples, and collect the data.

3.1.1 Research Question and General Objective

3.1.1.1 Research Question

From the perspective of keeping it concise, researchable, and relevant, our initial proposed research question was:

What is the role of knowledge dynamics and cultural intelligence in developing multicultural leadership?

After the first results of qualitative research, the question was reframed and also linked to the *organizational context (OC)*, as a tone setter for the work environment, which can either support or hinder ML practices.

3.1.1.2 General Objective

Current research indicates that cultural intelligence (CQ) is closely related to knowledge dynamics (KD), and they are components of ML and might impact the bottom-line results. Therefore, it is intended to model and evaluate the above fields in order to determine and assess the role of CQ and KD in developing multinational leadership.

3.1.2 Research Framework and Approach

The triangulation rule, as defined by Atif et al. (2013), involves analyzing the results of a study using multiple data collection methods. This technique is used

Developing Multicultural Leadership using Knowledge Dynamics and Cultural Intelligence, 25–46
Copyright © 2024 Dan Paiuc
Published under exclusive licence by Emerald Publishing Limited
doi:10.1108/978-1-83549-432-520241006

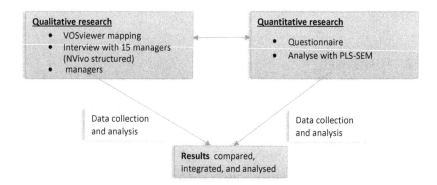

Fig. 1.   A Visual Diagram of the Mixed-Methods Concurrent
Triangulation Strategy. *Source:* Author's own research.

for three main purposes: to improve the validity of the research, to create a more comprehensive view of a research problem, and to explore different ways of interpreting it, as synthetized by Fig. 1.

For the qualitative part, we performed a comprehensive literature review and analyzed the correlations between basic concepts using VOSviewer, the most widely used software program for bibliometric data analysis (Colina Vargas et al., 2022). Also, we have performed semi-structured interviews with some multicultural leaders and analyzed the results via NVivo, one of the most popular software programs for Computer Assisted Qualitative Data Analysis (CAQDAS) (Zamawe, 2015), in order to build on it for the best ideas and questions to be valorized within our questionnaire.

For the quantitative research, based on the results mentioned above from our qualitative study, we designed a questionnaire that was addressed to managers working in multicultural environment companies based on the research model conceived in concordance with the Structural Equation Modeling (SEM) approach.

3.1.3 Research Models

Research models refer to frameworks or structures that guide the research process in order to support our research efforts. Below, we present the four stages to which we transitioned our model.

We have worked on the 15 interviews rooted in the first research model (model 1) and based just on CQ, KD, and ML – as presented in Fig. 2.

In Model 1, both KD and CQ scales are driven by the Knowledge Dynamic classifications (Bratianu & Bejinaru, 2019) with a clear split into three vectors: rational, emotional, and spiritual. Conceptual skills, interpersonal skills, and multicultural skills or values represent ML.

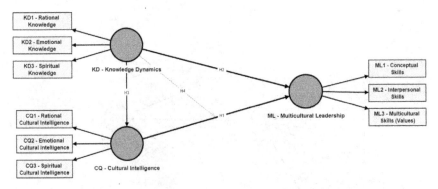

Fig. 2.   The Conceptual Model Utilized for the Interviews (Model 1).
Source: Author's own research.

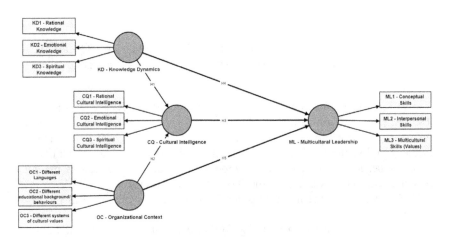

Fig. 3.   Enriched Model With Organizational Context (Model 2).
Source: Author's own research.

Following the interview results, we have enriched the original model with OC. In model 2 (presented below – Fig. 3), OC is structured in three categories: different languages, different educational backgrounds, and different systems of cultural values rooted in Edgar Schein's three levels of organizational culture: behavior and artifacts, espoused values, and basic or tacit assumptions (Hattangadi, 2021).

The next step in the transformation of the model was to replace the three vectors of CQ – utilized in the interviews (rational CQ; emotional CQ, and spiritual CQ) with four more precise ones: metacognitive CQ; cognitive CQ;

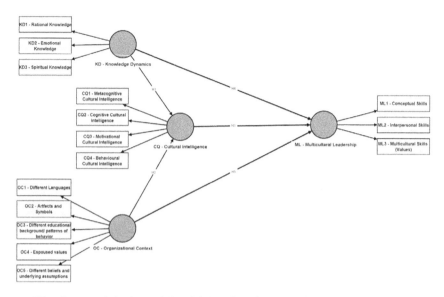

Fig. 4.   Enriched Model With Updated and Enhanced CQ and OC
Structure (Model 3). *Source:* Author's own research.

motivational CQ; and Behavioral CQ as synthesized by (Earley & Ang, 2003).
The OCA scale classification was adapted and utilized for OC that now is represented in the below model 3 (Fig. 4) with five vectors: different languages;
artifacts and symbols; different educational backgrounds; espoused values; and
different beliefs and underlying assumptions (Tama, 2019). Below is presented
model 3 with the described enhancements to CQ and OC.

The evolution of the model through its 4 phases is represented in the below
Table 1.

The last model (model 4 and Fig. 5) that was utilized to build the questionnaires has four vectors for ML: the three main ones identified by Robert Katz
(conceptual, interpersonal, and administrative or technical skills) (Rudd &
Fowler, 1989) and multicultural values (skills) as enhanced by Qu et al. (2017) and
underlined by Engelsberger et al. (2022). For OC, we have embedded OC1 (type
of company culture – represented by clan culture; adhocracy culture; market
culture; and hierarchy culture) as presented by Powers (2023) and rooted in the
work of professors Kim Cameron and Robert Quinn from the University of
Michigan. According to them, no corporate culture is as straightforward as being
good or *bad*, just distinct.

3.1.4 Research Hypothesis

Below are presented the hypotheses rooted in the research question that this study
focuses upon:

Table 1. The Evolution of Our Conceptual Model Through Its 4 Phases.

	Model 1 (interviews)	Model 2 (enhanced)	Model 3 (towards questionnaire)	Model 4 (questionnaire)	
KD — Knowledge Dynamics	KD1 Rational Knowledge	KD1 Rational Knowledge	KD1 Rational Knowledge	KD1 Rational Knowledge	KD scale
	KD2 Emotional Knowledge	KD2 Emotional Knowledge	KD2 Emotional Knowledge	KD2 Emotional Knowledge	
	KD3 Spiritual Knowledge	KD3 Spiritual Knowledge	KD3 Spiritual Knowledge	KD3 Spiritual Knowledge	
CQ — Cultural Intelligence	CQ1 Rational Cultural Intelligence	CQ1 Rational Cultural Intelligence	CQ1 Metacognitive Cultural Intelligence	CQ1 Metacognitive Cultural Intelligence	The 20-item, Four Factor Cultural Intelligence Scale (CQS)
	CQ2 Emotional Cultural Intelligence	CQ2 Emotional Cultural Intelligence	CQ2 Cognitive Cultural Intelligence	CQ2 Cognitive Cultural Intelligence	
	CQ3 Spiritual Cultural Intelligence	CQ3 Spiritual Cultural Intelligence	CQ3 Motivational Cultural Intelligence	CQ3 Motivational Cultural Intelligence	
			CQ4 Behavioural Cultural Intelligence	CQ4 Behavioural Cultural Intelligence	
ML — Multicultural Leadership	ML1 Conceptual Skills	ML1 Conceptual Skills	ML1 Conceptual Skills	ML3 Conceptual Skills	ML scale based on Robert Katz's structure
	ML2 Interpersonal Skills	ML2 Interpersonal Skills	ML2 Interpersonal Skills	ML2 Interpersonal Skills	
	ML3 Multicultural Skills (Values)	ML3 Multicultural Skills (Values)	ML3 Multicultural Skills (Values)	ML4 Multicultural Skills (Values)	
				ML1 Administrative Skills (Technical skills)	
OC — Organizational Context	Spoken languages; education level; cultural values: were treated within general and demographic questions	OC1 Different Languages	OC1 Different Languages	OC1 Type of company culture	Kim Cameron and Robert Quinn's company type
		OC2 Different educational backgrounds/ behaviours	OC2 Artifacts and Symbols	OC2 Strength Level of company's culture	
		OC3 Different systems of cultural values	OC3 Different educational backgrounds/ patterns of behaviour	OC3 Community and Connection level	
			OC4 Espoused values	OC4 Flexibility and Transparency level	Adaptation of OCA scale
			OC5 Different beliefs and underlying assumptions	OC5 Diversity, Equity and Inclusion level	
				OC6 Agility and Change level	
				OC7 Entrepreneurship, Autonomy and Innovation level	

Source: Author's own research.

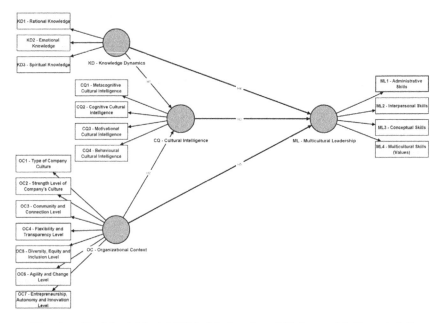

Fig. 5.   Enriched Model With Updated and Enhanced ML and OC Structure (Model 4) – Utilized for Questionnaires. *Source:* Author's own research.

H1. Knowledge dynamics (KD) has a positive impact on cultural intelligence (CQ).

H2. Organizational context (OC) has a positive impact on cultural intelligence (CQ).

H3. Cultural intelligence (CQ) has a positive impact on multicultural leadership (ML).

H4. Knowledge dynamics (KD) has a positive impact on multicultural leadership (ML).

H5. Organizational context (OC) has a positive impact on multicultural leadership (ML).

From this perspective, our study will enlarge its first scope to investigate the impact of CQ and KD on ML and analyze the possible positive correlations between OC-ML, KD-CQ, and OC-CQ.

3.2 Research Strategy: Qualitative Research

We drew upon the extensive specific literature review in order to design our interviews, choosing specific constructs, dimensions, and measurement methods based on our first theoretical model (Model 1). In the pages that follow, we outline our rationale for these choices.

3.2.1 Sample Size: Interviews

For qualitative research, Sandelowski (1995) recommends a sample size of 10 homogenous people interviews; Guest et al. (2006) insist on 15 as the minimum acceptable sample, while Hagaman (2014) found that thematic saturation varied depending on location and discussion order, ranging from 7 to 18 interviews, and Hennink et al. (2016) concluded that code saturation was reached at nine interviews.

The empirical part of this study was based on 15 interviews with multicultural managers that lead diverse origins and cultures teams. This number of interviewees was selected to simultaneously meet the above minimum standards of relevance of Sandelowski M., Guest G., Hagaman A., and Hennink M.

3.2.2 Sampling, Data Collection, and Interviewees Selection

The research was based on an empirical investigation that relied on a qualitative survey through online interviews administered between October 2022 and January 2023.

The selection of the interviewees was based on specific criteria presented below.

The first criterion was ensuring that the interviewee has experience leading multicultural teams. For these criteria, we have prescreened the possible candidates sourced mostly via LinkedIn using the filtering questions presented in Appendix B. On our theme-related resumes, if all three questions were answered with "yes", we moved to the next interview selection stage.

The second criterion was to ensure that the sample includes heterogeneous types of multicultural managers with expertise in various sectors within different business sizes.

Another criterion was geographical, to analyze whether the cultural background or location influences managers' ML views. In this case, interviewees from different continents and countries were recruited: Europe, Asia, North America, and Africa.

3.2.3 Interviews' Process

Potential interviewees were contacted and engaged via online social media and personal networks. They were contacted through social networks like LinkedIn, Facebook, or email. The first contact included a short presentation of the research context and aim and asked for a generic approval of participation from the potential interviewees. Once obtained, the screening filtering questions were shared (Appendix B) to ensure that interviewed candidates have the required knowledge and expertise.

If all questions from Appendix B were answered with "yes," we share the participation consent (Appendix C), and once returned signed, we prepare the interview deployment.

In Fig. 6, we present the data collection and interview process.

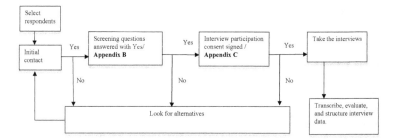

Fig. 6.   Interview Process. *Source:* Author's own research.

The contact process and the reminders were repeated numerous times until we reached a sufficient number of interviewees (15). Selected interviewees that passed the screening question test and shared their consent were sent in advance an email/message with grouped interview questions, presented below, the filtering questions (Appendix B) and the consent form (Appendix C) that explained their rights, the privacy protection of the collected data and how the data are going to be utilized. This way, the interviewees were provided with the opportunity to understand the context of the interview better, proceed to a reflection on its questions, if willing so, and feel complacent and satisfied about the privacy of their participation.

During the 4-month interview process, we initially contacted 140 managers, got refused at first introductory contact by 85, disqualified via screening questions 34, and got 6 refuses at General Data Protection Regulation (GDPR) and consent stage, thus leaving us with our 15 interviewees.

The time span of the interviews was between 30 and 45 minutes, and the process was structured as follows. The interviewer introduced himself and the context and frame of the research and then re-explained the actions and measures taken for the privacy of the collected information, the interviewees' rights to skip a question for data they wish not to disclose, and explained how the interview content would be used (Appendix C). The interviewer also requested the permission of the interviewee to start recording the interview. The next step was to inform the interviewee about the two parts or modules of the interview. The first module was related to collecting and accrual of demographic and generic data, and the second one was linked to our research questions. The language of the interview was English, and all real names were changed into mutually agreed pseudonyms.

The interviews were conducted online using various video platforms such as Zoom or Teams to make respondents more comfortable with the process.

3.2.4 Interview Design and Presentation

The final interview questions are structures into five sections: main demographics, research-specific demographics, CQ-related questions, KD-related questions, and ML-related questions (Table 2).

Table 2. Interview Presentation.

Demographics (General)

Description of Variable	Coding Instructions
Respondent number	Internal allocation
Name or pseudonym	Mutually agreed if pseudonym
Gender	Male = 1, Female = 2, Nonbinary = 3
Age	18–25 = 1, 26–40 = 2, 41–60 = 3, >61 = 4
Education	High School only = 1, University graduate = 2, Master graduate = 3, PhD graduate = 4
Geography	Europe = 1, Asia = 2, Africa = 3, North America = 4, South America = 5, Australia = 6
Country	

Research-Related Demographics

Description of Variable	Coding Instructions
Company sector	Retail = 1; Production = 2; Trade = 3; Services = 4; Others = 5
Company size (turnover)	<0.5 M. euro/year as turnover = 1, $0.5>=x < 1$ M. euro/year = 2, $1<=x < 5$ M. euro = 3, $5>=x < 10$ M. euro = 4, >10M = $x < 50M$ = 5, >=50 m euro = 6
Company size (employees' number)	1–10/11–50/51–100/101–500/501–1,000/ 1,001+ employees
Function	TOP management = 1/Middle Manage = 2/Lower management = 3/
Years of experience within the company	1–3 = 1/3–5 = 2/5–10 = 3/10–15 = 4/>16 = 5
Years of experience in total	1–3 = 1/3–5 = 2/5–10 = 3/10–15 = 4/16–20 = 5/21+ = 6
Number of nationalities managed	1–3 = 1/4–5 = 2/6–10 = 3/11–15 = 4/16–20 = 5/21–50 = 6/51–100 = 7/>100 = 8
Number of spoken languages	One = 1, Two = 2, Three = 3, More than 3 = 4
Number of continents in which the subject worked	One = 1, Two = 2, Three = 3, More than 3 = 4
Number of countries in which the subject worked	One = 1, Two = 2, Three = 3, More than 3 = 4

Table 2. *(Continued)*

(Cultural Intelligence) Questions

CQ	Questions
1.	How do you assess the cultural intelligence of your team members?
2.	How do you leverage your team members' cultural intelligence?
3.	Is there a relationship between the cultural intelligence of your team and your result as a multicultural manager? Please detail.
4.	What is your biggest challenge when dealing with cultural intelligence? Why?

(Knowledge Dynamics) Questions

KD	Questions
5.	Are your decisions based only on data and rational thinking?
6.	Do emotions play any role in your decisions?
7.	Do you consider their cultural values when interacting with people from different cultures? I consider their cultural values.
8.	Do you consider that it is useful to have a proper balance between rational thinking, emotions, and cultural values when making decisions?

(Multicultural Leadership) Questions

ML	Questions
9.	What is your leadership style with a multicultural team? Why?
10.	How do you create trust in your multicultural team?
11.	When assigning tasks, do you consider each team member's cultural background?

Source: Author's own research.

3.2.5 NVivo Methodology and Process – Based on Interviews' Data

Once the process of qualitative data gathering was done, we built a study framework, as shown in Fig. 7, which presents the applied analysis methodology using the NVivo 1.7.1 software, one of the most popular qualitative data management programs today and most pertinent for the exploration and categorization of text-based data, providing code-and-retrieve features (for thematic analysis), as well as functions that permit us to form and build interrelations and

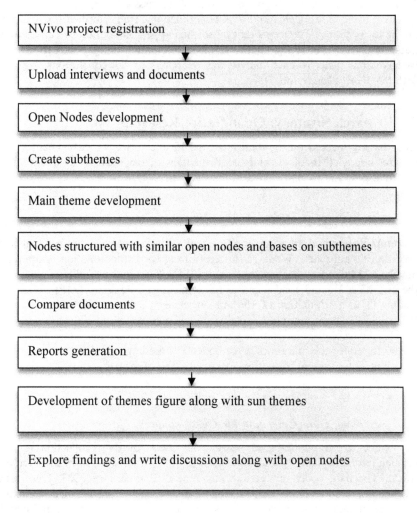

Fig. 7.   NVivo Data Analysis Process. *Source:* Author's own research.

connections between codes and categories of information, from which to construct conceptual frameworks and theories (Tang, 2023).

Finally, data in the form of metadata are preprocessed with Microsoft Excel/ Word and then analyzed using NVivo 1.7.1 software to automatically utilize and separate information in files with sentences, paragraphs, or unique text strings through code, directly decrypted by the abovementioned software. Via NVivo, we determined the pattern (themes, concepts) using emergent context and automatically performed coding and classification to fine-tune the relationships and generate an organized structure.

Below, we present the NVivo data analysis process:

Then, using *Word Cloud* and *TreeMap* functions, we performed text analysis on the list of terms or concepts that most often appear in relation to our research questions, which can reveal themes through automatic coding. Apart from that, we have done the cross-case analysis that supports our first conclusions, together with the *Word Clouds* and *TreeMaps*.

3.3 Research Strategy: Quantitative Research

After having worked on the data from the 15 interviews, we have finalized the research model (Model 4), and based on it, we have started our quantitative research, powered by 396 answered questionnaires.

3.3.1 Sample Size: Questionnaires

We utilized the standard procedure to establish the sample size and have taken a probabilistic approach. We have started from a working population of approximately 3.32 billion people, as reported by ILO (2021) and STATISTA (2021) at the end of 2021, and used a 5% average manager role share (ZIPPIA, 2022), leading us to a population of 166 million leaders. Using a standard confidence level of 95%, a basic margin of error of 5% and a common population proportion of 50%, the recommended sample size was 385. We have increased the sample size to 396 to reduce the margin of error under 5%, landing it at 4.92%.

In Fig. 8, we present the entire working process of the size estimation – backed by calculator.net (a sample size calculator software).

3.3.2 Sampling, Data Collection for Questionnaires

An online questionnaire-based survey was used for data collection among multicultural managers, gathering a number of 396 answers from all over the world. The data collection period was June 2022–February 2023. Our study reached out to potential participants for the questionnaire through targeted online social media and personal connections such as LinkedIn, Facebook, and email. For Romania, Malta, and Saudi Arabia, the three countries I worked and lived in during the last 5 years, the questionnaires were distributed via my professional network of multicultural managers, self-administered and without open-ended

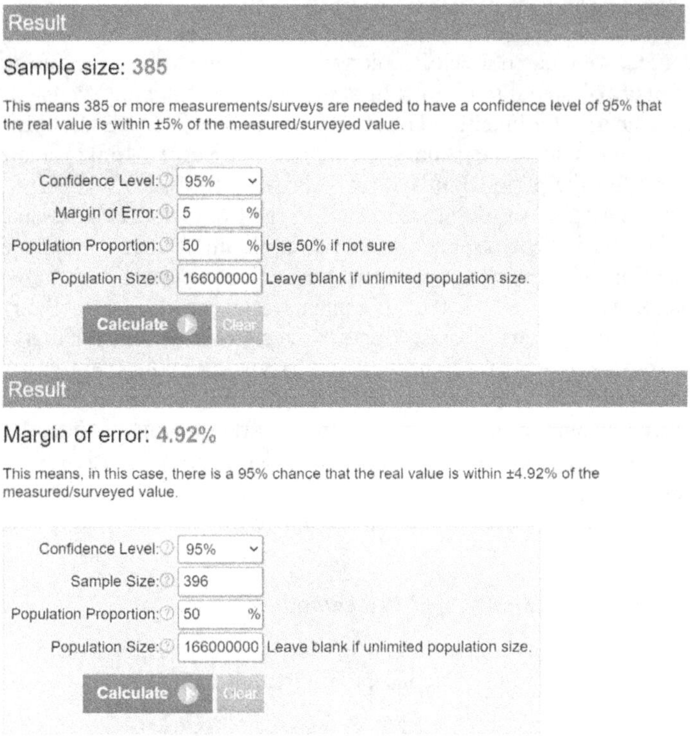

Fig. 8.   Sample Size Calculation Based on Calculator.net. *Source:*
Author's own analysis.

questions. Besides, the snowball technique was used to gather and register 42 valid responses (via Google Forms), accounting for 10.6% of our established sampling.

For the remaining 354 results, we have also utilized SurveyMonkey, a worldwide recognized platform for professional online surveys. The selected criteria for the SurveyMonkey data collection were age more than 18 years old, all continents mixed spread (excluding the already analyzed countries: Romania, Malta, and Saudi Arabia), and manager role.

The valid response recovery rate, all considered without any missing data, was 89.14% (396 valid and recorded answers from 439).

Before sending the questionnaire, a pretest was done to check it and eliminate any possible issues or misunderstandings.

The questionnaire was distributed to three coworkers with multicultural management roles and skills, who were also asked to provide feedback. Their suggestions were taken into account with respect to the clarity of instructions, question difficulty, and estimated completion time. As a result, minor adjustments were made. On average, it took them 10 minutes to finish the questionnaire.

3.3.3 Questionnaires' Process

As presented, we created an electronic version of the questionnaire using Google Forms and distributed it to multicultural managers in Romania, Malta, and Saudi Arabia via email or LinkedIn. The survey administration period began on June 20th, 2022, and ended on February 15th, 2023. The SurveyMonkey answers were collected within the period January 1st–February 3rd, 2023.

The questionnaire was developed based on the five hypotheses presented in this section. Each variable was represented by a minimum of three and a maximum of seven questions evaluating the intrinsic connections between each variable. The participants were given a set of statements and asked to rate their level of agreement or disagreement on a 7-point Likert scale (except demographic and Kim Cameron and Robert Quinn's company-type questions) (Fig. 9).

The questionnaire had an instruction part in which we mentioned the scope of the project and enhanced on the voluntary participation, confidentiality, and GDPR concerns and benefits of the study. A detailed presentation is exposed in addendum J, where we have stipulated that answering the questionnaire will represent the consent in regards to all the above mentions.

3.3.4 Questionnaire' Design and Presentation

The questionnaire, as presented in Fig. 10, has 76 questions divided into six sections that contribute to our conceptual research model.

Section 1	Section 2	Section 3	Section 4	Section 5	Section 6
Composed by 5 questions and supporting the building of the generic demographic variable (such as age, gender or education level).	Composed by 11 questions and supporting the building of the research-related demographic variable (such as number of managed nationalities or number of spoken languages).	Composed by 20 questions and supporting the building of the CQ variable.	Composed by 9 questions and supporting the building of the KD variable.	Composed by 12 questions and supporting the building of the ML variable.	Composed by 19 questions and supporting the building of the OC variable.
		Rooted on the Cultural Intelligence Scale (CQS).	KD scale rooted on the work developed by professor Bratianu.	ML scale based on Robert Katz's structure.	Kim Cameron and Robert Quinn's company type and adaptation of OCA scale.

Fig. 9.   Questionnaire – Building Phase. *Source:* Author's own research.

Demographics (general)

Description of variable	Coding instructions
Gender:	Male= **1**, Female=**2**, Non-binary=**3**
Age:	18-25= **1**, 26-40 =**2**, 41-60= **3**, >61=**4**
Education level:	High School only = **1**, University graduate =**2**, Master Graduate= **3**, PhD graduate = **4**
Geography (actual living continent):	Europe = **1**, Asia =**2**, Africa= **3**, North America = **4**, South America = **5**, Australia=**6**
Country (actual living country):	....

Research-related demographics

Description of variable	Coding instructions
Company's main sector:	Retail=**1**; Production =**2**; Trade =**3**; Services =**4**; Other =**5**
Company's size (company's yearly turnover in Millions €):	<0.5 M. €/year as turnover = **1**, 0.5>=x<1 M. €/year = **2**, 1 M. <=x<5 M. €/year =**3**, 5 M.>=x<10 M. €/ year =**4**, >10M=x<50M €/year =**5**, >=50 M. €/year = **6**
Company size (employees' number):	1-10 = **1** / 11-50 = **2**/ 51-100 =**3** / 101-500 = **4**/ 501 -1000 =**5**/ 1001+ employees =**6**
Function (from a management level point of view):	TOP management=**1** / Middle Manage=**2** / Lower management=**3** /
Years of experience within the company:	1-3 = **1**/ 4-5 =**2**/ 6-10=**3** / 11-15 = **4**/ >16=**5**
Years of experience in total	1-3 = **1**/ 4-5 =**2**/ 6-10=**3** / 11-15 = **4**/ 16-20 = **5** / 21+=**6**
Number of managed nationalities:	1-3 = **1**/ 4-5 =**2**/ 6-10=**3** / 11-15 = **4**/ 16-20 = **5** / 21-50=**6** / 51-100 =**7**/ >100 = **8**
Number of spoken languages:	One=**1**, Two= **2**, Three=**3**, More than 3 =**4and**
Number of continents in which you worked:	One=**1**, Two= **2**, Three=**3**, More than 3 =**4**
Number of countries in which you worked:	One=**1**, Two= **2**, Three=**3**, More than 3 =**4**
Experience in managing virtual teams:	No experience =**1** / 1-2 years' experience =**2** / 3-4 years' experience = **3** / 5+ years' experience = **4**

(Cultural Intelligence) scale
Instructions: select the response that best describes your capabilities.
Choose the answer that BEST describes you AS YOU REALLY ARE (1=strongly disagree; 7=strongly agree).

CQ	Description of variable	Coding instructions
Metacognitive CQ / CQ-Strategy		
MCQ1	I am aware of the cultural knowledge I should use when interacting with	1,2,3,4,5,6,7 (where 1 = strongly disagree and 7 = strongly agree)

Fig. 10.   The Utilized Questionnaire.
Source: Author's own research.

	people from different cultural backgrounds.	
MCQ2	I adjust my cultural knowledge as I interact with people from a culture that is unfamiliar to me.	1,2,3,4,5,6,7 (where 1 = strongly disagree and 7 = strongly agree)
MCQ3	I am conscious of the cultural knowledge I apply to cross-cultural interactions.	1,2,3,4,5,6,7 (where 1 = strongly disagree and 7 = strongly agree)
MCQ4	I check the accuracy of my cultural knowledge as I interact with people from different cultures.	1,2,3,4,5,6,7 (where 1 = strongly disagree and 7 = strongly agree)
Cognitive CQ / CQ Knowledge		
COCQ1	I know the legal and economic systems of other cultures.	1,2,3,4,5,6,7 (where 1 = strongly disagree and 7 = strongly agree)
COCQ2	I know the rules (e.g., vocabulary, grammar) of other languages.	1,2,3,4,5,6,7 (where 1 = strongly disagree and 7 = strongly agree)
COCQ3	I know the cultural values and religious beliefs of other cultures.	1,2,3,4,5,6,7 (where 1 = strongly disagree and 7 = strongly agree)
COCQ4	I know the marriage systems of other cultures.	1,2,3,4,5,6,7 (where 1 = strongly disagree and 7 = strongly agree)
COCQ5	I know the arts and crafts of other cultures.	1,2,3,4,5,6,7 (where 1 = strongly disagree and 7 = strongly agree)
COCQ6	I know the rules for expressing non-verbal behaviours in other cultures.	1,2,3,4,5,6,7 (where 1 = strongly disagree and 7 = strongly agree)
Motivational CQ / CQ Motivation		
MOTCQ1	I enjoy interacting with people from different cultures.	1,2,3,4,5,6,7 (where 1 = strongly disagree and 7 = strongly agree)
MOTCQ2	I am confident that I can socialize with locals in a culture that is unfamiliar to me.	1,2,3,4,5,6,7 (where 1 = strongly disagree and 7 = strongly agree)
MOTCQ3	I can deal with the stresses of adjusting to a culture that is new to me.	1,2,3,4,5,6,7 (where 1 = strongly disagree and 7 = strongly agree)
MOTCQ4	I enjoy living in cultures that are unfamiliar to me.	1,2,3,4,5,6,7 (where 1 = strongly disagree and 7 = strongly agree)
MOTCQ5	I am confident that I can get accustomed to the shopping conditions in a different culture.	1,2,3,4,5,6,7 (where 1 = strongly disagree and 7 = strongly agree)

Fig. 10. *(Continued)*.

Behavioural CQ/ CQ-Behaviour		
BEHCQ1	I change my verbal behaviour (e.g.,, accent, tone) when a cross-cultural interaction requires it.	1,2,3,4,5,6,7 (where 1 = strongly disagree and 7 = strongly agree)
BEHCQ2	I use pause and silence differently to suit different cross-cultural situations.	1,2,3,4,5,6,7 (where 1 = strongly disagree and 7 = strongly agree)
BEHCQ3	I vary the rate of my speaking when a cross-cultural situation requires it.	1,2,3,4,5,6,7 (where 1 = strongly disagree and 7 = strongly agree)
BEHCQ4	I change my non-verbal behaviour when a cross-cultural interaction requires it.	1,2,3,4,5,6,7 (where 1 = strongly disagree and 7 = strongly agree)
BEHCQ5	I alter my facial expressions when a cross-cultural interaction requires it.	1,2,3,4,5,6,7 (where 1 = strongly disagree and 7 = strongly agree)

(Knowledge Dynamics) scale
Instructions: select the response that best describes your capabilities.
Choose the answer that BEST describes you AS YOU REALLY ARE (1=strongly disagree; 7=strongly agree).

KD	Description of variable	Coding instructions
Rational Knowledge (RK) (reflective construct)		
RKD1	I use to take action starting from objective and data-based arguments.	1,2,3,4,5,6,7 (where 1 = strongly disagree and 7 = strongly agree)
RKD2	I rely on rational thinking when I am confronted with new business challenges.	1,2,3,4,5,6,7 (where 1 = strongly disagree and 7 = strongly agree)
RKD3	Whenever I have a strange feeling about a situation, I analyze the data and the methods used more systematically.	1,2,3,4,5,6,7 (where 1 = strongly disagree and 7 = strongly agree)
Emotional Knowledge (EK) [reflective construct]		
EKD1	I use to trust my feelings when dealing with different business issues.	1,2,3,4,5,6,7 (where 1 = strongly disagree and 7 = strongly agree)
EKD2	My intuition generates many good business ideas.	1,2,3,4,5,6,7 (where 1 = strongly disagree and 7 = strongly agree)
EKD3	I use empathy in dealing with people from other cultures.	1,2,3,4,5,6,7 (where 1 = strongly disagree and 7 = strongly agree)
Spiritual Knowledge (SK) [reflective construct]		
SK1	I am open to establishing sustainable professional connections/ agreements with business partners sharing the same cultural values.	1,2,3,4,5,6,7 (where 1 = strongly disagree and 7 = strongly agree)

Fig. 10. *(Continued).*

SK2	My personal values guide me in interpreting data and distinguishing between solutions.	1,2,3,4,5,6,7 (where 1 = strongly disagree and 7 = strongly agree)
SK3	My spiritual values and principles first screen my managerial decisions.	1,2,3,4,5,6,7 (where 1 = strongly disagree and 7 = strongly agree)

(Multicultural Leadership) scale

Instructions: select the response that best describes your capabilities.

Choose the answer that BEST describes you AS YOU REALLY ARE (1=strongly disagree; 7=strongly agree).

ML	Description of variable	Coding instructions
(Administrative skills)		
AS1	Managing people and resources is one of my strengths.	1,2,3,4,5,6,7 (where 1 = strongly disagree and 7 = strongly agree)
AS2	Filling out forms and working with details come easily to me.	1,2,3,4,5,6,7 (where 1 = strongly disagree and 7 = strongly agree)
AS3	I am effective at obtaining and allocating resources to support all business requirements.	1,2,3,4,5,6,7 (where 1 = strongly disagree and 7 = strongly agree)
(Interpersonal skills)		
IS1	Understanding the social fabric of the organization is important to me.	1,2,3,4,5,6,7 (where 1 = strongly disagree and 7 = strongly agree)
IS2	I use my emotional energy to motivate others.	1,2,3,4,5,6,7 (where 1 = strongly disagree and 7 = strongly agree)
IS3	I work hard to find consensus in conflict situations.	1,2,3,4,5,6,7 (where 1 = strongly disagree and 7 = strongly agree)
(Conceptual skills).		
CS1	I am effective at problem-solving.	1,2,3,4,5,6,7 (where 1 = strongly disagree and 7 = strongly agree)
CS2	Seeing the big picture comes easily to me.	1,2,3,4,5,6,7 (where 1 = strongly disagree and 7 = strongly agree)
CS3	Making strategic plans for my company appeals to me.	1,2,3,4,5,6,7 (where 1 = strongly disagree and 7 = strongly agree)
Multicultural leadership skills		
ML1	I actively recruit or wish to recruit persons of multicultural origins.	1,2,3,4,5,6,7 (where 1 = strongly disagree and 7 = strongly agree)

Fig. 10. *(Continued)*.

ML2	I encourage or wish to encourage in the proper context - persons of multicultural origin to develop professionally and lead.	1,2,3,4,5,6,7 (where 1 = strongly disagree and 7 = strongly agree)
ML3	I value multicultural diversity as a source of progress	1,2,3,4,5,6,7 (where 1 = strongly disagree and 7 = strongly agree)

(Organizational Context)

TC	Description of variable	Coding instructions
Type of company culture. According to business professors **Robert E. Quinn and Kim Cameron**, no corporate culture is as straightforward as being "good" or "bad", just distinct. They identified four types of cultures: clan culture, adhocracy culture, market culture, and hierarchy culture. Taking into account the below, please choose the company culture that best represents your organization:		
Type 1: Clan culture Clan cultures offer a friendly working environment where relationships, morale, participation, and consensus take center stage. In terms of leadership, managers are looked to as mentors. **Type 2: Adhocracy culture** This type of culture lives by that "move fast and break things" philosophy that's been popular among many startups. It is a very entrepreneurial environment where employees are encouraged to take risks and aggressively pursue off-the-wall ideas. As a result, much innovation, learning, and growth occur. **Type 3: Market culture** Emphasis is placed on results. Employees are highly goal-focused, and leaders are challenging and demanding to achieve the success metrics the company has defined. **Type 4: Hierarchy culture** A hierarchy applies to work environments that are more structured and process-oriented. Most activities and decisions are dictated by existing procedures rather than a lot of innovation and freethinking. Leaders are in place to ensure that their teams run like well-oiled machines, and they place the bulk of their focus on stability, results, and reliable delivery.		1,2,3,4 (where **1** = clan culture; **2** = adhocracy culture; **3** = market culture; **4** = hierarchy culture)
Instructions: select the response that best describes your capabilities.		
Choose the answer that BEST describes you AS YOU REALLY ARE (1=strongly disagree; 7=strongly agree).		

Fig. 10. *(Continued)*.

SL	Description of variable	Coding instructions
Strength level of the company's culture (the connection employees feel to their work)		
SL1	I feel connected to the work I do.	1,2,3,4,5,6,7 (where 1 = strongly disagree and 7 = strongly agree)
SL2	I am motivated by the mission of the company.	1,2,3,4,5,6,7 (where 1 = strongly disagree and 7 = strongly agree)
SL3	All managers share the same goals of/for the company as their teams.	1,2,3,4,5,6,7 (where 1 = strongly disagree and 7 = strongly agree)
Community and connection level		
CCL1	I do feel a sense of belonging at work.	1,2,3,4,5,6,7 (where 1 = strongly disagree and 7 = strongly agree)
CCL2	I am recognized and appreciated for my professional contributions.	1,2,3,4,5,6,7 (where 1 = strongly disagree and 7 = strongly agree)
CCL3	I do experience loyalty and trust while working at this company.	1,2,3,4,5,6,7 (where 1 = strongly disagree and 7 = strongly agree)
(Flexibility and transparency level		
FTL1	Leaders and managers are transparent in sharing all work-related information.	1,2,3,4,5,6,7 (where 1 = strongly disagree and 7 = strongly agree)
FTL2	My work schedule is flexible enough to meet family and personal responsibilities.	1,2,3,4,5,6,7 (where 1 = strongly disagree and 7 = strongly agree)
FTL3	I am always heard and understood at work.	1,2,3,4,5,6,7 (where 1 = strongly disagree and 7 = strongly agree)
Diversity, equity, and inclusion level		
DEIL1	The organization prioritizes diversity, equity, and inclusion.	1,2,3,4,5,6,7 (where 1 = strongly disagree and 7 = strongly agree)
DEIL2	I do know where and how to report concerns about harassment and discrimination.	1,2,3,4,5,6,7 (where 1 = strongly disagree and 7 = strongly agree)

Fig. 10. *(Continued)*.

DEIL3	Our company respects and values people from all cultures and backgrounds.	1,2,3,4,5,6,7 (where 1 = strongly disagree and 7 = strongly agree)
Agility and change level		
AC1	Things change fast enough in my company, placing us ahead of the average of our activity sector.	1,2,3,4,5,6,7 (where 1 = strongly disagree and 7 = strongly agree)
AC2	When managing change, I have the information and tools to adapt quickly and agilely.	1,2,3,4,5,6,7 (where 1 = strongly disagree and 7 = strongly agree)
AC3	The management teams are early change adopters in the organization.	1,2,3,4,5,6,7 (where 1 = strongly disagree and 7 = strongly agree)
Entrepreneurship, autonomy, and innovation level		
EAU1	The entrepreneurial spirit is encouraged.	1,2,3,4,5,6,7 (where 1 = strongly disagree and 7 = strongly agree)
EAU2	Employees and management take risks to achieve better results.	1,2,3,4,5,6,7 (where 1 = strongly disagree and 7 = strongly agree)
EAU3	Employees have the autonomy to complete tasks with little guidance.	1,2,3,4,5,6,7 (where 1 = strongly disagree and 7 = strongly agree)

Fig. 10. *(Continued)*.

3.3.5 Statistical Software Package for Social Sciences (SPSS) and Partial Least Squares (PLS)-SEM Methodology and Process – Based on Questionnaires' Data

The goal was to verify the previously described model by analyzing coded data statistically using IBM SPSS Statistics version 29 software. The questionnaires' responses were compared to the hypothesis via factor analysis and regression. Correlation computations between the original variables were performed to check the validity of variables, and Cronbach's Alpha's analysis was carried out for reliability testing or internal consistency (Walonick, 2010).

PLS-SEM is a statistical technique commonly used in academic research for modeling and testing complex structural relationships between variables. One advantage of PLS-SEM is that it can handle both reflective and formative measurement models, allowing for the analysis of both latent and observed variables (Hair et al., 2021). We have utilized PLS-SEM to test our five researched hypotheses and investigate the role and impact of CQ, KD, and OC on ML and the ones of OC on CQ and KD on CQ. First, the measurement model and model fit were evaluated, and then, the structural model estimation was analyzed using the bootstrapping method.

More in-depth analyses of the above two mentioned and utilized software sequence and applied methodology will be provided within the introductory parts of the study's results.

Chapter 4

Qualitative Research Results

4.1 Introduction and Technical Processes

This study investigates how cultural intelligence (CQ) and knowledge dynamics (KD) impact multicultural managers' decisions. We have adopted a thematic content investigation for the analysis of 15 interviews. After familiarization with the interview results, the data were imported into NVivo 1.7.1. Then, we proceeded with the coding, which involved assigning summative labels to the participants' responses. Next, we did the code review, ensuring that the appropriate summative labels were assigned to the participants' responses. The codes were themed deductively under the various constructs for the study. For KD, the constructs are rational knowledge, emotional knowledge, and spiritual knowledge. For CQ, the constructs are rational CQ, emotional CQ, and spiritual CQ. For multicultural leadership (ML), the constructs are conceptual skills, interpersonal skills, and multicultural skills (values). To be mentioned that organizational context (OC) construct was not part of this analyze but a result of the workings, and it will be integrated into the quantitative analyze. Codes that did not fall under these constructs were themed inductively. Lastly, the themes were reviewed and reported. The cross-case and network analyses were also performed.

4.2 First Findings and Results Using Content Analysis and Word Cloud

The results of the content analysis linked to word clouds will be treated bellow.

4.2.1 CQ-Related Results From Content and Word Cloud Analysis

This subtheme elaborates on how leaders leveraged their CQ for decision-making in a multicultural workspace.

4.2.1.1 Emotional CQ

This subtheme highlights the emotional CQ of the leaders in multicultural workspaces. It focuses on how multicultural leaders assess emotional cultural

Developing Multicultural Leadership using Knowledge Dynamics and Cultural Intelligence, 47–96
Copyright © 2024 Dan Paiuc
Published under exclusive licence by Emerald Publishing Limited
doi:10.1108/978-1-83549-432-520241008

Fig. 1.   Word Cloud of Emotional Cultural Intelligence. *Source:*
Author's own research.

intelligence through interaction and communication, leverage it for more significant results, and view emotional CQ issues as challenges (Fig. 1).

4.2.1.1.1 Assessing CQ Through Emotional Intelligence Metrics. Eleven of the participants spoke about how they assess the CQ of their participants through emotional intelligence metrics like acceptance, communication, and social interactions. Participant 6 said:

> We have included in our yearly evaluations a cultural intelligence tracker to identify progress and to be capable to assigned professional missions to the best and most agile colleagues. The tracker is based on . . . acceptance and adaptability as an answer to different business requirements.

Participant 6 assesses CQ based on metrics like acceptance and adaptability in order to be able to assign professional missions linked to the emotional CQ of team members. Although Participant 3 focuses more on skill sets, he still assesses his team's CQ based on the teams' interaction with clients. Participant 3 described his method of assessing CQ as follows: "I review their work and analyse the clients' feedback regarding each team member's actions and interactions. This gave me a global view of their work and applied cultural intelligence...I analyse the clients' feedback regarding each team member's actions and interactions." Participant 7 also evaluates CQ through personal interactions. To assess the CQ of team members, Participant 7 has "... targeted 1:1 evaluations and coaching sessions with them every quarter." Participant 9 assesses team members' CQ through "personal interactions" on a "daily and weekly basis." Participant 1 described how the 360' review by coworkers is his preferred mode of assessing the team members' emotional CQ. In the words of Participant 1:

> I used to work with the cultural intelligence scale developed by Yang, but nowadays, I use a 360' review (developed by Gallup) that helps me assess the cultural and emotional intelligence level of all my team members. Meaning that each employee in our company is assessed by matrix colleagues, direct managers and subordinates.

In the same light, Participant 15 states, "by interacting with other colleagues during any project, I can see how quickly they are making new friends and how fast they are adopting new foods." This means that Participant 15 also assesses team members' CQ based on the team member's interactions with others. Conversations with team members are also a method of assessing CQ, as Participant 2 said: "I used to do Conversations with the team members to assess their experience and knowledge...." Participant 8 also assesses the CQ of team members through her interactions with her team, "I approach my team members in a friendly and informal way to learn about their cultural values and develop my understanding and their regard." Communication is a main way of assessing the team member's skills and experience, as stated by Participant 13: "I used to heavy communicate with the team members to assess their experience and skills. Never insisted on assessing their cultural intelligence on a routine basis." According to Participant 11: "Our company has a specific questionnaire, and everyone must fill it out while hiring ... As a team head, I have got a clear idea through the results report of the questionnaire about the cultural and emotional intelligence level of my team members." Participant 11's company assesses employees' CQ based on a questionnaire's emotional and CQ metrics.

4.2.1.1.2 Leverage Emotional CQ for Company Result. Five participants spoke about leveraging the emotional CQ of their team for assigning tasks and, subsequently, for generating better results for their companies. The emotional CQ of team members is used to allocate tasks to the team members based on their strengths in the aspect as elaborated by Participant 1: "After assessing each team member's cultural and emotional intelligence level, I allocate them the tasks and roles based on their cultural agility, experience and expertise." The tasks are allocated to the team members based on their cultural agility experience and resultant expertise. Participant 6 spoke on leveraging CQ in interacting with clients in cross-cultural encounters for best results. Participant 6 said: "The same goes for my multinational team; we all use appropriate verbal and nonverbal behaviour in cross-cultural encounters. This will allow us to be agile and ready to overpass any cultural differences that might appear with various business partners." Participant 15 leverages the CQ of his team "through social events. ..." Most social events create opportunities for informal interaction where emotional CQ would be needed. Firms leverage the emotional CQ of team members to enable better results for the company. Participant 15 expatiated on this: "Yes, I think so. Being respectable and conscious of every culture enhances both my and the company's global results." Participant 2 explained how the various members of his team and himself respect every cultural background and tradition for better results. Participant 2 said: "Yes, my team members always care about each other's cultural values, and I always consider their cultural backgrounds. Taking cultural heritage into account helps my business succeed," for better performance and improved overall results.

4.2.1.1.3 Viewing Emotional CQ Issues as Challenges. When asked about the most significant challenge faced with CQ, seven participants focused on emotional CQ issues as a challenge. This latently shows that the participants prioritize emotional CQ. This subtheme delves into the view of the leaders of multicultural workspaces on challenges faced in terms of the emotional CQ of team members. Participant 10 highlighted that the biggest issue encountered in dealing with CQ is accepting the opinions of others, as he stated: "The biggest challenge when dealing with cultural intelligence is accepting others' opinions." Being able to accept and respect others' opinions is integral for successful interaction with people and is, therefore, an "emotional cultural intelligence issue."

People from various cultural backgrounds react and respond to situations in different ways. It becomes challenging to make these people of diverse CQ work together. Participant 2 said: "My biggest challenge is a behavioural difference. I have a small, diverse team, and each team member reacts differently to the same situation based on their culture. Nevertheless, I am always telling the team that customers expect the best services from us – no matter our cultural intelligence." Similarly, Kristain Skovrider commented that: "My biggest challenge is to get different people to work together for the same common goal." Participant 7's challenge is based on communication. For Participant 7, providing the right feedback to his team members in regards Canadian work practices and Canadians' feelings might pose a challenge. Participant 7 said his biggest challenge as regards CQ is: "Providing the right feedback to my team members so that they understand Canadian work practices or how Canadian people are feeling." This cultural and emotional barrier poses a challenge to the results of the team and might impact the results of the company. The varying attitude of individual team members toward work due to their cultural differences serves as a challenge, as said by Participant 13: "This is not a big challenge, but I must mention that all the members have different temperaments regarding work and attitudes toward other colleagues." This is an emotional intelligence issue as it requires emotional CQ to work with people from diverse cultures with diverse temperaments. Managing the diversity of the various team members may also pose a challenge, as stated by Participant 12: "So, my biggest challenge would be managing diversity." Managing the various ethnic diversity can be challenging, according to the participant. In dealing with CQ interconnections, the level of conscious cultural awareness of various members of the team poses a challenge. This was detailed by Participant 6: "The level of conscious cultural awareness during interactions is my biggest challenge when dealing with CQ interconnections." Individual team members possess varying levels of CQ, which can become more evident in direct interactions.

4.2.1.2 Rational CQ

This subtheme focuses on rational CQ concerning multicultural leaders assessing CQ through knowledge of other cultures, assigning tasks based on knowledge of culture and leveraging team members' CQ by actively learning about their culture (Fig. 2).

4.2.1.2.1 Assessing CQ Through Knowledge and Experience of Other Cultures. Six participants focused on being knowledgeable about clients' and team members' cultures. Participant 12 sought more knowledge about the culture of employees from the internet: "I research on the internet about his/her cultural, social and religious background. So, I like to know their values and culture before I meet them or start working with them. That helps me in assessing their cultural intelligence but also in leveraging it." Knowing about the culture of his team helps

Fig. 2.   Word Cloud of Rational Cultural Intelligence. *Source:* Author's own research.

Participant 12 assess their CQ. Participant 2 spoke on how he engages in conversations with team members to assess their knowledge of culture: "I used to do conversations with the team members to assess their experience and knowledge. during these conversations, we also touch base with the cultural differences and see how this could be best utilised in the business's needs." Participant 6 uses yearly evaluations based on knowledge to evaluate the CQ of team members. "We have included in our yearly evaluations a CQ tracker to identify progress and to be capable to assigned professional missions to the best and most agile colleagues. The tracker is based on knowledge." Experiencing others' cultures can make team members more knowledgeable about the cultures. Participant 10 elaborated on this, saying: "Saudi Arabia is a country with many cultural backgrounds due to a state talent attraction policy from all over the world. I asses my team members' cultural intelligence and skills by giving them the same task and evaluating their different results. This will allow me to see how cultural background influences business outcomes and results." Participant 5 assesses CQ by checking team members' experience and knowledge. In her words: "I check their skills, experiences and knowledge on an everyday basis. Their culture should impact and influence in smaller or bigger proportions all the above." Participant 7 also focuses on knowledge for assessment as he asks for their "cultural background and prior experiences – and give them an overview of clients' situations and Canadian work culture." Participant 7, therefore, focuses on being knowledgeable about team members' cultural backgrounds and further educates his team members on the Canadian work culture and mandatory professional ground base.

4.2.1.2.2 Leverage Rational CQ for Results. Nine participants leveraged rational CQ for a better result for the company. Seven of these participants assign tasks or clients to their team based on their knowledge and experience of other cultures. Participant 3 mentioned that: "After I check their skill sets and past experiences, I assign the best capability to tasks/clients." In the case of Participant 4, he indicated that since their business is done internationally, they allocate team members to familiar regions: "We do international business so try to get them involved in a country or region with familiar cultural background." To illustrate this point, Participant 8 said: "By giving them the tasks, they are good at" and added "or engaging them with clients they are more likely from a cultural point of view" in order to show how tasks are assigned to team members. Participant 9 simply said: "By trying to align their cultural strengths with tasks to be allocated." This is an effective allocation method as it focuses on each team member's individual CQ strengths. Participant 10 assigns the right task to the right cultural backgrounds. Participant 10 leverages CQ: "By allocating the right culture and skills to the right task." Still, on the subject, Participant 11 added: "After this questionnaire, as I know the cultural ... level of any of my team members – I might try to leveraged added value in the task allocation process. However, the main principles in the task's allocations are experience and expertise." This shows that to Participant 11, experiencing other peoples' cultures, one would be more knowledgeable and fitter for a task with clients of the experienced culture. Participant 12 expressed how the CQ of team members is leveraged to allocate tasks to members of the team: "I leverage the cultural intelligence of my team by assessing what every team member brings to the table from a cultural point of view and then by allocating tasks accordingly to these added value competencies."

Learning about the individual cultures of team members and clients is a way of leveraging rational CQ for results. This method was spoken about by Participant 6 as he stated: "First, I take an active interest in learning about other cultures; and seek information on any required local context." The acquired knowledge can then be leveraged for better performance and results. Leveraging rational CQ for results is an effective method of optimizing performance as a multicultural manager, as explained by Participant 11: "Yes, it is a clear relationship between the cultural intelligence of my team and my result as a multicultural manager. Not understanding the cultural needs of our customers – will impact my results – so my team should be skilled in tracking, understanding and accomplishing all clients' needs." The significance of leveraging rational CQ as a multicultural manager was expatiated on by Participant 12 as he explained that: "It is a significant relationship – because I believe that not everyone is suitable for a particular job, so I have to choose specific jobs to allocate to certain people. The mix between the right choice of tasks and the right cultural intelligence background will determine my success as a manager." This relationship was also described by Participant 4: "Yes, I need to learn about my business partners' cultures to gain their trust; also, my clients are multicultural, and I know that they are doing the same. Also, I encourage my team to follow international news from the regions where we have developed partnerships. This will bring better mutual understanding and better bottom-line results." Speaking on how being a multicultural manager can be leveraged in terms of rational CQ, Kristain Skovrider stated that: "I believe that you learn from the differences, and better results will appear if leveraged." Participant 6 explained how leveraging on the diverse CQ of team members can make for better results as he stated: "Yes – As an inclusive leader, I empower individuals as well as leverage the thinking of diverse cultural and social groups. This is not only the company's internal policy but also better results enhancer" to this end. Leveraging the thinking of diverse cultural and social groups shows that one has learned about the thought patterns of others' cultures and social groups.

4.2.1.2.3 Viewing Rational CQ Issues as Challenges. When asked about the biggest challenge faced with CQ, six participants focused on rational CQ issues as a challenge. This latently shows that the participants prioritize rational CQ. Participant 4 identified stereotyping as major and generalized belief as a major cultural intelligence issue.: "Stereotypes and generalized beliefs about a particular group or class of people are the most significant changes when dealing with CQ." This challenge is based on knowledge of others' cultures, as generalized belief is having surface knowledge of other people's cultures without really researching for proper and structured information. Educating team members on Canadian work culture is the biggest challenge faced by Participant 7. He said, "Providing the right feedback to my team members so that they understand Canadian work practices" is the biggest challenge. Lack of knowledge of different cultures is a challenge when dealing with CQ for Participant 9. To him, the biggest challenge is: a "Lack of knowledge of respective cultures. You do not know how to get the maximum out of a person at the beginning unless you understand a bit about their culture and social background." Understanding the language of other cultures is a challenge to Participant 8. She said, "Language, sometimes things are lost in translations. So specific actions/moments/plans need to be explained in detail, and feedback from team members is a must in order to check their understanding level."

Managing diversity is a problem because different people understand the task differently. A significant challenge may arise as different people from different cultural backgrounds understand the same task differently, as described by Participant 11 saying: "While working with different nationalities, the different personalities management and the various understandings of the same procedure are my significant challenges." Similarly, Participant 12 commented on this subject, expressing that: "...various understandings of the same task. That is why I let my team members know from the very beginning what is expected so that everyone can work towards the same goals, despite cultural background" as he endeavors to bypass this by eloquently stating what is expected of them from the task at hand.

4.2.1.3 Spiritual CQ

This subtheme describes how multicultural leaders leverage spiritual CQ for results and view spiritual CQ issues as in their multicultural workspace (Fig. 3).

4.2.1.3.1 Leverages on Spiritual CQ. Explicitly, only one participant leveraged the team's spiritual CQ. Participant 15 said he leverages the CQ of the team members "...monitored team ambiance." "Ambience" could be extrapolated and considered as spiritual as it focuses on the "aura" or "feel" of an environment.

4.2.1.3.2 View Spiritual CQ Issues as Challenges. When asked about the biggest challenge faced with CQ, four participants focused on spiritual CQ issues as a challenge. This latently shows that the participants prioritize spiritual CQ. Participant 15 focused on the "value" as a CQ challenge. Participant 15 expressed his fear of hurting team members' personal beliefs. He was quoted saying: "My biggest challenge when dealing with cultural intelligence is not to hurt any personal beliefs ... It is important not to disrespect any cultural experiences because it is linked to previous roots and might affect productivity in the actual workplace." For Participant 1, the difference in personal intrinsic values is the biggest challenge: "My biggest challenge is portrayed by the business etiquette differences between Arab culture & European culture. Leading a team composed mainly of Arabic country members and dealing with European customers – forced me to learn and develop specific European business tactics and approaches. One is the pricing construct, where Europeans prefer a less negotiated option – so my first proposal is close to my target price." The difference in work value is a challenging face of the topic, according to Participant 14. He expressed this: "...I must say, because people have different mindsets regarding work. So, Asian people like to work harder than Europeans, but on the other hand, Europeans are generally considered more honest regarding the work done than Asians. Asian people waste

Fig. 3.   Word Cloud of Spiritual Cultural Intelligence. *Source:*
Author's own research.

more time not effectively working while European people are strict on time and very efficient. So, it is a challenge to understand each individual approach toward work." Therefore, understanding individual team members' approaches toward work might address and solve a problem in dealing with CQ.

4.2.1.3.3 Downplays CQ for Team Culture. Some multicultural leaders downplay CQ by focusing on skill sets and shared understanding of tasks rather than leveraging the CQ of team members (Fig. 4).

According to Participant 13, "…all the members should have the same skill set, so it does not matter where they belong or what are their cultural values." The CQ of the team is not of importance to Participant 13. "I've never had to do that" was the response of Participant 13 to the question of how he leverages the CQ of the team members. Similarly, Participant 14 stated that he does not assess or leverage the CQ of team members but focuses on their skills. In Participant 14's words, "I prepare assessment tasks, allocate them to team members, and evaluate everyone's results … We do not judge people on their personality. We do an assessment based on skill." According to Participant 7, individual CQ is not

Fig. 4.   Word Cloud of Downplays Cultural Intelligence for Team
Culture. *Source:* Author's own research.

integral to task performance: "Through the work that we carry out via meetings, workshops, and sessions – we are trying to give the best service to our customers. Individual cultural intelligence should not play a pivotal role as we must act like a team." Similarly, Participant 3 spoke about having a common understanding of tasks as a team and focusing on abilities: "I face no challenge when dealing with cultural intelligence because we have the same scales to test abilities, to develop them, and we all have a common understanding of the tasks." The participant expressed that there is no challenge experienced in dealing with the varying CQ of team members as there is a standard to test ability and a common understanding of the task. Participant 3 believed that the relationship between the results of the team and the CQ of team members is negligible as "there is no need for too much cultural intelligence enhancements as my team works equally based on the same skill set, I have developed and transmitted." Participant 7 could not speak definitively on the relationship between the CQ of the team members and the results of the team as he expressed that "I've never really measured, nor have I given much thought to that." The participant claimed that CQ was not a parameter that has been monitored by him or his firm.

4.2.2 KD-Related Results From Content and Word Cloud Analysis

This theme details the KD leveraged by the participants for decision-making. Participants used spiritual knowledge, rational knowledge, emotional knowledge but also balanced rational, emotional, and cultural values for decision-making.

4.2.2.1 Emotional Knowledge

This subtheme focuses on the role emotions or feelings played in the decision of six of the leaders in a multicultural workplace (Fig. 5).

4.2.2.1.1 Emotions Play a Role in the Decision-Making Process. Six of the participants believed that emotions play a role in decision-making. Participant 6 believes that emotions play a significant role in decision-making. According to Participant 6, emotions "absolutely" play a role in decision-making; "emotions

Fig. 5.   Word Cloud of Emotional Knowledge. *Source:* Author's own research.

like caring for people as individuals, not resources – are part of my daily management routine." Similarly, Participant 8 believes that emotions play a role in decision-making because "we are all humans. We cannot perform without taking into account the emotions of our team members and clients." To Participant 15, emotions "sometimes" play a role in his decision-making. Participant 5 believes that "50% of all decisions integrate emotions." However, Krian Skovrider is "trying to reduce the percentage."

4.2.2.1.2 Emotions Play a Minimal Role in the Decision-Making Process. According to Participant 9, emotions play a minimal role in decision-making. Participant 9 said, "To a minimal extent. Emotions play a reduced role in my decision-making process but are not to be neglected." Similarly, Participant 3 said: "emotions play a less than 1% part/role in my decisions." For Participant 12, emotions have very little influence on his decision-making process: "emotions do play little role in my decisions." Participant 10 believes that emotions play a minimal role but not in business. In Participant 10's words, emotions play a role "more in human-related topics than business." To Participant 10, work should be focused on "respecting procedures and sticking to KPIs and deadlines." Similarly, Dean Watson believes that emotions should not play an integral role in decision-making. He believes that "as a human, emotions are involved in all processes. But I ensure that I am not influenced only by emotions when making decisions. Emotions are there but should not be dominant."

4.2.2.2 Rational Knowledge

This subtheme focuses on adopting data and logical reasoning as one of the main drivers in the decision-making of 14 leaders in a multicultural workplace, with emotions playing minimal or no role in the above process (Fig. 6).

4.2.2.2.1 Data and Rational Thinking Is the Main Driver in Decision-Making. Some of the participants made their decisions based on data and facts. According to Participant 13, "…my decisions are based on data only." Participant 14 also appreciates making his decisions on data: "Always on data. You cannot miss targets with the correct data." Similarly, Participant 1's decision-making is based on data. However, Participant 1 also bases his decision on past experiences: "Depending on the situation – my decisions are based on data (rational thinking) or experience. If a situation is urgent and there is no data or no time for getting the data, I rely on my experience." Similarly, Participant 5 said: "My decisions are 50% based on data and rational thinking – according to situations." Combining data and rational thinking work for Participant 15 in decision-making as he said: "I can say my decisions are a mixture of data and rational thinking." Participant 13 considers his decisions to be based mostly on rational thinking. "Rational thinking is the main driver" was his answer to the question of what drives his decision-making process.

4.2.2.2.2 Emotions Have No Role in the Decision-Making Process. Five participants believe emotions do not play any role in their decision-making process or this role is quite neglectable. According to Participant 14, "…emotions are not

Fig. 6.   Word Cloud of Rational Knowledge. *Source:* Author's own research.

included in any kind of decision-makings." The decision-making process does not involve emotion. Participant 4 also disagreed on emotions playing a role in his decision-making process. "No, emotions do not play any role in my decisions." Similarly, Participant 13 confirms that emotions do not influence his decisions. "No, not really. I go with data outcomes." Participant 1 does not believe emotions should play any role in business decisions. Participant 1 believes decisions made in business should not be influenced by emotions "Yes, I really do, but mostly between rational thinking and cultural values. I do not think that emotions are to be involved in the business."

4.2.2.2.3 Does Not Consider Cultural Values as the Focus When Interacting With People of Different Cultures. Individual CQ is negligible when interacting with a group of people of diverse cultures. As Dean Watson said, the cultural value "does not come to mind as something that I should plan and prepare." Despite not considering cultural values as a focus when interacting with people, Dean added that he shows his respect regardless. "However, based on my education, I show respect, engage properly with them and even try to understand their cultural values if the subject is raised." Participant 13 also mentioned his focus on skills is more than that on cultural values when interacting with people. "Sometimes, I do not think I have to keep their culture in mind when speaking with people from different countries. We just need to see and address his or her skills."

4.2.2.2.4 Business Should Be Prioritized When Making a Decision. Prioritizing business when making a decision is essential to the growth of the business. Participant 4 expressed that individual cultural values should not affect decisions beneficial to the business "Yes – I think this should not be a game stopper as the business should be prioritized, and win-win partnerships should prevail on any cultural differences." Participant 14 is also of the opinion that individual cultural values should not be imposed in a work environment: "...what I am trying to say is that according to the work environment what we need from people who recently joined our company is that they understand the company's culture rather than imposing their own. ..." Decisions that are sustainable and progressive for the business should always come first.

4.2.2.3 Spiritual Knowledge

This subtheme focuses on the adoption of values as main driver in the decision-making of some of the leaders in a multicultural workplace, with emotions playing minimal or no role (Fig. 7).

Fig. 7.   Word Cloud of Spiritual Knowledge. *Source:* Author's own research.

4.2.2.3.1 Understanding the Values of Others Is Needed for Decision-Making When Interacting with Business Partners and Team Members. In decision-making, participants think of cultural value for a better relationship with business clients. Participant 12 considers the cultural value of business partners to show respect for the cultural origin of business partners. According to Participant 12, thinking of cultural values is:

> ...essential to me because I belong to a different culture and work in a different country, so I recognize the importance that people respect your cultural background. I tend to do the same with my team and business partners, meaning to respect everyone's beliefs, culture and background and to have empathy and knowledge that everyone is different and you cannot treat everyone the same way.

The value of respect is also important to Participant 1. Participant 1 believes that knowing the cultural value "will show my business partners that I respect their origins and cultures, and this will help the professional partnership between our companies." While conversing with people of various cultural backgrounds, it is imperative to take into account their cultural values for an optimal business relationship. This was emphasized by Participant 8, who thinks of cultural value as "a primary step to make good business relations with customers ... construct friendships with people." Awareness of other team members cultures can enhance communication by eliminating potential misunderstandings. Cultural value enables accessible communication and easy understanding. According to Participant 3, "when running a multicultural team, it's important to research their cultural values. This will give you an extensive understanding of how they perceive any situation." For Participant 11, developing an understanding of team members' cultural values creates an avenue to have meaningful interactions. Participant 11 said: "I just want to know everything about new people or members in my team."

4.2.2.3.2 Making Decisions Based on Common Sense. Few of the participants spoke about relying on common sense for decision-making. Participant 1 believes that "if a situation is urgent and there is no data or no time for getting the data. I rely on my experience and common sense to make the best decision., I cannot lose a contract because I need 2 days to get the exact numbers." Similarly, Participant 9 states that "I try to but do not succeed every time due to lack of time. In these time-sensitive cases I rely on universal common sense." In this context mentioned above, relying on common sense in a time-constrained situation is more beneficial than waiting for data.

4.2.2.3.3 Authentic Decision-Making. A flexible yet authentic approach is used for decision-making by Participant 6. Instead of relying on data and rational thinking, Participant 6 tries "to be flexible yet consult data for authenticity" when making decisions.

4.2.2.4 Combining Rational, Emotional, and Cultural Values for Decision-Making

This subtheme explains how 13 of the participants ultimately believe in balancing rational, emotional, and cultural values for decision-making (Fig. 8).

A sustainable decision-making process needs a proper balance between emotions, cultural and spiritual values, and rational thinking in order to attain a high level of productivity. Participant 1 says: "yes, otherwise, the proper balance between rational thinking and cultural values smooths the decision-making process and increases the overall productivity of the teamwork." Decision-making "was carried out only based on data, and rational thinking could be interpreted from his perspective as a bit rigid. Other factors surrounding the topic must be considered to allow a more agile and improved result." According to Participant 2: "no, decisions are not made only based on data and rational analysis. The environment, principles, values, and emotions come into account when to take a business and even a personal decision."

As a manager, Participant 12 sees the essence of balancing rational thinking, emotions, and cultural values when deciding. "Yes, it is essential, you cannot just make decisions based on one factor, so you have to consider everything." He

Fig. 8.   Word Cloud of Combing All Forms of Knowledge Dynamics for Decision. *Source:* Author's own research.

furthered his point with: "When allocating tasks to specific team members, we must consider again what strengths and weaknesses they bring to the table and how their rational thinking, emotions and cultural values will transform the task into a success." Equally incorporating all three factors in the decision-making process will leave no table unturned. Just as Participant 2 said: "...You have to have all 3 (rational thinking, emotions and cultural values), and if you cut one off or ignore it, you aren't operating at your best, and the decision is not great. However, it would be best if you managed the rhythm and share of each element – so that one is not always dominant." Similarly, Participant 5 also agreed that the balance of all three factors is useful in decision-making progress. "Absolutely, it's very important to have a good balance between rational, emotional and cultural."

Emotions, rational thinking, and cultural values are all great mechanisms for the approach of the decision-making process. Participant 8 states: "yes, it is a success key factor, this balance helps me take the best decisions." Participant 10 simply said: "yes, it should be but not in place as a standardised tool, at the time being at my job." Rational thinking, emotions, and cultural values are the key factors in decision-making. Participant 8 said: "this balance helps me take the best decisions." In agreement, Participant 9 said: "the combination of all these is the correct base to make the right decision at the right time." As per above, decision-making cannot rely only on data; the coalition of the other mentioned factors balances the process toward the right decision.

4.2.3 ML-Related Results From Content and Word Cloud Analysis

This subtheme talks about the ML attributes that leaders possess while working in a multicultural work environment.

4.2.3.1 Conceptual Skills

The conceptual skills of the leaders in a multicultural work group are enveloped in this subtheme as it describes the application of conceptual skills in the leadership of multicultural teams or workforce (Fig. 9).

4.2.3.1.1 Identifying Practices That Lead to Productivity. Identifying practices that lead to increased productivity is an important skill to possess as a leader. One of the participants, Participant 11, detected how friendliness and openness make her team more productive: "I am very open and friendly with my team because its increases productivity and builds performance." Her openness with her team members boosts productivity. Best practices can also be picked up from team members for all-round implementation, as is the case of Participant 12: "I pick up good practices from any of my team members and try to implement them across the board just to increase productivity and the quality of our output." Participant 15 spoke on how he delegates to boost productivity with an example: "Usually, I prefer to give a task that requires a short and fast answer to Asian people because they are more adapted to working under pressure." Participant 4 employs a similar strategy in client acquisition: "I also try to find clients from the same

Fig. 9. Word Cloud of Conceptual Skills. *Source:* Author's own research.

culture as the team – to simplify the process or when there is not enough time. This is leading my business to success."

4.2.3.1.2 Leveraging Cultural Background for Company Success. Managers in leadership positions in multicultural workspaces in Canada leverage their cultural background for the company's success. Participant 1 iterated: "I always do because every different cultural team member mostly has a different skill set that I always want to leverage to optimize results." Participant 12 perfectly described this: "Yes, I do, as whenever I meet a new team member for the first time, I do my own research on his/her cultural background. So, I think it helps me to establish what kinds of strengths and weaknesses the team members will bring to our team and then assign tasks on that basis, so they can also maximize their potential while best serving the business needs." Participant 4 explained how he learns from the cultural background of staff and how it can benefit the company: "I try to learn from the cultures I deal with; I look into history, art, sports, food, political systems and people's behaviours. I often speak about what goes on in the business partners' countries and continents. And I am pushing my team to do the same. I also try to find clients from the same culture as the team – to simplify the process or when there is not enough time. This is leading my business to success." He then added how he leverages the cultural background in assigning tasks: "...I leverage my team members' cultural background when assigning a task, mostly related to export activity." Participant 5 iterated: "Yes, I have to remember the team members' cultural values and backgrounds when assigning a task, but all this is within a fixed perimeter, as everyone has his/her own predefined areas of responsibility" while speaking on how he considers the cultural background of staff while assigning tasks.

4.2.3.1.3 Strategic Planning. Strategic planning is a tool that Participant 15 employs to facilitate trust sharing climate among team members, as he iterated this point that: "Through mission, vision, and breaking those into short-term/long-term goals," he creates trust among his multicultural team. The laid-out plans in terms of long- and short-term goals yield a sense of security among team members. Participant 3 also builds trust by "assigning ... clear duties." Participant 10 also creates trust by giving "roles and duties and tracking them."

4.2.3.2 Interpersonal Skills

This subtheme focuses on the interpersonal skills of multicultural leaders in the multicultural workspace for building trust and leading a multicultural workforce (Fig. 10).

4.2.3.2.1 Coaching and Empowering Team Members. Coaching and empowerment are interpersonal methods being employed by multicultural team leaders, as evident from the words of Participant 1: "I create and develop trust within the team by coaching each member. I am also insisting on the company values – as a trust generator." Speaking on this subject, Participant 10 stated that: "Leading by example is my leadership style. In this way, I show my team members what commitment in retail looks like." This practice helps in building trust among the multicultural team. Participant 7 adopts an empowerment leadership style by "encouraging him/her (team member) to assume decisions and results." Participant 9 empowers team members by "making everyone responsible for the whole business."

4.2.3.2.2 Collaboration. Collaboration among members of the team is a tool being employed by some participants of the survey. Participant 9 described his leadership style as: "Collaborative, as it gives the maximum output, reduces the work in silos and brings everyone together." This practice brings all members of the team together and fosters a healthy relationship among members of the team. Participant 6 also credited "collaboration" as part of his leadership style in his multicultural team. Participant 2 believes that collaboration with team members is needed for trust building: "trusting team members and working alongside them is consolidating the trust in our company."

4.2.3.2.3 Communication. Communication among the multicultural team is essential in the managerial style of participants. Participant 14 stated that her strategy for leading a multicultural team is based on communication: "... as everyone has a different kind of thinking to lead the company and to lead people. Regarding my strategy, I am pretty straightforward in my thinking. I sit with team members and plan the day during early morning meetings. We talk, we

Fig. 10.   Word Cloud of Interpersonal Skills. *Source:* Author's own research.

communicate, and the more we communicate, the more we solve problems" as this approach helps in problem-solving among the team. Participant 13 attributed good communication to building trust among his multicultural team as he said: "We are communicating with them and giving them a comfort zone to work with much freedom and trust." This enables comfort and freedom of expression among the multicultural team. Similarly, Participant 6 credited good communication and contribution among team members to facilitating trust among said team members in a multicultural group: "We are establishing a set of guiding principles that encourage people to contribute without fear. We all learn and build on our mistakes." In the same light, Participant 7 iterated that: "...ensuring feedback mechanisms are in place" also helps to create trust among the multicultural team.

4.2.3.2.4 Empathy and Kindness. Some of the participants have the interpersonal skill of empathy. Participant 7 adopts an empathetic style of leadership. Describing her leadership style, Participant 7 stated that: "It is a mix of empathetic..." and added that: "I care about each team member." Participant 6 is also empathetic because he was of the opinion that team members and leaders make mistakes and can learn from them: "We all learn and build on our mistakes." Participant 3 highlighted how he creates trust and cohesion among team members by being kind: "not being heavy-handed in the oversight."

4.2.3.2.5 Friendliness and Openness. Friendliness increases productivity and makes team members feel comfortable, according to Participant 11: "I am very open and friendly with my team because its increases productivity and builds performance. I work with my team members side by side and support them on all topics." She added that this friendly approach is effective in building trust among team members: "...I create trust by being friendly and open with my team members, so they do not fear talking to me about any of their successes or failures." Participant 4 simply stated that: "I think I have a friendly and open leadership style – if this exists" when asked about his ML style. In the same manner, Participant 8 iterated that: "Friendliness is my guiding principle because it makes the team comfortable and members can share anything with me" was his leadership style and added that: "This creates trust" among the team members. He also credited creating a friendly environment as a catalyst for building trust among team members. Participant 11 and Participant 13 stated openness as the characteristic of their leadership style. Participant 9 similarly iterated that openness and honesty enable the trust to grow among team members as he expressed that: "By being honest and open. Also, by sharing the information, " he creates trust among his multicultural team.

4.2.3.2.6 Building an Environment With a Sense of Belonging. Creating a sense of belonging among team members in a multicultural workspace will help to create trust among teammates. According to Participant 12: "...you have to identify that everyone comes from a different background and environment. So, I have to create team bonding and the right environment which will develop trust and federate all energies towards the same goal." This will facilitate more synergy among the team toward their shared goal. Participant 6 also mentioned building "a sense of belonging" as a leadership style to adopt in a multicultural workplace.

4.2.3.3 Multicultural Skills (Values)

This subtheme focuses on participants' values and intercultural competence that is used in building trust and leading a multicultural workforce (Fig. 11).

4.2.3.3.1 Equal Treatment. Equal treatment is an essential quality to possess in the leadership of a multicultural team, according to Participant 15: "I do not differentiate between any employee based on ethnicity while giving any responsibility or job opportunity because every member comes with different valuable ideas." Participant 5 similarly added more to this subject, saying: "Everyone has his/her own areas of responsibility; my leadership style is equality-oriented." This leadership style gives every member a sense of belonging and equality.

4.2.3.3.2 Finding Common Grounds. A prominent of creating trust among multicultural teams, according to Participant 4, is to find common ground between each member of the team. "I have a conversation about familiar cultural topics for my team. I try to bond the culture governing my company to the one

Fig. 11.   Word Cloud of Multicultural Skills (Value). *Source:*
Author's own research.

from clients and employees. I find common grounds that build trust." Finding
common ground within various cultures helps to build trust within multicultural
workspaces.

4.2.3.3.3 Respecting Cultural Differences. Some participants adopted respect
for cultural differences as a leadership style or a way to create trust in the team. In
his inclusive leadership style,

Participant 6 stated that his leadership style is based on: "acknowledging and
leveraging cultural or social differences." Participant 8 believed that understanding and respect for various cultures might build trust among members of a
multicultural team. Participant 8 builds trust: "by trying to understand each one's
cultural background." Participant 9 also respects his team members' cultural
background by considering their cultural background when allocating tasks: "I
try to be conscious of the cultural background of each team member when
allocating tasks."

*4.2.3.3.4 Leadership Focuses on Uniformity Skill Set or Task Completion, Not
Cultural Background.* Although most multicultural leaders have either conceptual, interpersonal, or multicultural skills, some of them focus more on task
uniformity and completion and do not consider the cultural background of their
staff when assigning tasks or in their leadership style (Fig. 12).

Fig. 12.   Word Cloud of Focus on Uniformity, Skill Set, or Task, Not
Cultural Background. *Source:* Author's own research.

4.2.3.3.5 Assign Tasks Based on Skill Set and Not Cultural Background. Some
of the participants stated that they do not consider the cultural background of
their team members when assigning tasks. According to Participant 13: "I do not
have to keep their cultural background in mind as it has nothing to do with their
job and tasks." Similarly, Participant 14 does not consider the cultural background of team members in assigning tasks as he said "all I know is that this team
member is here to do the assigned task, and he or she should do it well."
Participant 2 focuses on the *best hands* and does not consider the cultural background. He said: "...it is who is the best person for the task, who can bring
maximum satisfaction to the client, and who can maximise revenues for my
company." According to Participant 3, the focus should be on the task to be done
and not on cultural background: "...we work as a team toward the common goal
with no cultural bias and only focusing on the task at hand." Reni Senan reit-
erated the point that the cultural backgrounds of team members are not a
necessary factor to be considered in the allocation of tasks as he said: "...I think
we do not need it as we are fully trained in order to best serve the clients, and our
job is relatively standardised and automatized." He believed that the training and
acquired skill set were the prerequisites for task allocation as the work process is
standardized.

4.2.3.3.6 Focus on Uniformity Rather Than Understanding the Cultural Background. Leaders focus on uniformity as opposed to the cultural background of team members. This was illustrated by Participant 1: "My leadership style is bureaucratic and transactional, and all my employees are strictly advised to follow the established rules. This will ensure predictability and uniformity, and these are important characteristics when dealing with multicultural teams." Speaking on the subject, Participant 2 expressed that: "leads by my own value and principles." This shows that the values adopted in his workplace are mostly uniform to his.

4.3 First Findings and Results Using Cross-Case Analysis

4.3.1 CQ-Related Results From Cross-Case Analysis

Both male and female subjects were more influenced by emotional CQ and rational CQ. Spiritual CQ was reported on third position to male subjects. Emotional CQ had the highest percentage, followed by rational CQ. Male subjects had higher emotional CQ than females but a lower downplay of cultural differences (Fig. 13).

Subjects aged 26–40 and 41–60 were highly influenced by emotional CQ. For those age groups – emotional CQ was the highest driver, followed by rational CQ. Emotional CQ increased with increasing age while downplaying cultural differences for the team, and spiritual intelligence decreased with increasing age. Participants aged >61 were equally influenced by rational intelligence and emotional CQ (Fig. 14).

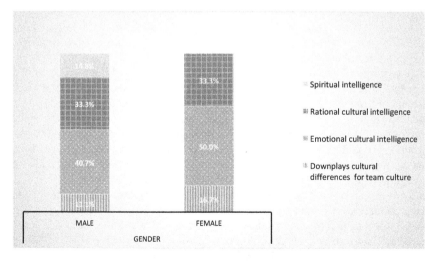

Fig. 13.   Cultural Influence Between Male and Female Participants.
Source: Author's own research.

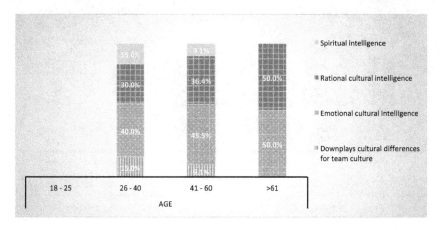

Fig. 14.   Cultural Influence Between Age Groups. *Source:* Author's
own research.

In equal terms, participants with high school only were influenced by rational
CQ and emotional CQ, while university graduates and master's graduates were
mostly driven by emotional CQ. Rational and emotional CQ decreased with
increased education, while spiritual CQ increased (Fig. 15).

Based on continents, Europe was influenced in equal terms by emotional CQ
and rational CQ, respectively: 41.7%. Asia was equally influenced by emotional
CQ and rational CQ (50%) each, while Africa and North America were most
influenced by emotional CQ (50%) and rational CQ (36.4%). All studied continents, but Asia, had emotional CQ, rational CQ, and spiritual intelligence and

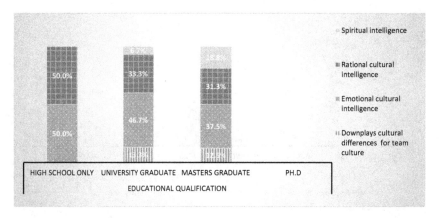

Fig. 15.   Cultural Differences Based on Educational Qualifications.
Source: Author's own research.

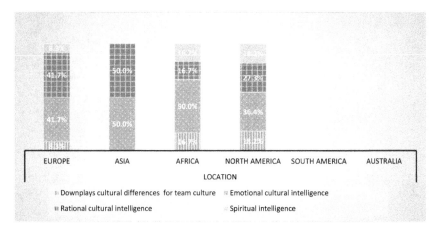

Fig. 16.   Cultural Differences Among Participants Based on
Continental Experiences. *Source:* Author's own research.

downplayed cultural differences for team culture. Spiritual intelligence is highest
in North America (18.2%) compared to Africa (16.7%) and Europe (8.3%). Asia
and Africa were influenced mainly by emotional CQ (50%), followed by Europe
and North America (Fig. 16).

For countries, Saudi Arabia, Iran, Denmark, and Georgia were influenced, in
an equal manner, by emotional CQ and rational CQ (50%/50%), while Egypt,
Canada, and England were influenced mainly by emotional CQ. In contrast, the
United States were influenced equally by emotional CQ, rational CQ, and
downplayed cultural differences for team culture (Fig. 17).

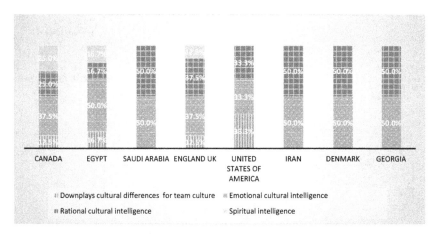

Fig. 17.   Cultural Differences Among Participants Based on Country
of Experience. *Source:* Author's own research.

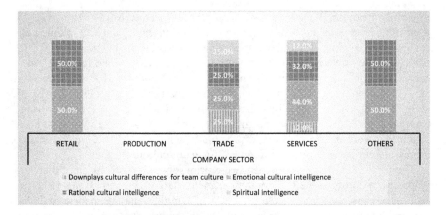

Fig. 18.   Cultural Differences Among Participants Based on
Company Sector. *Source:* Author's own research.

Retail and others were influenced in equal terms by emotional CQ and rational
CQ, while trade had equal influence from spiritual CQ, rational CQ, emotional
CQ, and downplayed cultural differences for team culture. Services were mainly
influenced by emotional CQ, even though other variables are present (Fig. 18).

Companies sized <0.5M and 1M- <5M were equally influenced by rational
CQ and emotional CQ, while companies sized 0.5M- <1M were primarily
influenced by emotional CQ. Companies sized 5M- <10M were influenced
equally by rational CQ and emotional CQ, while the ones sized 10M- <50M were
driven by spiritual CQ. Companies sized 50M and above were mainly influenced
by emotional CQ (Fig. 19).

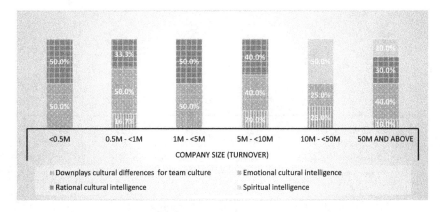

Fig. 19.   Cultural Differences Among Participants Based on
Company Size (Turnover). *Source:* Author's own research.

Companies sized (from a number of employees' perspective) 1–10 and 101–500 were influenced in equal terms by rational CQ and emotional CQ. While companies sized (from same above-mentioned perspective) 11–50, 51–100, and 1,001+ were mainly influenced by emotional CQ, although not in a size-dependent manner, as it was highest in 1–10 and 101–500 and lowest in 51–100. Rational emotional intelligence was highest in companies sized 1–10 and 101–500, followed by companies sized 51–100, while 11–50 had the lowest score. Companies sized 1,000+ have the highest spiritual intelligence compared to 11–50 as the two were the only groups expressing it, while sized 51–100 expressed the biggest downplay of cultural differences for team culture (Fig. 20).

The top and middle management were primarily influenced by emotional CQ, followed by rational CQ. Top management had higher emotional CQ and rational CQ than middle management, while middle management had higher spiritual intelligence and downplays cultural differences for team culture than top management (Fig. 21).

All categories of years of experience within the company were mostly influenced by emotional CQ, followed by rational CQ. Emotional CQ was highest in 5–10 years of experience within the company compared to others, while rational CQ was highest for 10–15 years of experience within the company. All but 5–10 years of experience within the company displayed spiritual CQ. Similarly, 10–15 years of experience within the company was the only group that did not present downplay cultural differences for team culture (Fig. 22).

Groups with 1–3, 6–10, and 11–15 managed nationalities were mostly driven by emotional CQ, while the group with 4–5 lead nationalities was influenced in equal terms by emotional CQ and rational CQ. Group 16–20 nationalities was equally influenced by emotional CQ, rational CQ, and spiritual CQ (Fig. 23).

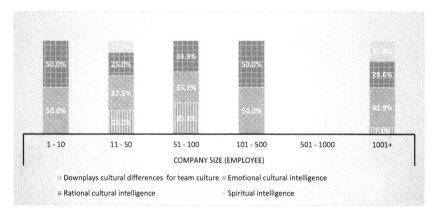

Fig. 20.   Cultural Differences Among Participants Based on Company Size (Employee). *Source:* Author's own research.

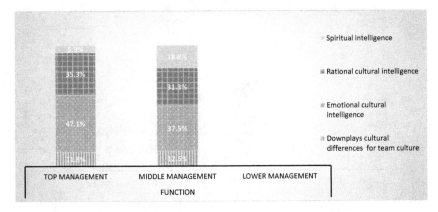

Fig. 21. Cultural Differences Among Participants Based on Management Role. *Source:* Author's own research.

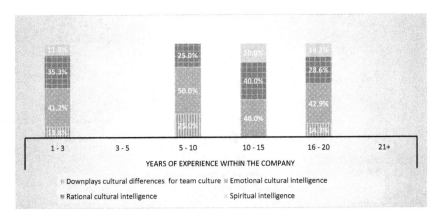

Fig. 22. Cultural Differences Among Participants Based on Years of Experience Within the Company. *Source:* Author's own research.

One language group was influenced in equal proportion by rational CQ and emotional CQ. For two and three spoken language groups, emotional CQ had the dominant influence. Spiritual intelligence and emotional CQ had equal influence in more than three languages group (Fig. 24).

Subjects with one, two, and three countries' working experiences were predominantly influenced by emotional CQ, while those with more than three countries of work that were influenced by spiritual intelligence (Fig. 25).

All subjects, irrespective of the number of continents of work, were influenced by emotional CQ except those of three continents, equally influenced by rational

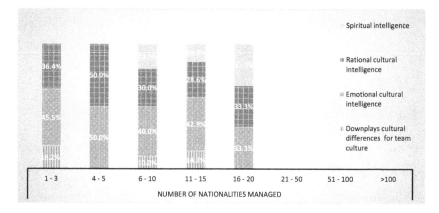

Fig. 23.   Cultural Differences Among Participants Based on the
Number of Managed Nationalities. *Source:* Author's own research.

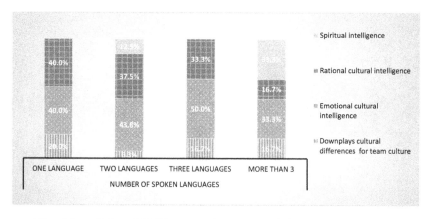

Fig. 24.   Cultural Differences Among Participants Based on the
Number of Spoken Languages. *Source:* Author's own research.

CQ and emotional CQ. Emotional CQ and downplayed cultural differences for
team culture decreased with increasing numbers of continents on which subjects
have worked on. Spiritual intelligence and rational CQ increased with a growing
number of continents with work experience (Fig. 26).

Subjects with 3–5 and 5–10 years of experience were influenced equally by
rational CQ and emotional CQ, while subjects 10–15 and 21+ years of total
experience were mainly influenced by emotional CQ. Subjects with 3–5 years of
total experience had the biggest emotional CQ impact, followed by subjects with
21+ and subjects with 10–15 years of total experience (Fig. 27).

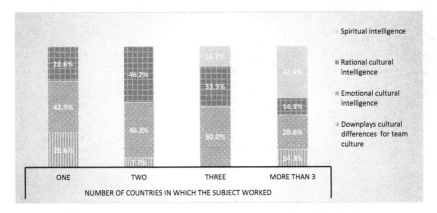

Fig. 25.   Cultural Differences Among Participants Based on the
Number of Countries the Participants Worked in. *Source:* Author's own
research.

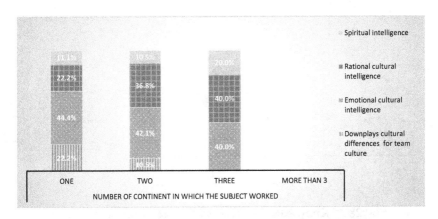

Fig. 26.   Cultural Differences Among Participants Based on the
Number of Continents the Participants Worked in. *Source:* Author's own
research.

4.3.2 KD-Related Results From Cross-Case Analysis

Male participants made more use of the need to balance rational, emotional, and
cultural values for decision-making, even as they expressed spiritual knowledge
and emotional knowledge in decision-making, while female participants displayed
more rational knowledge. Male participants employed more emotional knowledge than females (Fig. 28).

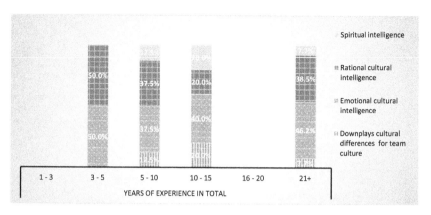

Fig. 27. Cultural Differences Among Participants Based on Years of
Experience in Total. *Source:* Author's own research.

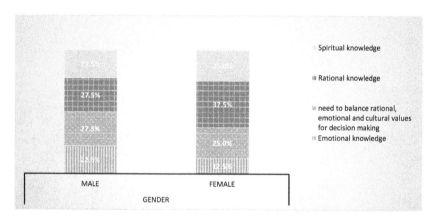

Fig. 28. Knowledge Differences Between Male and Female
Participants. *Source:* Author's own research.

Participants within the age bracket 26–40 employed spiritual knowledge and
rational knowledge in equal terms, while those of 41–60 years old employed with
same weight rational knowledge and the need to balance rational, emotional, and
cultural values for decision-making. Moreover, those >61 years old utilized all
the KD equally in decision-making. Rational knowledge and the need to balance
rational, emotional, and cultural values for decision-making is highest among
participants aged 41–60 compared to other age groups (Fig. 29).

Participants with high school only as their educational qualification employed
in equal terms rational knowledge need to balance rational, emotional, and

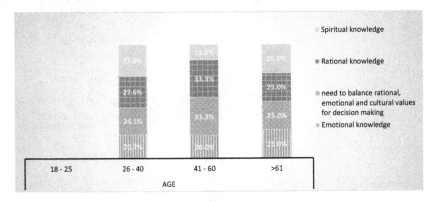

Fig. 29.   Knowledge Differences Between Age Groups. *Source:*
Author's own research.

cultural values for decision-making and emotional knowledge. At the same time, those with university degrees were influenced more by rational knowledge. Those with master's degrees were more influenced by spiritual knowledge. High school only had the need to balance rational, emotional, and cultural values for decision-making at higher levels than other levels of educational qualification (Fig. 30).

KD based on continents and countries showed that Asia and Africa were more influenced by rational knowledge. At the same time, North America had equal influence from spiritual knowledge, the need to balance rational, emotional, and cultural values for decision-making, and emotional knowledge (Fig. 31).

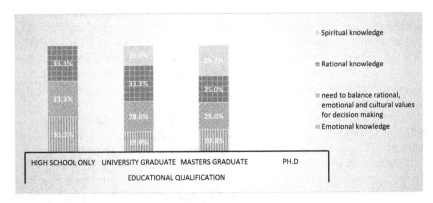

Fig. 30.   Knowledge Differences Among Participants Based on
Educational Qualifications. *Source:* Author's own research.

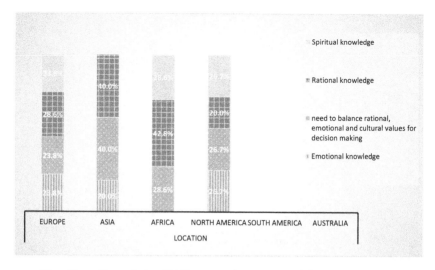

Fig. 31.   Knowledge Differences Among Participants Based on
Continents. *Source:* Author's own research.

Saudi Arabia was equally influenced by rational knowledge, the need to balance rational, emotional, and cultural values for decision-making, and emotional
knowledge. Canada was influenced at the same level by emotional knowledge, the
need to balance rational, emotional, and cultural values for decision-making, and
spiritual knowledge. Egypt was influenced by rational knowledge and, to a lesser
extent, by spiritual knowledge and the need to balance rational, emotional, and
cultural values for decision-making. England was mainly influenced by rational
knowledge; the United States, Denmark, and Georgia had equal influence from
spiritual knowledge, rational knowledge, emotional knowledge, and the need to
balance rational, emotional, and cultural values for decision-making (Fig. 32).

The spiritual knowledge, rational knowledge, and emotional knowledge had
an equal influence on Retail and Others, while spiritual knowledge and rational
knowledge had a driven influence on Trade. Services were influenced by rational
knowledge and the need to balance rational, emotional, and cultural values for
decision-making (Fig. 33).

Companies sized (structured by annual turnover in Euro) <0.5M had an equal
influence of rational knowledge and the need to balance rational, emotional, and
cultural values for decision-making. Companies sized 0.5M- <1M were most
influenced by rational knowledge, while the batch 1M- <5M were equally driven
by the four variables. Companies sized 5M- <10M were influenced equally by
spiritual knowledge, rational knowledge, and the need to balance rational,
emotional, and cultural values for decision-making, while companies sized 10M-
<50M were impacted in equal terms by spiritual knowledge and rational
knowledge. Those of 50M and above were influenced in equal terms by spiritual

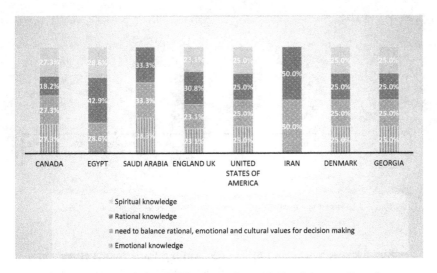

Fig. 32.   Knowledge Differences Among Participants Based on
Countries. *Source:* Author's own research.

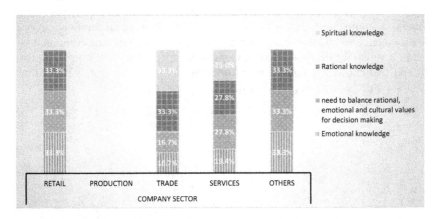

Fig. 33.   Knowledge Differences Among Participants Based on
Company Sector. *Source:* Author's own research.

knowledge, the need to balance rational, emotional, and cultural values for
decision-making, and emotional knowledge (Fig. 34).

Companies sized (as the number of employees) 1–10 were influenced in equal
terms by rational knowledge and the need to balance rational, emotional, and
cultural values for decision-making, while companies sized 11–50 were influenced

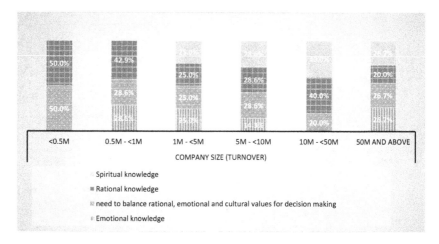

Fig. 34.   Knowledge Differences Among Participants Based on
Company Size (Turnover). *Source:* Author's own research.

mainly by rational knowledge. Companies sized 51–100 were influenced in equal
terms by spiritual knowledge, rational knowledge, emotional knowledge, and the
need to balance rational, emotional, and cultural values for decision-making.
Similarly, companies sized 101–500 were influenced in equal terms by spiritual
knowledge, rational knowledge, and the need to balance rational, emotional, and
cultural values for decision-making. Companies sized 100+ were mostly impacted
by spiritual knowledge and the need to balance rational, emotional, and cultural
values for decision-making (Fig. 35).

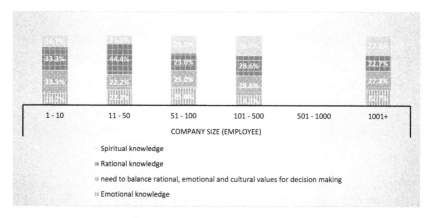

Fig. 35.   Knowledge Differences Among Participants Based on
Company Size (Number of Employees). *Source:* Author's own research.

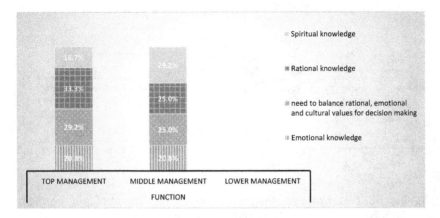

Fig. 36.   Knowledge Differences Among Participants Based on
Management Level. *Source:* Author's own research.

Top management was influenced by rational knowledge, followed by the need
to balance rational, emotional, and cultural values for decision-making, while
middle management was influenced by spiritual knowledge, followed by rational
knowledge, and the need to balance rational, emotional, and cultural values for
decision-making (Fig. 36).

For batches of years of experience within the companies: 1–3 years and 5–10
years, knowledge was mainly influenced by rational knowledge; the 10–15 years
group was driven by spiritual intelligence, emotional knowledge, and the need to
balance rational, emotional, and cultural values for decision-making. 16–20 years
batch was influenced primarily by rational knowledge and the need to balance
rational, emotional, and cultural values for decision-making (Fig. 37).

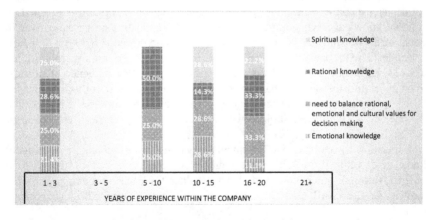

Fig. 37.   Knowledge Differences Among Participants Based on Years
of Experience With the Company. *Source:* Author's own research.

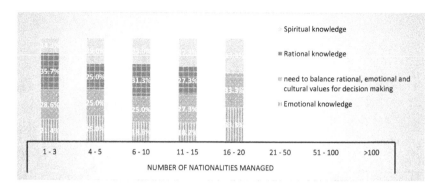

Fig. 38.   Knowledge Differences Among Participants Based on the Number of Managed Nationalities. *Source:* Author's own research.

The number of managed nationalities groups 1–3 and 6–10 were influenced by rational knowledge, 4–5 group was influenced equally by spiritual knowledge, rational knowledge, the need to balance rational and cultural values for decision-making, and emotional knowledge. The 11–15 group was equally impacted by spiritual knowledge, rational knowledge, and the need to balance rational, emotional, and cultural values for decision-making, while the 16–20 group was driven in equal terms by spiritual knowledge, emotional knowledge, and the need to balance rational, emotional, and cultural values for decision-making (Fig. 38).

One spoken language group was influenced in equal terms by rational knowledge, the need to balance rational, emotional, and cultural values for decision-making, and emotional knowledge. Two spoken languages group was mostly influenced by the need to balance rational, emotional, and cultural values for decision-making. The three spoken languages group was mainly impacted by rational knowledge, while more than three spoken languages group was driven in equal terms by spiritual knowledge and rational knowledge (Fig. 39).

Subjects with one country experience were influenced mainly by rational knowledge; those of two and three countries had an equal influence of rational knowledge and the need to balance rational, emotional, and cultural values for decision-making though the percentages in those of three countries is higher than the ones in two countries. Subjects with more than three countries were driven by spiritual knowledge (Fig. 40).

Subjects with one and two continents experience were influenced by rational knowledge, while those with three continents were influenced by the need to balance rational, emotional, and cultural values for decision-making. Rational knowledge decreased with an increasing number of worked on continents (Fig. 41).

The 3–5 years of experience group was equally co-influenced by spiritual knowledge, rational knowledge, and the need to balance rational, emotional, and

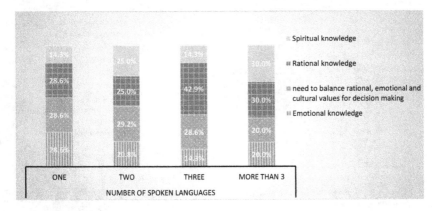

Fig. 39.   Knowledge Differences Among Participants Based on the
Number of Spoken Languages. *Source:* Author's own research.

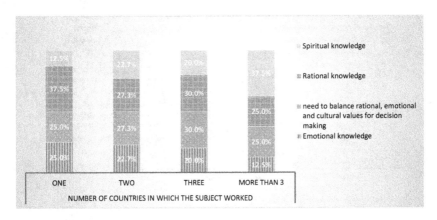

Fig. 40.   Knowledge Differences Based on the Number of Countries
Participants Worked in. *Source:* Author's own research.

cultural values for decision-making; 5–10 years of experience group was
co-influenced by spiritual and rational knowledge. The 10–15 years of experience
segment was equally impacted by spiritual knowledge, rational knowledge,
emotional knowledge, and the need to balance rational, emotional, and cultural
values for decision-making. In contrast, 21+ experience was co-influenced by
rational knowledge and the need to balance rational, emotional, and cultural
values for decision-making (Fig. 42).

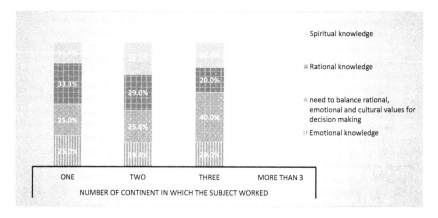

Fig. 41. Knowledge Differences Among Participants Based on the Number of Worked on Continents. *Source:* Author's own research.

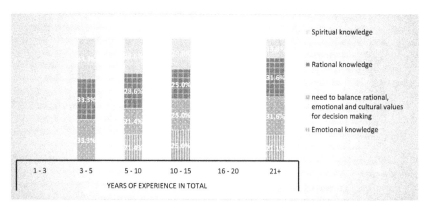

Fig. 42. Knowledge Differences Among Participants Based on Years of Experience in Total. *Source:* Author's own research.

4.3.3 ML-Related Results From Cross-Case Analysis

Male participants displayed more interpersonal skills than other skills, while females displayed more of the equally balanced combination of leader focuses on uniformity and task completion, and interpersonal skills. All skills except conceptual skills were more displayed in females than in males (Fig. 43).

Ages 26–40 years displayed more interpersonal skills than other skills, 41–60 years displayed a main focus on uniformity and task completion, while >61 years displayed equally multicultural skills, interpersonal skills, and conceptual skills. Conceptual skills were age-dependent (Fig. 44).

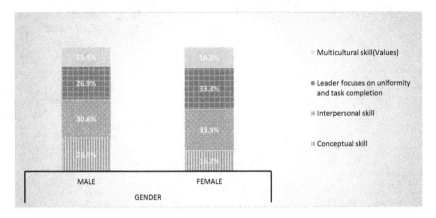

Fig. 43.   Leadership Differences Between Male and Female
Participants. *Source:* Author's own research.

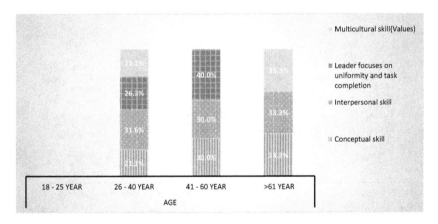

Fig. 44.   Leadership Differences Between Age Groups. *Source:*
Author's own research.

Subjects with high school only displayed leader focused on uniformity and task
completion concept; university graduates focused mainly on an equal balance
combination of focus on uniformity and task completion and interpersonal skills,
while master's graduates based themselves more on interpersonal skills. Focus on
uniformity and task completion decreased with increased educational qualifications (Fig. 45).

ML based on continents showed that Africa displayed no multicultural skills,
while Asia displayed conceptual and interpersonal skills in equal terms. In
contrast, North America and Europe displayed all four forms of ML skills
(Fig. 46).

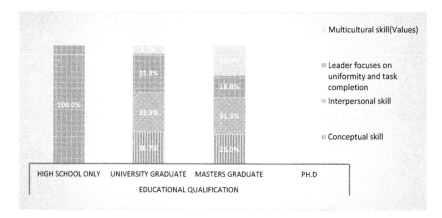

Fig. 45.   Leadership Differences Among Participants Based on
Educational Qualifications. *Source:* Author's own research.

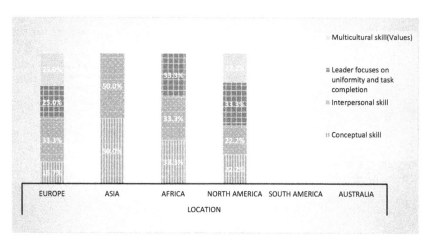

Fig. 46.   Leadership Differences Among Participants Based on
Continents. *Source:* Author's own research.

Canada displayed conceptual, interpersonal, uniformity-focused, and multi-cultural skills in equal terms. At the same time, Iran displayed conceptual and interpersonal skills in equal terms. The United States displayed a full focus on uniformity and task completion. Denmark displayed conceptual, interpersonal, and multicultural skills in the same proportions, while Georgia portrayed in equal terms interpersonal skills, leader focus in uniformity and task completion, and multicultural skills (Fig. 47).

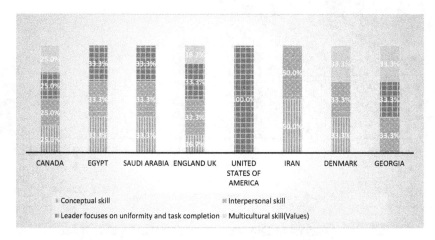

Fig. 47.   Leadership Differences Among Participants Based on
          Countries. *Source:* Author's own research.

Retail displayed in equal terms conceptual skills, interpersonal skills, and
leader focus on uniformity and task completion, Trade displayed in equal terms
conceptual skills, interpersonal skills, leader focus on uniformity and task
completion, and multicultural skills, Services focused on interpersonal skills while
Others presented only leader focus on uniformity and task completion (Fig. 48).

Companies sized (as annual turnover in Euro) < 0.5M displayed in equal
terms interpersonal and conceptual skill, 0.5M- <1M and 10- <50M were driven

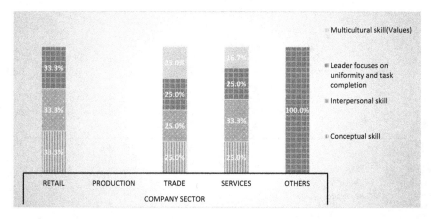

Fig. 48.   Leadership Differences Among Participants Based on
          Company Sector. *Source:* Author's own research.

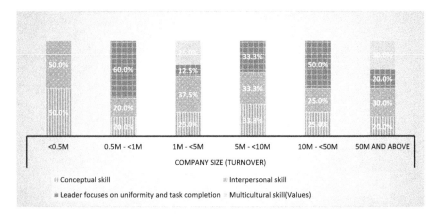

Fig. 49.   Leadership Differences Among Participants Based on
Company Size (Turnover). *Source:* Author's own research.

by leader focus on uniformity and task completion, 1M- <5M displayed mostly
interpersonal skills, 5- <10 portrayed in equal terms leader focuses on uniformity
and task completion and conceptual skills while 50M and above displayed in
equal terms multicultural skills and interpersonal skills (Fig. 49).

Company size (number of employees) 1–10 displayed in equal terms interpersonal skills and conceptual skills, 11–50 was driven by leader focuses on uniformity and task completion concept, 51–100 displayed leader focuses on uniformity
and task completion only, while 101–500 and 1,001+ focused on interpersonal
skills (Fig. 50).

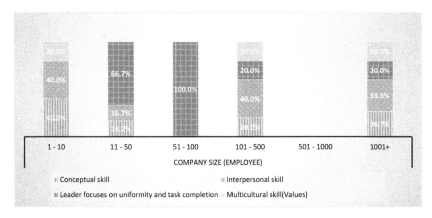

Fig. 50.   Leadership Differences Among Participants Based on
Company Size (Number of Employees). *Source:* Author's own research.

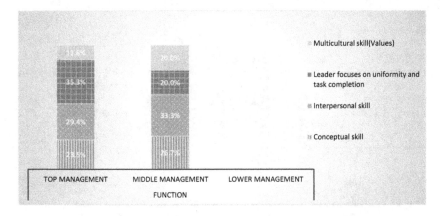

Fig. 51.   Leadership Differences Among Participants Based on
Management Level. *Source:* Author's own research.

Top management displayed mostly the leader focus on uniformity and task
completion concept, while middle management focused on interpersonal skills.
All but leaders focus on uniformity and task completion, increased from top
management to middle management (Fig. 51).

Participants with 1–3 years of experience displayed leading interpersonal skills,
5–10 years presented mostly the leader focuses on uniformity and task completion
concept, 10–15 years displayed in equal terms multicultural skills, interpersonal
skills, and conceptual skills, while 16–20 years presented with equal shares leader
focus on uniformity and task completion, interpersonal skills, and conceptual
skills (Fig. 52).

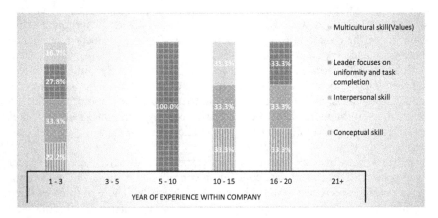

Fig. 52.   Leadership Differences Among Participants Based on Years
Within the Company. *Source:* Author's own research.

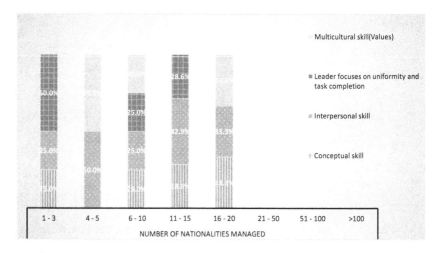

Fig. 53.   Leadership Differences Among Participants Based on the Number of Nationalities Managed. *Source:* Author's own research.

Participants with 1–3 numbers of managed nationalities displayed a dominant leader focus on uniformity and task completion concept, 4–5 nationalities presented multicultural skills and interpersonal skills equally. 6–10 nationalities exposed in equal terms multicultural skills, leader focuses on uniformity and task completion, interpersonal skills, and conceptual skills, 11–15 years of experience were driven by interpersonal skill while 16–20 years of experience shared in equal parts multicultural skills, interpersonal skill, and conceptual skills (Fig. 53).

One spoken language group displayed leader focuses on uniformity and task completion concept only. Two languages group displayed primarily interpersonal skills; three languages were driven by interpersonal skills and conceptual skills, while more than three languages group mainly displayed leaders focusing on uniformity and task completion (Fig. 54).

Subjects with work experience in one country exclusively displayed leader focus on uniformity and task completion, those of two countries displayed mainly multicultural skills, and those of three countries focused on conceptual skills. In contrast, those of more than three countries portrayed in equal leading shares leader focus on uniformity and task completion, interpersonal skills, and conceptual skills (Fig. 55).

Subjects with one continent working experience displayed leading leader focuses on uniformity and task completion concept, while those with two continents working experience were led by interpersonal skills. Those of three working experience continents showed in equal terms leading interpersonal skills and conceptual skills (Fig. 56).

Subjects with 3–5 years of experience displayed in equal terms interpersonal skills and conceptual skills, 5–10 years of experience focused more on

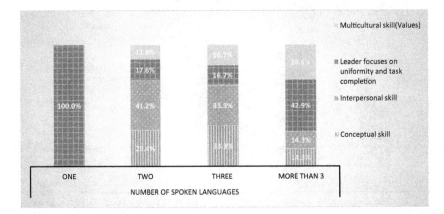

Fig. 54.   Leadership Differences Among Participants Based on the Number of Spoken Languages. *Source:* Author's own research.

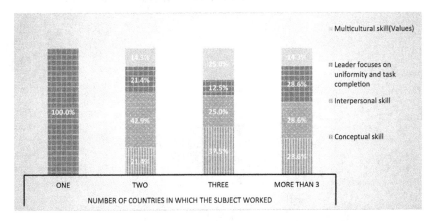

Fig. 55.   Leadership Differences Based on the Number of Countries Participants Worked in. *Source:* Author's own research.

interpersonal skills, 10–15 years of experience was driven by leader focusing on uniformity and task completion concept while those with more than 21 years' experience displayed in an equal manner leader focuses on uniformity and task completion, interpersonal skills, and conceptual skills (Fig. 57).

4.4 Summary and Conclusions of Our Qualitative Research

The research was conducted to investigate the content and connections within the relationship between CQ, KD, and ML.

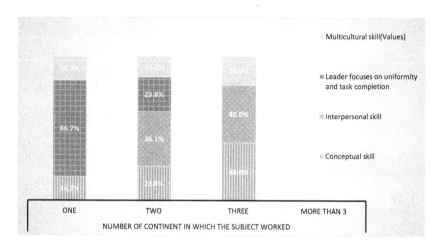

Fig. 56.   Leadership Differences Based on the Number of Continents
Participants Worked in. *Source:* Author's own research.

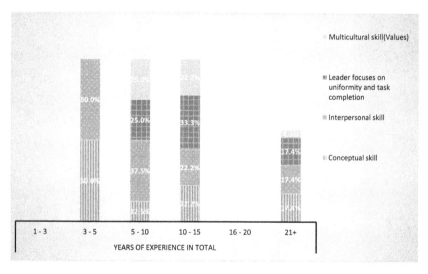

Fig. 57.   Leadership Differences Among Participants Based on Years
of Experience in Total. *Source:* Author's own research.

Emotional CQ was the participants' highest form of CQ, followed by rational CQ. While most interviewees spoke about emotional and rational CQ, only a few people spoke of spiritual CQ. Some of the participants also downplayed individual cultural differences for team culture.

Most participants based their decision-making on rational knowledge, followed by spiritual knowledge. Few interviewees based their decisions on emotional knowledge, believing that emotional knowledge should play only a minimal role in decision-making. Most participants also believed in combining all forms of KD – rational, emotional, and spiritual – in order to make the most agile and appropriate decisions.

Most of the participants displayed interpersonal skills of ML. Some of the participants displayed conceptual skills and multicultural skills (values). However, some leaders focus on uniformity and task completion rather than cultural values or differences.

The cross-case analysis of CQ, KD, and ML based on the demographic variables also revealed how these concepts were expressed comparatively. Female participants expressed more emotional CQ than male participants, while only male participants expressed spiritual CQ. Male and female participants had the same response percentage for rational CQ. Participants above 60 years expressed only rational and emotional CQ, while only participants of age groups 26–40 and 41–60 expressed spiritual CQ minimally.

Participants with a master's degree expressed more spiritual intelligence than participants with a university degree. In contrast, participants with a university degree expressed more emotional and rational intelligence than participants with a master's graduate. Participants from Africa and Asia mostly expressed emotional CQ, while participants from North America expressed spiritual CQ more than participants from any other continent.

Participants in Trade expressed all forms of CQ equally, while Participants in Services displayed primarily emotional CQ. Those in Retail expressed only rational and emotional CQ and no spiritual CQ. Only participants whose company size (turnover) is 10 million and above expressed spiritual CQ. Top and middle management expressed mostly emotional CQ. Participants whose company size (employees) was 1,001+ mostly focused on spiritual CQ. Participants who had worked for 5–10 years within the company expressed emotional CQ more than any other age group. Participants who had worked for 10–15 years expressed rational and spiritual CQ the most. Only participants who had managed six or more nationalities expressed spiritual CQ. Participants who spoke more than three languages expressed spiritual CQ the most. Participants who spoke three languages expressed mostly emotional CQ. Participants who spoke only one language expressed more rational CQ than those who spoke two or more languages. Participants who worked in more than three countries expressed more spiritual CQ than those who worked in three countries or less. Participants who worked in three countries and less displayed more rational CQ than others. Participants with work experience in three continents displayed the highest spiritual and rational CQ expression. Participants with work experience in two or one continent(s) expressed more emotional CQ than participants who worked in three continents.

Female participants expressed more spiritual knowledge and rational knowledge than male participants, while male participants expressed more emotional knowledge. Male participants also combined all forms of KD for decision-making *n* a more balanced way than female participants.

Participants with a master's degree expressed more spiritual knowledge than others, while high school graduates expressed emotional knowledge more than university and master's graduates. Only participants in Trades and Services expressed the use of spiritual knowledge for decision-making. Only participants whose company turnover is 1 million and above expressed spiritual knowledge. Participants who worked in companies that made less than 1 million used rational knowledge more for decision-making. Participants in middle management expressed the use of more spiritual knowledge, while participants in top management used more rational knowledge for decision-making. Participants who managed 16 to 20 nationalities expressed more spiritual and emotional knowledge than the interviewees who managed less than 15 nationalities. Participants whose number of nationalities managed is 1–3 used more rational knowledge for decision-making.

Participants who speak more than three languages use more spiritual knowledge, while participants who speak three languages use more rational knowledge for decision-making. Participants who speak one language use emotional knowledge most. Participants who worked in more than three countries used spiritual knowledge the most, while those who worked in one country used rational and emotional knowledge the most. Participants who had work experience in three continents combined different forms of KD most, while the most while participants who worked in one continent used rational and emotional knowledge the most. Only participants who had worked 5 years and above used emotional knowledge. Participants who worked less than 5 years displayed spiritual and rational knowledge the most.

Male participants expressed higher conceptual skills, while female participants expressed higher interpersonal skills. More of the participants from 41–60 years of age focused on uniformity and task completion instead of cultural differences. Participants with a master's degree expressed more multicultural skills (value), while participants in high school only focused on uniformity and task completion, not cultural differences. Only participants from Europe and North America displayed multicultural skills (values). Only participants who worked in Trade and Services expressed multicultural skills (values). Participants in middle management expressed more multicultural skills (values) than participants from top management. Participants who spoke more than three languages expressed the highest multicultural skill (values). Only participants with a total work experience of 5 years and above expressed multicultural skills (values). Participants with work experience in three continents expressed more conceptual, interpersonal, and multicultural skills (values). Only participants who worked in one or two countries focused on uniformity and task completion instead of cultural differences.

The result supported the study's conceptual model on the relationship of the concepts. It was found that KD directly influenced CQ and ML. CQ also had a direct influence on ML. Furthermore, the result showed that KD indirectly influenced ML through CQ.

Chapter 5

Quantitative Research

As presented in detail in the methodology chapter, the questionnaire, developed based on the six hypotheses, regrouped 396 valid answers from all over the world.

5.1 Demographical Information – As Resulted From the Questionnaires

Demographical information describes the personal and professional information of the current sample. It includes gender, age, education, continent, and country affiliation. In the context of professional information, it includes the company's main sector, company's size (company's yearly turnover in millions €), company size (employees' number), function (from a management level point of view), years of experience within the company, years of experience in total, number of managed nationalities, number of continents in which you worked, number of countries in which you worked, and experience in managing virtual teams. The Descriptive Analysis of Statistical Package for Social Sciences (SPSS) provides each demographic's stepwise frequency and percentages.

Gender. The gender is comprised of male, female, and nonbinary categorization. The descriptive results are described in Fig. 1. It showed that male ($n = 200$, 50.5%) samples were most probably the leading category of the sample. While a substantial number of females ($n = 188$, 47.5%), the least represented gender sample is the nonbinary group ($n = 8$, 2.0%). Fig. 1 represents the gender mapping percentage as a result of the interview.

Age. The sample's age ranges from 18 to more than 61 years for a valid number of answers of $N = 396$. The descriptive results reported that 65 participants (16.41%) had ages ranging from 18 to 25 years, 136 participants (34.34%) had an age of 26–40 years, 160 participants (40.4%) had an age that ranged between 41 and 60 years, and only 35 (8.84%) had an age of more than 61 years old (Fig. 2).

Education. In the academic context, the education of the sample was categorized into High School only, University Graduate, Master Graduate, and PhD Graduate. Fig. 3 represents the frequency and percentage of each educational group. It was found that most of the participants could be associated with

Developing Multicultural Leadership using Knowledge Dynamics and Cultural Intelligence, 97–138
Copyright © 2024 Dan Paiuc
Published under exclusive licence by Emerald Publishing Limited
doi:10.1108/978-1-83549-432-520241010

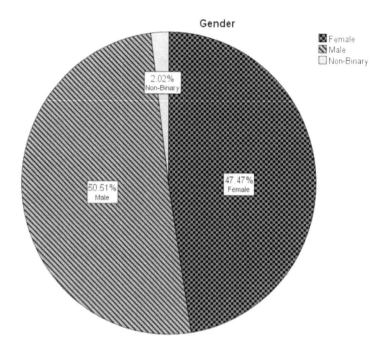

Fig. 1. Gender Groups by Percentage (For Questionnaires). *Source:*
Author's own research.

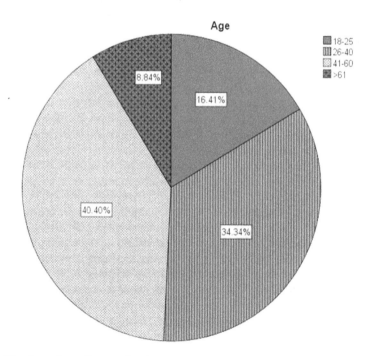

Fig. 2. Age Groups by Percentage (For Questionnaires). *Source:*
Author's own research.

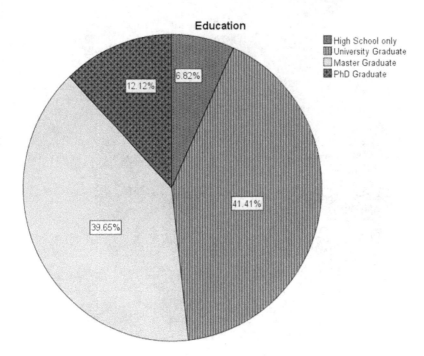

Fig. 3.   Education Groups by Percentage (For Questionnaires).
Source: Author's own research.

University Graduates ($n = 164$, 41.4%). In the second place, we found the Master Graduates ($n = 157$, 39.6%), followed by PhD Graduates ($n = 48$, 12.1%) and High School only ($n = 27$, 6.8%); Fig. 3.

Continent. The geographical affiliation of the sample was also assessed. It includes highly populated continents such as Africa, Asia, Australia, Europe, North America, and South America. The descriptive results showed that 47 (11.9%) participants were Africans, 79 (19.9%) were Asians, 38 (9.6%) were Australians, 130 (32.8%) Europeans, 73 (18.4%) were North Americans, while only 29 (7.3%) were South Americans. It can be seen in Fig. 4 that Europeans (32.8%) were the most commonly found population, followed then by Asians, North Americans, Africans, Australians, and South Americans (Fig. 4).

Country. The country affiliation was also analyzed using descriptive analysis of SPSS. In the current context, more than 50 diverse country affiliations were reported by the sample. However, US ($n = 28$, 7.1%) and Australia ($n = 27$, 6.8%) respondents had higher numbers and percentages than other country affiliations. Furthermore, 9 (2.3%) respondents came from Malta, 17 (4.3%) from Romania, and 16 (4.1%) respondents had Saudi Arabia affiliation (Fig. 5).

Company Main Sector. The professional information search category first analyzed the participants' affiliation with the company's main sectors of activity.

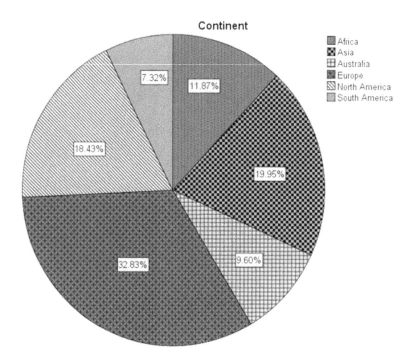

Fig. 4.   Continent Groups by Percentage (For Questionnaires).
Source: Author's own research.

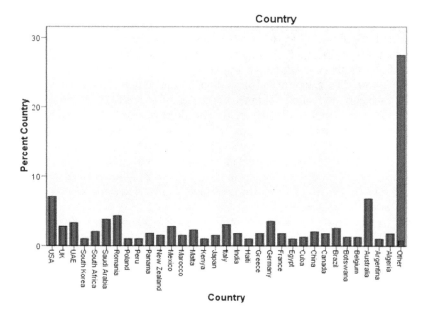

Fig. 5.   Country Groups by Percentage (For Questionnaires With
Collapsed Countries Less Than 1%). *Source:* Author's own research.

We have summarized five sectors: Production, Retail, Services, Trade, and *Other Sectors*. The descriptive results described that 87 (22%) respondents had production-sector affiliation, 95 (24%) had retail sector, 115 (29%) had service-sector, 92 (23.2%) had trade sector, and only 7 (1.8%) had other sectors affiliation. Fig. 6 shows that most participants had service-sector (29%) affiliation, while *other sectors* (1.8%) represent the lowest affiliated sector among the sample (Fig. 6).

Company's size (company's yearly turnover in millions €.). Secondly, the assessed demographic was related to the company's size concerning yearly turnover in millions €. The results presented in the further down figure showed that the number of respondents associated with <0.5M €/year turnover was 50, ≥0.5M but <1 M€/year was 72, ≥1M but <5M €/year as turnover - 102, ≥5M but <10M €/yearly turnover – 107. Similarly, ≥10M but <50M €/year as turnover was 48, and ≥50M €/yearly turnover was reported by 17 participants. The most frequent yearly turnover was ≥5M but <10M €/yearly (27.02%). In

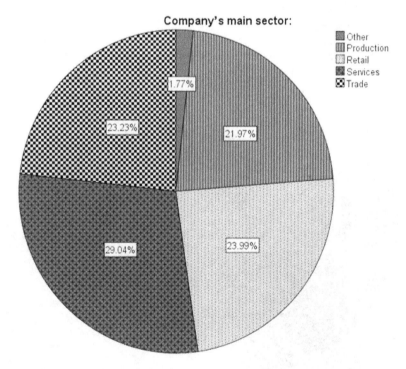

Fig. 6.   Company's Main Sector Groups by Percentage (For Questionnaires). *Source:* Author's own research.

contrast, ≥50M €/year (4.3%) was the least probable company's yearly turnover reported by the sample (Fig. 7).

Company size (employees' number). Thirdly, company size concerning employees' number was analyzed also using descriptive analysis. It is comprised of employee numbers ranging from 1 to more than 1,000 employees. The results explained that 53 (13.4%) participants had 1–10 employee-based company size, 65 (16.4%) had 11 to 50 employees, 84 (21.2%) had 51–100 employees, and 116 (29.3%) had 101–500 employee-based company dimensions. Moreover, 60 (15.2%) participants reported 501–1,000 employees, with only 18 (4.5%) participants reporting more than 1,000 employee-based company size. In short, 101–500 (29.2%) employee-based company size was the most common, with more than 1,000 (4.5%) employee-based company size as the least common employee-based company size reported by the sample (Fig. 8).

Function (from a management-level point of view). The next assessed demographic is the managerial function of the sample. It comprised lower, middle, and top managerial functions. The descriptive results reported that top managerial functions (*n* = 205, 51.8%) were most probable than middle managerial functions

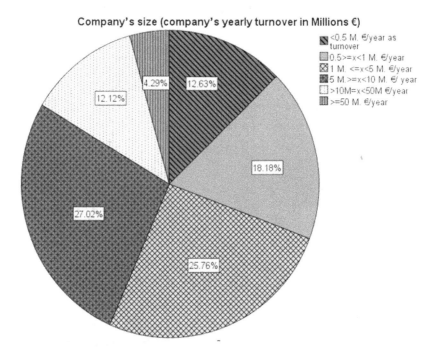

Fig. 7.   Company's Size (Company's Yearly Turnover in Millions €) Groups by Percentage (For Questionnaires). *Source:* Author's own research.

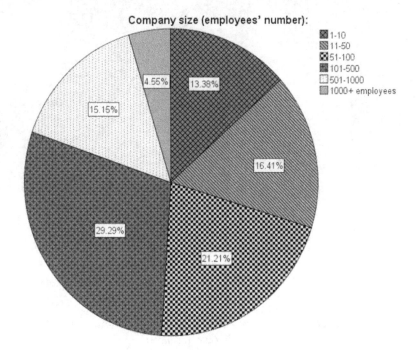

Fig. 8.   Company's Size (Employees' Number) Groups by Percentage
(For Questionnaires). *Source:* Author's own research.

(n = 145, 36.6%), with the least probable the lower managerial roles (n = 46,
11.6%) (Fig. 9).

Years of experience within the company. The company-specific experience of
the sample was also analyzed. It comprised five categorizations ranging from 1 to
more than 16 years of experience within the company. It can be seen further down
that 33 (18.2%) participants had 1–3 years of working experience within their
actual company, 82 (20.7%) had 4–5 years, 100 (25.3%) had 6–10 years, 116
(29.3%) had 11–15 years, and 26 (6.6%) had more than 16 years of work experience within the actual job. Thus, the most commonly reported work experience
within the company was 11–15 years (29.3%) (Fig. 10).

Years of experience in total. The total work experience (in years) was also
assessed. The results in Fig. 11 showed the frequency and percentages of categorization of total work experience years. It was found that most of the participants had total work experience of 11–15 years (n = 116, 27.8%), then 6–10 years
(n = 88, 22.2%), and 16–20 years (n = 72, 18.2%) of work experience. In contrast,
over 21 years of work experience (n = 30, 7.6%) was the least reported total work
experience (Fig. 11).

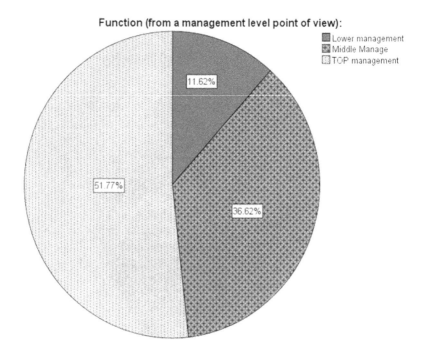

Fig. 9.   Function Groups by Percentage (For Questionnaires). *Source:*
Author's own research.

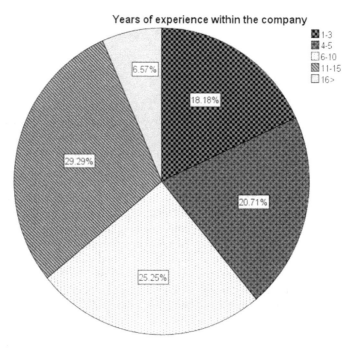

Fig. 10.   Year of Experience Within Company Groups by Percentage
(For Questionnaires). *Source:* Author's own research.

Years of experience in total

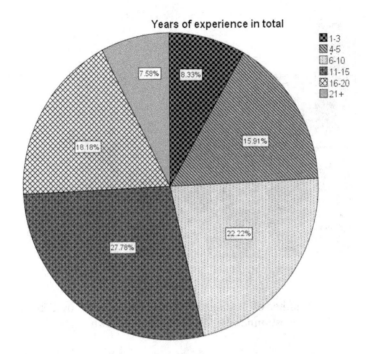

Fig. 11.   Year of Experience in Total Groups by Percentage (For Questionnaires). *Source:* Author's own research.

Number of managed nationalities. The managed nationalities by the sample were another assessed demographic. The descriptive results found that 23.2% of respondents had 1–3 managed nationalities, 18.2% 4–5, 16.7% had 11–15, and 13.6% had 6–10 leaded nationalities. These were the highest reported managed nationalities of the sample. However, only 2% had more than 100, 6.1% had 50 to 100, and 8.8% had 6 to 10 managed nationalities. These were the least reported nationalities managed by the sample. In short, 1 to 3 (n = 92, 23.2%) nationalities were the most probable leaded nationalities of our sample (Fig. 12).

Spoken Languages. The linguistic characteristics of the sample were assessed by measuring the number of spoken languages. It was categorized into One, Two, Three, or More than three spoken languages. The results in Fig. 13 reported that 45 (11.4%) participants can speak one language, 147 (37.1%) can speak two languages, 139 (35.1%) can speak three languages, and 65 (16.4%) can speak more than three languages. It means most of the participants easily speak two or three languages (Fig. 13).

Number of continents in which interviewees worked. Another assessed demographic is the number of worked continents. It was reported that One (n = 166,

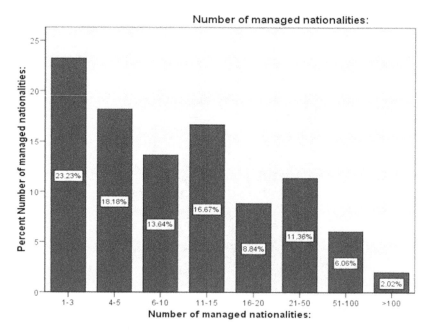

Fig. 12. Number of Managed Nationalities Groups by Percentage (For Questionnaires). *Source:* Author's own research.

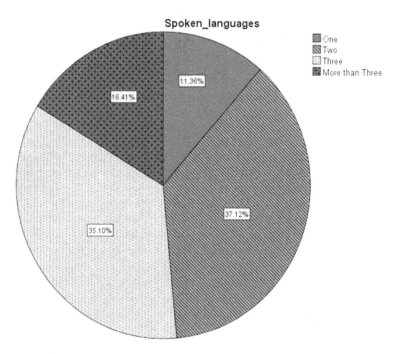

Fig. 13. Spoken Languages Groups by Percentage (For Questionnaires). *Source:* Author's own research.

41.9%) and Two (*n* = 128, 32.3%) worked continents were the most commonly encountered sample answers. In contrast, the lowest frequencies represented by Three (*n* = 62, 15.7%) or *More than three* (*n* = 40, 10.1%) worked continents (Fig. 14).

Number of countries in which interviewees worked. Further in the professional information, the other assessed demographic is the number of worked countries. The descriptive results explained that Three (*n* = 104, 26.3%), More than three (*n* = 100, 25.3%), and Two (*n* = 99, 25%) worked countries were more highly reported than One (*n* = 90, 23.5%) worked country (Fig. 15).

Experience in managing virtual teams. Lastly, the experience related to virtual team management was assessed. It was categorized from no experience to more than 5 years of experience. The descriptive results highlight the frequency and percentage of these demographics. It was found that 51 (12.9%) participants had no experience, 99 (25%) had 1–3 years, 142 (35.9%) had 4–5 years, and 104 (26.3%) had more than 5 years of experience in managing virtual teams. In short, 4–5 years (35.9%) of work experience managing virtual teams was the most encountered answer (Fig. 16).

Table 1 synthesizes all the captured demographic answers with enhancing on their frequencies and percentages.

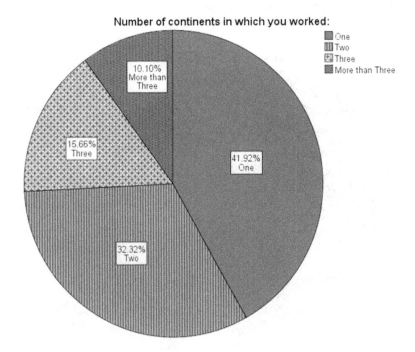

Fig. 14. Number of Worked Continents Groups by Percentage (For Questionnaires). *Source:* Author's own research.

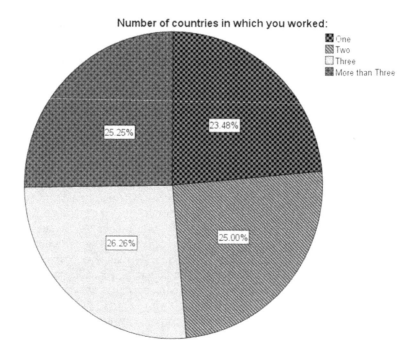

Fig. 15.   Number of Worked Countries Groups by Percentage (For Questionnaires). *Source:* Author's own research.

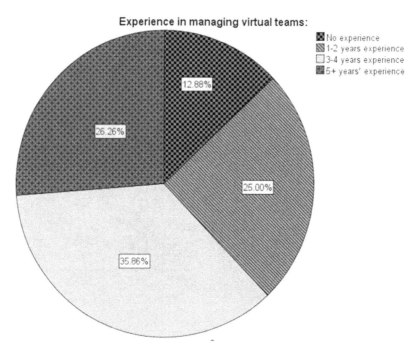

Fig. 16.   Experience in Managing Virtual Team Groups by Percentage. *Source:* Author's own research.

Table 1. Demographic Information Synthesis (Except the Countries).

Demographic Variables	Group	Category	Frequency	Percentage (%)
Gender	1	Female	188	47.5
	2	Male	200	50.5
	3	Nonbinary	8	2.0
Education	1	High School only	65	16.4
	2	University Graduate	35	8.8
	3	Master Graduate	136	34.3
	4	PhD Graduate	160	40.4
Continent affiliation	1	Asia	79	19.9
	2	Africa	47	11.9
	3	Australia	38	9.6
	4	Europe	130	32.8
	5	North America	73	18.4
	6	South America	29	7.3
Company sector	1	Production	87	22.0
	2	Retail	95	24.0
	3	Services	115	29.0
	4	Trade	92	23.2
	5	Other	7	1.8
Company's size (company's yearly turnover in millions €)	1	<0.5M €/year as turnover	50	12.6
	2	≥0.5 to<1M €/year as turnover	72	18.2
	3	≥1M to < 5M €/year as turnover	102	25.8
	4	≥5M to <10M €/year as turnover	107	27.0
	5	≥10M to <50M	48	12.1
	6	≥50M €/year as turnover	17	4.3

(Continued)

Table 1. *(Continued)*

Demographic Variables	Group	Category	Frequency	Percentage (%)
Company size (employees' number)	1	1–10	53	13.4
	2	11–50	65	16.4
	3	51–100	84	21.2
	4	101–500	116	29.3
	5	501–1,000	60	15.2
	6	1,000+ employees	18	4.5
Function (from a management level point of view)	1	Lower management	46	11.6
	2	Middle management	145	36.6
	3	Top management	205	51.8
Years of experience within the company	1	1–3 years	72	18.2
	2	4–5 years	82	20.7
	3	6–10 years	100	25.3
	4	11–15 years	116	29.3
	5	≥16 years	26	6.6
Years of experience in total	1	1–3 years	33	8.3
	2	4–5 years	63	15.9
	3	6–10 years	88	22.2
	4	11–15 years	110	27.8
	5	16–20 years	72	18.2
	6	≥21 years	30	7.6
Number of managed nationalities	1	1–3	92	23.2
	2	4–5	72	18.2
	3	6–10	54	13.6
	4	11–15	66	16.7
	5	16–20	35	8.8
	6	21–50	45	11.4

Table 1. *(Continued)*

Demographic Variables	Group	Category	Frequency	Percentage (%)
	7	51–100	24	6.1
	8	>100	8	2.0
Spoken languages	1	One	45	11.4
	2	Two	147	37.1
	3	Three	139	35.1
	4	More than three	65	16.4
Number of continents in which you worked	1	One	166	41.9
	2	Two	128	32.3
	3	Three	62	15.7
	4	More than three	40	10.1
Number of countries in which you worked	1	One	93	23.5
	2	Two	99	25.0
	3	Three	104	26.3
	4	More than three	100	25.3
Experience in managing virtual teams	1	No experience	51	12.9
	2	1–2 years' experience	99	25.0
	3	3–4 years' experience	142	35.9
	4	5+ years' experience	104	26.3

Source: Author's own research.

5.2 Descriptive Statistics

In the second step of the research, we utilized IBM's SPSS Statistics version 22 to analyze survey data, and we have presented in Appendix K the descriptive statistics for all the constructs. The survey received 396 replies, and the scale used was a Likert one, with answers ranging from one to seven, with one being "Strongly disagree" and seven being "Strongly agree."

5.3 Descriptive Statistics – Assessing Normality (Mean, Standard Deviation, Minimum and Maximum Ranges, Median, Skewness and Kurtosis)

Descriptive statistics were further assessed to analyze the central tendencies, data dispersion, and normality of current data. It gives statistics on the mean, standard deviation, and minimum and maximum ranges. It also provides skewness and kurtosis statistics for the respective items of the construct. This was also done using SPSS version 22. Appendix L shows the indicators' descriptive statistics, the 76 items' skewness, and kurtosis results for normality. In SmartPLS, the Partial Least Squares Structural Equation Modeling (PLS-SEM) was a nonparametric statistical analysis. It does not entail data to be normal. Thus, it was not based on CB-SEM (Confirmatory Factor Analysis-based Structural Equation Modeling) and variate from Maximum Likelihood (Hair, Hollingsworth, et al., 2017).

According to the literature, the criterion for the higher mean is the positive mean value within the range of minimum to maximum statistics of data. A higher standard deviation is about a standard deviation in the ± 1 range and lower than the mean. Similarly, the skewness value greater than 1 or less than -1 is interpreted as highly skewed, 0.5 to 1 or -0.5 to -1 shows moderately skewed, and -0.5 to 0.5 is explained fairly symmetrical distribution (Hair, Hollingsworth, et al., 2017). Other specialized literature suggests that skewness and kurtosis values ranging between ± 1 define the normal distribution of data. An extreme positive or negative value results in positive or negative distribution of data other than the normal distribution (Livingston, 2004).

The first subscale of cultural intelligence (CQ) is metacognitive CQ. The descriptive analysis reported the positive range, while the standard deviation was lower than the mean. It suggests the central distribution of data, following significant criteria of central tendency. Furthermore, the skewness value of metacognitive CQ was -9.66, while the kurtosis value was 0.411. Both values were within the range of ± 1, thus suggesting the normal distribution of data. The second subscale of CQ is the cognitive CQ. It comprised 6 items whose mean range was from 4.94 to 5.10 with a standard deviation of 1.575 to 1.719, respectively. The skewness value ranged from -0.488 to -0.721, being in the range of ± 1. Similarly, the kurtosis ranges from -0.244 to -0.800, also lower than -1, indicating central dispersion of respective items. The third subscale is about motivational CQ. The descriptive results indicated that the mean and standard deviation was higher for the items of motivational CQ. As it ranges from 5.03 to 5.24 with a standard deviation ranging from 1.653 to 1.710, respectively, this subscale also showed normal dispersion of data in terms of skewness and kurtosis, which lied within the range. The other subscales of CQ also showed normal central tendencies and dispersion of data (see Appendix L and K). The scales of knowledge dynamics (KD), organizational context (OC), and multicultural leadership (ML) are also shown in Appendix K, where their items showed normal dispersion.

5.4 Descriptive Statistics – Assessing Normality (Kolmogorov-Smirnov and Shapiro-Wilk Tests)

Other tests of normality were also discussed in this section. It includes Kolmogorov-Smirnov and Shapiro-Wilk tests for normality. Both tests indicated – as a general rule of thumb – that the data are normally distributed if its significance value (p) falls above 0.05 ($p > 0$ .05). Otherwise, the distribution is not statistically normal ($p < 0$ .05) (Hair, Hollingsworth, et al., 2017). The sequential analysis of all the items is given in Appendix M.

In our specific case, it was found that the Kolmogorov-Smirnov test of all the items indicated the statistics with a p-value less than 0.05. Hence, it indicates the non-normal distribution of data. Similarly, the Shapiro-Wilk test for normality indicated that all the data items were not normally distributed, as all the current p-value was found to be less than 0.05 (see Appendix M). In the wholesome, the data assessing study constructs were not statistically normal, according to the results of normality tests.

The further section of this chapter indicates the assessment of current data using PLS-SEM as the data were found to be different from the normal distribution. Hence, nonparametric tests were used for further analysis. Majorly focused assessments were made using the PLS-SEM of SmartPLS. The in-detail explanation of model assessment is provided in the below subchapters.

5.5 Evaluation of Measurement Models

The first step in the examination of PLS-SEM involves the assessment of the measurement model where the constructs' reliability, validity, and collinearity are discussed in the light of the predefined rule of thumb (Diamantopoulos & Winklhofer, 2001; Hair, Risher, et al., 2019).

The main measurement analysis includes the reliability and validity analysis assessing current model accuracy and consistency. In the PLS-SEM, PLS Algorithm provides the statistics of concerned reliabilities and validities of the model. Firstly, the reliability analysis was analyzed. It includes indicator reliability, explained in the current section. Secondly, the discriminant validity and convergent validity of the model were analyzed and explained.

5.5.1 Reliability Evaluation

In the reliability context, outer loadings are typically measured for each item within the latent variable. In PLS-SEM, outer loading is the standardized estimate, which is identified as factor loading (Benitez et al., 2020). Generally, it is suggested that the significant factor loadings should be above 0.70 (Hair, Risher, et al., 2019). Benitez et al. (2020) discussed that lower than 0.70 values are not problematic if the construct reliability and validity threshold is met. Table 2 shows the outer loadings of each indicator. Since all factor loadings were above 0.70, it can be observed that study indicators were highly reliable for all latent

Table 2. Evaluation of Measurement Model.

Indicators	Code	FL	Cronbach's Alpha	rho_a	Composite Reliability	AVE
Cultural Intelligence (CQ)			0.962	0.962	0.965	0.582
MCQ			0.846	0.847	0.897	0.685
	MCQ1	0.837				
	MCQ2	0.839				
	MCQ3	0.817				
	MCQ4	0.816				
COCQ			0.907	0.907	0.928	0.682
	COCQ1	0.825				
	COCQ2	0.808				
	COCQ3	0.844				
	COCQ4	0.843				
	COCQ5	0.824				
	COCQ6	0.811				
MOTCQ			0.895	0.895	0.923	0.705
	MOTCQ1	0.850				
	MOTCQ2	0.861				
	MOTCQ3	0.829				
	MOTCQ4	0.820				
	MOTCQ5	0.837				
BEHCQ			0.876	0.876	0.910	0.668
	BEHCQ1	0.821				
	BEHCQ2	0.818				
	BEHCQ3	0.801				
	BEHCQ4	0.823				
	BEHCQ5	0.824				
Knowledge Dynamics (KD)			0.905	0.906	0.922	0.569
RKD			0.819	0.822	0.892	0.735
	RKD1	0.868				
	RKD2	0.833				
	RKD3	0.870				

Table 2. *(Continued)*

Indicators	Code	FL	Cronbach's Alpha	rho_a	Composite Reliability	AVE
SKD			0.824	0.824	0.895	0.740
	SKD1	0.872				
	SKD2	0.844				
	SKD3	0.864				
EKD			0.795	0.795	0.880	0.709
	EKD1	0.833				
	EKD2	0.851				
	EKD3	0.842				
Multicultural Leadership (ML)			0.920	0.921	0.932	0.532
AS_ML			0.792	0.793	0.878	0.706
	AS_ML1	0.833				
	AS_ML2	0.855				
	AS_ML3	0.834				
IS_ML			0.765	0.767	0.865	0.681
	IS_ML1	0.813				
	IS_ML2	0.807				
	IS_ML3	0.855				
CS_ML			0.766	0.776	0.865	0.682
	CS_ML1	0.863				
	CS_ML2	0.845				
	CS_ML3	0.766				
MLS_ML			0.769	0.772	0.867	0.684
	MLS_ML1	0.844				
	MLS_ML2	0.784				
	MLS_ML3	0.851				
Organizational Context (OC)			0.940	0.941	0.946	0.495
ACL_OC			0.723	0.723	0.844	0.643
	ACL_OC1	0.809				
	ACL_OC2	0.789				
	ACL_OC3	0.809				

(Continued)

Table 2. *(Continued)*

Indicators	Code	FL	Cronbach's Alpha	rho_a	Composite Reliability	AVE
CCL_OC			0.803	0.803	0.884	0.717
	CCL_OC1	0.863				
	CCL_OC2	0.844				
	CCL_OC3	0.834				
DEIL_OC			0.742	0.742	0.853	0.660
	DEIL_OC1	0.832				
	DEIL_OC2	0.812				
	DEIL_OC3	0.792				
EAIL_OC			0.736	0.736	0.850	0.654
	EAIL_OC1	0.800				
	EAIL_OC2	0.810				
	EAIL_OC3	0.817				
FTL_OC			0.764	0.764	0.864	0.679
	FTL_OC1	0.819				
	FTL_OC2	0.820				
	FTL_OC3	0.834				
SL_OC			0.729	0.737	0.846	0.648
	SL_OC1	0.823				
	SL_OC2	0.765				
	SL_OC3	0.825				

Source: Author's own research.

Note: FL: Factor Loadings, MCQ: Metacognitive Cultural Intelligence, COCQ: Cognitive Cultural Intelligence, MOTCQ: Motivational Cultural Intelligence, BEHCQ: Behavioral Cultural Intelligence, RKD: Rational Knowledge Dynamics, SKD: Spiritual Knowledge Dynamics, EKD: Emotional Rational Knowledge Dynamics, AS_ML Administrative Skills, IS_ML: Interpersonal Skills, CS_ML Conceptual Skills, MLS_ML: Multicultural Leadership Skills, ACL_OC: Agility and Change Level, CCL_OC: Community and Connection Level, DIEL_OC: Diversity, Equity, and Inclusion Level, EAIL_OC: Entrepreneurship, Autonomy, and Innovation Level, FTL_OC: Flexibility and Transparency Level, SL_OC: Strength Level of the Company's Culture.

factors in the measurement model. Thus, it leads to the retention of all the items concerning their respective construct.

Indicator reliability is about the internal consistency of the overall used scale items. It also includes the dimensions of constructs. Literature reported that

Cronbach's alpha of ≥0.70 was categorized as good construct reliability (Hoelzle & Meyer, 2013). Other specific literature reported that Cronbach's alpha was considered statistically significant when the alpha value lay above 0.70 and was considered to have a high internal consistency when the value ranges above 0.80. Thus, in order to have a result that indicates significant construct reliability (Goodhue et al., 2012), Table 2 incorporates the above analysis into the current construct reliability summary.

It was found that all the constructs and their sub-constructs had excellent reliability, according to the criterion of Goodhue et al. (2012). According to our workings, all constructs and their sub-constructs meet the significant construct reliability threshold ($\alpha >0.80$).

Meanwhile, composite reliability and rho_a are other measurements used to determine internal consistency. According to the literature, the composite reliability and rho_a must be above the 0.70 threshold (Nunnally & Bernstein, 1994). The results of composite reliability and rho_a are also reported in Table 2. All independent and dependent constructs of the measurement model had good indicator reliability.

Furthermore, indicator reliability assesses the amount to which each indicator associates with a variable. The value of average variance extracted (AVE) was also considered typically to determine the reliability of a latent variable (Hair, Risher, et al., 2019). An AVE above 0.50 is suggested for the empirical evidence of the convergent validity, and Table 2 also represents the AVE values for all latent variables of the model. The indicator reliability was empirically proved good as all the AVE values lie above 0.50. In contrast, the AVE value of organizational context (AVE = 0.495) (see Table 2) was somewhat equal to 0.50. Thus, the overall model shows an acceptable range of internal consistency. In short, the measurement model had significant relevance with their respective constructs. The pictorial representation of the measurement model evaluation is shown in Fig. 17.

5.5.2 Discriminant Validity Measurement

Discriminant validity requires that the latent factors that are aimed to signify different theoretical concepts are also statistically different (Benitez et al., 2020). In other words, it shows that theoretically different constructs were also found statistically different. Specific literature reported three types of methods to assess discriminant validity, and those are: the Cross loading, Fornell and Larcker (1981), and the Heterotrait-Monotrait Ratio (HTMT). The step-wise explanation of each method is given below.

5.5.2.1 Cross Loadings

Cross loadings is considered the first method of analyzing discriminant validity. It provides information about the indicators having loadings on their respective construct and with multiple constructs using PLS-SEM. The threshold of significant discriminant validity is the cross loading of construct items that were higher

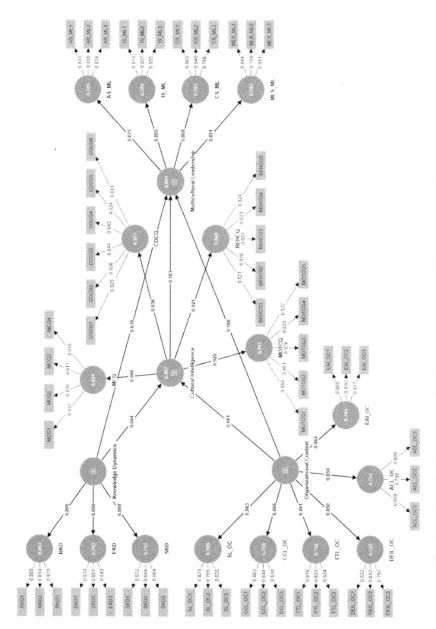

Fig. 17.   The Evaluation of the Measurement Model. *Source:* Author's own research.

within its construct than other constructs. Generally, it is suggested for the cross loadings to be above 0.70 – thus interpreted as statistically significant (Hair, Sarstedt, et al., 2019). Table 3 shows the results of cross loadings of each construct. It was found that all the indicators had higher cross loading in their respective constructs. The criterion for significant cross loading was fulfilled as the loading of each indicator was greater than its loading on other constructs – thus indicating the discriminant validity of constructs. It means theoretically different constructs were also statistically different.

5.5.2.2 (Fornell and Larcker Criterion)

The second method for assessing discriminant validity is the Fornell and Larcker Criterion. This criterion suggested the comparison of latent constructs correlations with the square root of the AVE value (Fornell & Larcker, 1981). The AVE value must be above 0.50. It means the constructs' AVE square roots must be greater than its correlation with other constructs (Hair, Hult, et al., 2017). The current correlations and square root of the AVE value were also obtained using PLS Algorithm. The results of the Fornell and Larcker Criterion are shown in Table 4. It was found that all the items had a higher correlation index. Thus, significant discriminant validity was observed. It gives more statistical strength to the current measurement model having a discrimination index.

5.5.2.3 The Heterotrait-Monotrait Ratio (HTMT)

The third method of assessing discriminant validity is the HTMT Ratio. Literature reported that HTMT attains great specificity and sensitivity rates across all analyses than the Fornell Larcker criterion. It estimates the average HTMT correlations across constructs measuring different phenomena (Hair et al., 2018; Henseler et al., 2015). To reach out the statistical empirical evidence using HTMT for the discriminant validity, Henseler et al. (2015) suggested the HTMT value must be less than 0.85 (strict rule of thumb) or less than 0.90 (lenient rule of thumb), or significantly lower than 1 (Franke & Sarstedt, 2019; Henseler et al., 2015). PLS Algorithm provides the HTMT results, as shown in Table 5. It demonstrates that all items meet the criteria (e.g., HTMT <0.85).

In the wholesome, current measurement model assessment suggested that each indicator had a statistical difference in their underlying measures as compared to other constructs measurements, thus indicating an excellent set of discriminant validity of the current measurement model following cross loading, Fornell and Larcker Criterion, and HTMT Ratio criteria.

Further sections explained the structural model analysis using PLS-SEM. If all tests are passed, the model goes statically valid and reliable.

Table 3. Indicator Cross Loading.

	MCQ	BEH CQ	MOT CQ	CO CQ	RKD	SKD	EKD	AS	IS	CS	MLS	ACL	CCL	DEIL	EIAL	FTL	SL
MCQ1	**0.837**	0.634	0.719	0.477	0.484	0.460	0.511	0.477	0.460	0.534	0.484	0.324	0.386	0.293	0.302	0.303	0.343
MCQ2	**0.839**	0.644	0.704	0.479	0.478	0.435	0.517	0.479	0.431	0.491	0.455	0.314	0.349	0.256	0.280	0.287	0.298
MCQ3	**0.817**	0.636	0.647	0.434	0.462	0.459	0.556	0.434	0.484	0.480	0.495	0.331	0.392	0.306	0.293	0.255	0.349
MCQ4	**0.816**	0.658	0.622	0.513	0.503	0.515	0.541	0.513	0.463	0.510	0.525	0.309	0.380	0.248	0.245	0.308	0.322
COCQ1	0.646	**0.825**	0.628	0.646	0.368	0.423	0.432	0.378	0.429	0.463	0.445	0.291	0.306	0.294	0.307	0.304	0.331
COCQ2	0.640	**0.808**	0.629	0.644	0.444	0.433	0.470	0.466	0.477	0.459	0.506	0.353	0.370	0.375	0.339	0.352	0.390
COCQ3	0.674	**0.844**	0.634	0.678	0.470	0.465	0.498	0.445	0.473	0.509	0.503	0.312	0.349	0.319	0.310	0.349	0.315
COCQ4	0.719	**0.843**	0.720	0.729	0.550	0.482	0.519	0.474	0.518	0.532	0.506	0.350	0.365	0.344	0.324	0.353	0.370
COCQ5	0.647	**0.824**	0.653	0.665	0.472	0.486	0.476	0.425	0.478	0.519	0.492	0.296	0.334	0.299	0.285	0.315	0.303
COCQ6	0.703	**0.811**	0.668	0.643	0.450	0.458	0.491	0.486	0.486	0.549	0.480	0.341	0.358	0.287	0.310	0.311	0.334
MOTCQ1	0.631	0.659	**0.850**	0.443	0.408	0.397	0.486	0.443	0.445	0.432	0.442	0.315	0.394	0.295	0.285	0.276	0.330
MOTCQ2	0.665	0.670	**0.861**	0.471	0.425	0.415	0.442	0.471	0.483	0.477	0.450	0.297	0.331	0.300	0.249	0.259	0.313
MOTCQ3	0.661	0.686	**0.829**	0.480	0.422	0.441	0.535	0.480	0.489	0.517	0.435	0.362	0.395	0.324	0.276	0.346	0.333
MOTCQ4	0.683	0.667	**0.820**	0.477	0.479	0.452	0.520	0.477	0.505	0.495	0.473	0.331	0.382	0.339	0.328	0.311	0.357
MOTCQ5	0.667	0.709	**0.837**	0.505	0.449	0.451	0.506	0.505	0.509	0.482	0.505	0.311	0.330	0.329	0.296	0.323	0.339
BEHCQ1	0.631	0.641	0.663	**0.821**	0.488	0.505	0.529	0.507	0.548	0.490	0.478	0.350	0.357	0.303	0.264	0.340	0.322
BEHCQ2	0.615	0.688	0.665	**0.818**	0.515	0.507	0.520	0.465	0.515	0.531	0.450	0.305	0.344	0.340	0.306	0.358	0.317
BEHCQ3	0.626	0.655	0.622	**0.801**	0.451	0.454	0.487	0.449	0.453	0.468	0.459	0.263	0.271	0.254	0.272	0.318	0.263
BEHCQ4	0.650	0.671	0.699	**0.823**	0.450	0.437	0.488	0.446	0.518	0.497	0.427	0.309	0.353	0.314	0.299	0.336	0.320
BEHCQ5	0.653	0.652	0.652	**0.824**	0.494	0.486	0.513	0.402	0.510	0.488	0.491	0.290	0.328	0.246	0.237	0.314	0.276

RKD1	0.545	0.537	0.528	0.626	**0.868**	0.617	0.665	0.626	0.601	0.549	0.676	0.432	0.409	0.422	0.410	0.455	0.425
RKD2	0.462	0.475	0.428	0.620	**0.833**	0.546	0.556	0.620	0.516	0.576	0.577	0.355	0.381	0.327	0.396	0.373	0.372
RKD3	0.486	0.494	0.473	0.605	**0.870**	0.520	0.613	0.605	0.541	0.554	0.586	0.447	0.465	0.450	0.429	0.461	0.421
SKD1	0.498	0.551	0.526	0.561	0.580	**0.872**	0.502	0.561	0.550	0.565	0.557	0.427	0.428	0.337	0.379	0.418	0.379
SKD2	0.480	0.474	0.449	0.524	0.502	**0.844**	0.628	0.524	0.562	0.587	0.565	0.400	0.411	0.360	0.356	0.379	0.396
SKD3	0.477	0.485	0.457	0.600	0.610	**0.864**	0.545	0.600	0.571	0.570	0.574	0.452	0.409	0.367	0.364	0.428	0.392
EKD1	0.559	0.527	0.483	0.554	0.588	0.573	**0.833**	0.554	0.573	0.635	0.579	0.457	0.493	0.413	0.395	0.430	0.449
EKD2	0.530	0.528	0.480	0.562	0.576	0.526	**0.851**	0.562	0.569	0.622	0.577	0.417	0.487	0.426	0.439	0.461	0.465
EKD3	0.531	0.513	0.509	0.576	0.641	0.540	**0.842**	0.576	0.597	0.595	0.637	0.391	0.414	0.402	0.425	0.416	0.454
AS_ML1	0.511	0.462	0.465	0.429	0.568	0.538	0.549	**0.833**	0.538	0.564	0.626	0.389	0.408	0.372	0.347	0.427	0.398
AS_ML2	0.469	0.461	0.484	0.497	0.624	0.566	0.581	**0.855**	0.613	0.556	0.638	0.389	0.478	0.427	0.390	0.408	0.411
AS_ML3	0.470	0.439	0.479	0.472	0.623	0.542	0.559	**0.834**	0.531	0.539	0.618	0.463	0.461	0.400	0.364	0.446	0.415
IS_ML1	0.448	0.510	0.510	0.485	0.489	0.538	0.535	0.485	**0.813**	0.592	0.557	0.409	0.422	0.449	0.390	0.397	0.426
IS_ML2	0.464	0.509	0.491	0.591	0.530	0.535	0.539	0.591	**0.807**	0.593	0.622	0.418	0.426	0.409	0.417	0.442	0.408
IS_ML3	0.461	0.522	0.433	0.573	0.577	0.542	0.628	0.573	**0.855**	0.637	0.588	0.449	0.453	0.446	0.363	0.420	0.434
CS_ML1	0.507	0.525	0.506	0.538	0.581	0.596	0.693	0.591	0.656	**0.863**	0.593	0.456	0.482	0.389	0.422	0.445	0.472
CS_ML2	0.558	0.516	0.476	0.509	0.570	0.585	0.562	0.585	0.633	**0.845**	0.578	0.487	0.433	0.353	0.402	0.417	0.439
CS_ML3	0.437	0.475	0.434	0.447	0.454	0.460	0.556	0.440	0.526	**0.766**	0.480	0.442	0.366	0.346	0.362	0.353	0.410
MLS_ML1	0.534	0.522	0.551	0.652	0.708	0.564	0.582	0.652	0.630	0.552	**0.844**	0.386	0.404	0.393	0.384	0.480	0.441
MLS_ML2	0.479	0.395	0.440	0.567	0.484	0.461	0.571	0.567	0.542	0.528	**0.784**	0.394	0.401	0.365	0.370	0.368	0.487
MLS_ML3	0.455	0.476	0.475	0.630	0.579	0.600	0.609	0.630	0.598	0.582	**0.851**	0.461	0.469	0.431	0.444	0.421	0.489
ACL_OC1	0.264	0.286	0.332	0.283	0.322	0.348	0.387	0.376	0.411	0.435	0.317	**0.809**	0.523	0.565	0.567	0.567	0.562
ACL_OC2	0.348	0.321	0.317	0.321	0.468	0.461	0.452	0.433	0.455	0.508	0.451	**0.789**	0.549	0.471	0.570	0.575	0.540

(Continued)

Table 3. (Continued)

	MCQ	BEH CQ	MOT CQ	CO CQ	RKD	SKD	EKD	AS	IS	CS	MLS	ACL	CCL	DEIL	EIAL	FTL	SL
ACL_OC3	0.318	0.338	0.277	0.290	0.369	0.385	0.366	0.374	0.375	0.402	0.438	**0.809**	0.523	0.523	0.553	0.561	0.556
CCL_OC1	0.408	0.359	0.391	0.366	0.401	0.441	0.447	0.483	0.461	0.442	0.456	0.542	**0.863**	0.623	0.524	0.561	0.635
CCL_OC2	0.354	0.346	0.372	0.349	0.419	0.406	0.498	0.415	0.398	0.448	0.376	0.569	**0.844**	0.537	0.582	0.622	0.661
CCL_OC3	0.394	0.364	0.345	0.313	0.419	0.381	0.456	0.460	0.478	0.432	0.473	0.571	**0.834**	0.578	0.589	0.538	0.635
DEIL_OC1	0.250	0.291	0.317	0.263	0.361	0.320	0.376	0.343	0.403	0.371	0.345	0.555	0.531	**0.832**	0.581	0.537	0.575
DEIL_OC2	0.246	0.272	0.286	0.274	0.363	0.288	0.390	0.378	0.423	0.352	0.388	0.512	0.563	**0.812**	0.570	0.514	0.607
DEIL_OC3	0.316	0.381	0.319	0.333	0.416	0.397	0.431	0.439	0.458	0.348	0.438	0.511	0.573	**0.792**	0.567	0.553	0.554
EAIL_OC1	0.263	0.313	0.284	0.310	0.426	0.364	0.452	0.384	0.411	0.402	0.428	0.545	0.532	0.548	**0.800**	0.635	0.550
EAIL_OC2	0.292	0.321	0.283	0.261	0.354	0.347	0.423	0.340	0.367	0.409	0.377	0.602	0.561	0.589	**0.810**	0.526	0.592
EAIL_OC3	0.266	0.284	0.261	0.247	0.386	0.322	0.334	0.336	0.368	0.353	0.367	0.556	0.526	0.573	**0.817**	0.533	0.544
FTL_OC1	0.320	0.356	0.369	0.449	0.419	0.440	0.452	0.449	0.426	0.415	0.411	0.591	0.559	0.533	0.568	**0.819**	0.566
FTL_OC2	0.293	0.366	0.357	0.415	0.402	0.375	0.452	0.415	0.421	0.437	0.429	0.560	0.537	0.523	0.585	**0.820**	0.582
FTL_OC3	0.249	0.288	0.268	0.390	0.422	0.362	0.378	0.390	0.413	0.370	0.429	0.598	0.579	0.571	0.574	**0.834**	0.602
SL_OC1	0.353	0.338	0.368	0.455	0.487	0.431	0.490	0.455	0.474	0.465	0.572	0.613	0.689	0.619	0.642	0.698	**0.823**
SL_OC2	0.241	0.218	0.255	0.273	0.236	0.295	0.345	0.273	0.344	0.368	0.314	0.496	0.525	0.528	0.467	0.479	**0.765**
SL_OC3	0.352	0.319	0.362	0.426	0.397	0.352	0.458	0.426	0.406	0.448	0.462	0.545	0.606	0.566	0.553	0.509	**0.825**

Source: Author's own research.

Table 4. Discriminant Validity (Fornell and Larcker Criterion).

Items	ACL_OC	AS_ML	BEHCQ	CCL_OC	COCQ	CS_ML	DEIL_OC	EAIL_OC	EKD	FTL_OC	IS_ML	MCQ	MLS_ML	MOTCQ	RKD	SKD	SL_OC
ACL_OC	0.802																
AS_ML	0.491	0.841															
BEHCQ	0.371	0.555	0.817														
CCL_OC	0.662	0.534	0.405	0.847													
COCQ	0.392	0.540	0.809	0.420	0.826												
CS_ML	0.559	0.658	0.605	0.520	0.613	0.826											
DEIL_OC	0.648	0.476	0.357	0.684	0.387	0.440	0.812										
EAIL_OC	0.703	0.437	0.337	0.667	0.379	0.480	0.705	0.809									
EKD	0.501	0.670	0.621	0.551	0.583	0.733	0.491	0.499	0.842								
FTL_OC	0.708	0.507	0.408	0.678	0.401	0.493	0.658	0.698	0.517	0.824							
IS_ML	0.516	0.668	0.623	0.526	0.578	0.737	0.526	0.472	0.689	0.509	0.825						
MCQ	0.386	0.575	0.777	0.455	0.814	0.609	0.333	0.339	0.642	0.348	0.555	0.827					
MLS_ML	0.501	0.747	0.564	0.513	0.592	0.670	0.480	0.483	0.710	0.513	0.714	0.591	0.827				
MOTCQ	0.385	0.566	0.808	0.436	0.795	0.573	0.378	0.342	0.593	0.361	0.580	0.788	0.550	0.839			
RKD	0.481	0.720	0.587	0.488	0.558	0.652	0.468	0.480	0.715	0.503	0.646	0.582	0.717	0.521	0.857		
SKD	0.496	0.653	0.585	0.484	0.555	0.667	0.412	0.426	0.649	0.475	0.653	0.564	0.657	0.514	0.656	0.860	
SL_OC	0.690	0.485	0.367	0.760	0.412	0.534	0.713	0.696	0.542	0.708	0.512	0.396	0.570	0.398	0.475	0.452	0.805

Source: Author's own research.

Table 5. Discriminant Validity (HTMT).

Items	ACL_OC	AS_ML	BEHCQ	CCL_OC	COCQ	CS_ML	DEIL_OC	EAIL_OC	EKD	FTL_OC	IS_ML	MCQ	MLS_ML	MOTCQ	RKD	SKD	SL_OC
ACL_OC																	
AS_ML	0.651																
BEHCQ	0.467	0.666															
CCL_OC	0.870	0.670	0.482														
COCQ	0.485	0.637	0.907	0.493													
CS_ML	0.752	0.838	0.736	0.660	0.734												
DEIL_OC	0.884	0.621	0.442	0.887	0.473	0.583											
EAIL_OC	0.963	0.572	0.420	0.868	0.463	0.638	0.954										
EKD	0.661	0.844	0.744	0.691	0.686	0.938	0.640	0.651									
FTL_OC	0.952	0.653	0.499	0.864	0.483	0.643	0.874	0.932	0.665								
IS_ML	0.694	0.855	0.761	0.671	0.695	0.957	0.700	0.630	0.881	0.666							
MCQ	0.495	0.702	0.902	0.553	0.928	0.753	0.421	0.429	0.783	0.434	0.690						
MLS_ML	0.673	0.955	0.685	0.654	0.708	0.870	0.635	0.642	0.908	0.667	0.929	0.734					
MOTCQ	0.479	0.672	0.912	0.515	0.881	0.690	0.464	0.421	0.704	0.437	0.700	0.905	0.661				
RKD	0.625	0.894	0.691	0.602	0.643	0.819	0.599	0.619	0.884	0.634	0.813	0.698	0.897	0.608			
SKD	0.643	0.808	0.689	0.595	0.642	0.834	0.527	0.546	0.802	0.599	0.822	0.676	0.823	0.599	0.796		
SL_OC	0.943	0.629	0.453	0.985	0.502	0.709	0.964	0.939	0.704	0.935	0.678	0.499	0.748	0.491	0.599	0.575	

Source: Author's own research.

5.6 Evaluation of the Structural Model in PLS-SEM

PLS-SEM also measures linear association between two or more latent constructs (Becker, 2021). The assessment of the structural model was done after the statistical support for constructs was valid and reliable. In this section, according to Hair, Risher, et al. (2019), the structural model must be assessed by the overall model fit, standardized path coefficients, their level of significance, collinearity statistics (Inner VIF), F^2 value, Q^2 (predictive relevance), the effect size (F-square), and the determination coefficient (R-square). The step-wise explanation is given below.

5.6.1 Collinearity Statistics (Inner VIF)

Collinearity statistics give statistical strength to the composite model. The composite model is tested concerning the multicollinearity (Chin, 1998), as the situation where two or more independent variables in the model are highly correlated with each other, since high multicollinearity can lead to unexpected weight signs and insignificant estimates. Thus, the collinearity among constructs' indicators should be assessed with the Variance Inflation Factor (VIF) (Wong, 2013). Generally, the VIF values greater than 5 are interpreted as the presence of multicollinearity among constructs' indicators (Hair et al., 2011). Table 6 represents the VIF values for the items or indicators of composite models. In summarizing the whole statistics of VIF, it was indicated that there is an absence of multicollinearity among the construct's indicators as all the VIF values of the current structural model lie below 5. Thus, no association is found between the construct's indicators of the current structural model.

5.6.2 R-*Square* (R²) *Value*

R-square, as a statistical measure, the variance in the endogenous variable as portrayed by the exogenous variable(s). Simply, it means how much change in the dependent variable can be accounted for by one or more independent variable(s). The significant threshold for the R-square value range from 0 to 1. According to Falk and Miller (1992), 0.10 is the lowest level of acceptability of the R^2 value. Moreover, Chin (1998) explained that the highest R-square value must be greater than 0.67, 0.33 to 0.67 are interpreted as moderate, 0.19 to 0.33 are considered weak, and lower than 0.19 are unacceptable. However, Henseler et al. (2015), Hair, Risher, et al. (2019) and Hair, Sarstedt, et al. (2019) presented a different variation/tolerance for the criterion for the R-square value. According to them, R^2 of 0.75 is considered as high, 0.50 is considered moderate, and 0.25 is interpreted as weak variance among dependent variables explained by independent variables.

The current scenario results are explained in Table 6. Hence, the predefined criterion of significant R-square estimation was fulfilled (Henseler et al., 2015). All the R-squares explain the highest level of variance in their respective dependent variable.

Table 6. Structural Model Results.

Constructs	VIF	R^2	R-Square Adjusted	F^2	Q^2
MCQ	1.000	0.821(High)	0.820(High)	4.580	0.558
COCQ	1.000	0.877(High)	0.876(High)	7.110	0.594
MOTCQ	1.000	0.847(High)	0.847(High)	5.542	0.592
BEHCQ	1.000	0.848(High)	0.848(High)	5.576	0.562
RKD	1.000	–	–	4.047	0.584
SKD	1.000	–	–	3.046	0.552
EKD	1.000	–	–	3.825	0.557
AS_ML	1.000	0.765(High)	0.765(High)	3.263	0.536
IS_ML	1.000	0.784(High)	0.783(High)	3.620	0.527
CS_ML	1.000	0.755(High)	0.754(High)	3.080	0.508
MLS_ML	1.000	0.793(High)	0.793(High)	3.832	0.538
ACL_OC	1.000	–	–	2.597	0.461
CCL_OC	1.000	–	–	2.995	0.532
DIEL_OC	1.000	–	–	2.612	0.471
EAIL_OC	1.000	–	–	2.886	0.480
FTL_OC	1.000	–	–	2.869	0.500
SL_OC	1.000	–	–	3.546	0.497

Source: Author's own research.

5.6.3 F^2 *Value*

Effect size measures how the latent construct is affected by other constructs. It was done to analyze the removal of exogenous variable results in changes in the dependent variable. In PLS-SEM, F^2 estimation was used to analyze the removal of the exogenous variable and relevant change in the dependent variable. According to previous literature, it was reported that an F-square equal to 0.02 suggest small, 0.15 suggested medium, and an F-square of 0.35 or larger is interpreted as a larger effect size of the exogenous variable on the endogenous variables of the structural model (Chin, 1998; Cohen, 1988).

Table 6 presents the effect size estimations of the current structural model using PLS Algorithm. It can be seen that significant effect sizes were observed for the current structural model.

5.6.4 *Predictive Relevance* Q^2

The structural model assessment further indicates the predictive power of the model using Q^2. It was analyzed by Blindfold analysis in which construct cross-validated redundancy was considered. In this redundancy, the Q-square value is considered.

Henseler et al. (2015) described that $Q^2 < 0.15$ depicts a weak predictive effect, $Q^2 < 0.35$ shows a moderate predictive effect, and $Q^2 \geq 0.35$ dictates a strong predictive effect of the structural model constructs. Further literature explained the cutoff for Q-square greater than 0 interpreted as predictive relevance of a respective construct. In another way, 0 or below 0 Q-square value highlights no predictive relevance of the construct (Chin, 1998). Indeed, other literature described that Q-square values – 0–0.2; 0.2–0.25, and >0.50 – represent low, moderate, and high predictive power of the PLS model (Hair, Risher, et al., 2019).

Table 6 shows the Q-square of the current path model as the Q-square value lies above 0.35 (Henseler et al., 2015). Thus, we are showing the stronger predictive power of the construct with the path model (Henseler et al., 2015).

5.6.5 Assessment of Prediction Employing PLSpredict

PLSpredict estimations give other assessment measures for assessing predictive power and predictive performance evaluation within PLS path models (Shmueli et al., 2016). It was estimated using a linear regression model (LM). The MAE was calculated before and after LM using the PLSpredict function of PLS-SEM. It results in predictions for the dependent variable's indicators on the exogenous constructs' indicators in the PLS-SEM evaluation.

According to Shmueli et al. (2019), the criterion for predictive power is if all the indicators PLS-SEM (MAE) were lower than the LM (MAE) of indicators. It was interpreted as the model lacking predictive power. Secondly, if a small number of indicators had PLS-SEM (MAE) lower than LM (MAE) of indicators – it represents a lower predictive effect. Thirdly, if the most or the same number of indicators PLS-SEM (MAE) was lower than LM (MAE), it indicates moderate predictive power of the model. Lastly, if all the indicators had PLS-SEM (MAE) lower than LM (MAE), it means the model had high predictive power.

Table 7 presents PLSpredict for current model indicators. It was explained as half of the indicators had PLS-SEM (MAE) lower than LM (MAE). Thus, dictating indicators had a moderate predictive effect, following Shmueli et al. (2019) threshold.

5.6.6 Assessment of Path Coefficient Using Bootstrapping (Hypothesis Testing)

Hypothesis testing is the final step in structural model assessment. It was done to see the statistical significance of the path model through path coefficients, as the data are not normally distributed. Thus, as mentioned, PLS-SEM as a nonparametric approach was used to analyze also the current hypothesis. All the hypotheses consist of a two-tailed scenario. Thus, the Bootstrapping using a two-tailed test was used to obtain path coefficients and their significance. The path coefficient is about t-statistics which show the magnitude of association among variables. However, the *p*-value gives statistical significance to accept or reject the hypothesis. The criterion for the significance of path coefficients is based

Table 7. PLSpredict Assessment of Manifest Variables (Original Model).

Items	PLS-SEM			PLS-SEM-LM
	Q^2 predict	MAE	LM MAE	MAE**
MCQ1	0.298	1.089	1.119	−0.03**
MCQ2	0.285	1.09	1.15	−0.06**
MCQ3	0.305	1.063	1.058	0.005**
MCQ4	0.333	1.074	1.094	−0.02**
COCQ1	0.208	1.162	1.194	−0.032**
COCQ2	0.261	1.076	1.114	−0.038**
COCQ3	0.289	1.15	1.179	−0.029**
COCQ4	0.338	0.997	1.013	−0.016**
COCQ5	0.287	1.146	1.209	−0.063**
COCQ6	0.276	1.144	1.201	−0.057**
MOTCQ1	0.235	1.211	1.22	−0.009**
MOTCQ2	0.227	1.156	1.209	−0.053**
MOTCQ3	0.277	1.151	1.143	0.008**
MOTCQ4	0.299	1.103	1.135	−0.032**
MOTCQ5	0.278	1.144	1.198	−0.054**
BEHCQ1	0.323	1.109	1.17	−0.061**
BEHCQ2	0.331	1.121	1.128	−0.007**
BEHCQ3	0.27	1.15	1.17	−0.02**
BEHCQ4	0.267	1.134	1.178	−0.044**
BEHCQ5	0.306	1.019	1.049	−0.03**
RKD1	0.656	0.71	0.000	0.71**
RKD2	0.533	0.851	0.000	0.851**
RKD3	0.57	0.804	0.000	0.804**
SKD1	0.54	0.863	0.000	0.863**
SKD2	0.549	0.831	0.000	0.831**
SKD3	0.575	0.757	0.000	0.757**
EKD1	0.562	0.814	0.000	0.814**
EKD2	0.539	0.912	0.000	0.912**
EKD3	0.578	0.802	0.000	0.802**
AS_ML1	0.39	0.994	1.048	−0.054**
AS_ML2	0.447	0.939	0.95	−0.011**
AS_ML3	0.43	0.907	0.939	−0.032**
IS_ML1	0.359	1.014	1.049	−0.035**
IS_ML2	0.378	0.932	0.99	−0.058**

Table 7. *(Continued)*

Items	PLS-SEM			PLS-SEM-LM
	Q^2 predict	MAE	LM MAE	MAE**
IS_ML3	0.439	0.905	0.92	−0.015**
CS_ML1	0.498	0.807	0.81	−0.003**
CS_ML2	0.425	0.961	0.974	−0.013**
CS_ML3	0.316	1.105	1.113	−0.008**
MLS_ML1	0.483	0.899	0.839	0.06**
MLS_ML2	0.336	1.017	1.031	−0.014**
MLS_ML3	0.465	0.921	0.927	−0.006**
ACL_OC1	0.476	0.899	0.000	0.899**
ACL_OC2	0.452	0.896	0.000	0.896**
ACL_OC3	0.458	0.87	0.000	0.87**
CCL_OC1	0.531	0.846	0.000	0.846**
CCL_OC2	0.548	0.806	0.000	0.806**
CCL_OC3	0.528	0.836	0.000	0.836**
DEIL_OC1	0.482	0.906	0.000	0.906**
DEIL_OC2	0.474	0.905	0.000	0.905**
DEIL_OC3	0.468	0.907	0.000	0.907**
EAIL_OC1	0.484	0.827	0.000	0.827**
EAIL_OC2	0.501	0.875	0.000	0.875**
EAIL_OC3	0.465	0.856	0.000	0.856**
FTL_OC1	0.494	0.862	0.000	0.862**
FTL_OC2	0.486	0.89	0.000	0.89**
FTL_OC3	0.526	0.864	0.000	0.864**
SL_OC1	0.619	0.744	0.000	0.744**
SL_OC2	0.393	0.96	0.000	0.96**
SL_OC3	0.484	0.904	0.000	0.904**

Source: Author's own research.

Note: *PLS-SEM < LM for none of the indicators. If the PLS-SEM analysis (compared to the LM) yields lower prediction errors in terms of the MAE (or the RMSE) for none of the indicators, this indicates that the model lacks predictive power.

**PLS-SEM < LM for a minority of the indicators. If the minority of the dependent construct's indicators produces lower PLSSEM prediction errors compared to the naïve LM benchmark, this indicates that the model has a low predictive power.

***PLS-SEM < LM for a majority of the indicators. If the majority (or the same number) of indicators in the PLS-SEM analysis yields smaller prediction errors compared to the LM, this indicates a medium predictive power.

****PLS-SEM < LM for all indicators. If all indicators in the PLS-SEM analysis have lower MAE (or RMSE) values compared to the LM benchmark, the model has high predictive power.

on ***$p < 0.001$, **$p < 0.01$, and *$p < 0.05$ (Hair, Hollingsworth, et al., 2017). The current structural model derived respective second-order components (Lower-Order Components) relationships:

- KD positively associates with CQ.
- There is an insignificant causal relationship present between OC and CQ.
- CQ was a significant positive predictor of ML.
- KD significantly predicts ML.
- There is a positive significant causal–effect relationship was present between OC and ML.

Furthermore, the following hypothesis can be reported concerning Bootstrapping result of the current structural model:

H1. There is a significant relationship present between knowledge dynamics and cultural intelligence.

H2. There is a significant relationship present between organizational context and cultural intelligence.

H3. There is a significant relationship present between cultural intelligence and multicultural leadership.

H4. There is a significant relationship present between knowledge dynamics and multicultural leadership.

H5. There is a significant relationship present between organizational context and multicultural leadership.

Table 8 also shows Std Beta, Std Error, *t*-value, *P*-value, 5% lower bounds, and 95% upper bounds of second-order components variables. The pictorial representation of the structural model evaluation is shown in Fig. 18.

Table 8. Analysis of Second-Order Components Variables.

HOC	LOCs	SB	SE	*t* statistics	*P* values	Supported	5%BCa	95%BCa
CQ	KD	0.664	0.053	12.456	0.000***	Yes	0.555	0.762
CQ	OC	0.061	0.051	1.186	0.236	No	−0.038	0.162
ML	CQ	0.183	0.043	4.204	0.000***	Yes	0.100	0.269
ML	KD	0.639	0.044	14.480	0.000***	Yes	0.548	0.721
ML	OC	0.168	0.041	4.084	0.000***	Yes	0.089	0.250

Source: Author's own research.

Note: HOC: Higher order component; LOCs: Lower order components; SB: Standard Beta; SE: Standard Error; BCa: Bias-corrected and accelerated, *P*: Significance Level, ***P < 0.001, **P < 0.01, *P < 0.05.

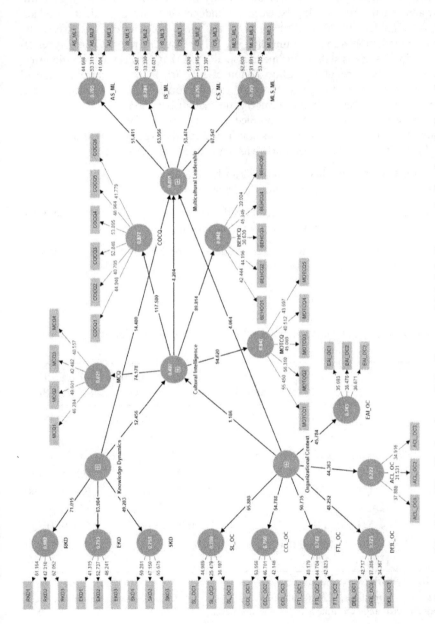

Fig. 18. The Evaluation of the Structural Model. *Source:* Author's own research.

5.7 Mediation Analysis

Testing the mediational effects is about analyzing the indirect effect of the third variable on the relationship between the independent and dependent variables (Hair, Hult, et al., 2017). Furthermore, the mediational effect can effectively change prediction stability (Shmueli et al., 2019). Thus, there are various types of mediation – such as state-of-art mediation analysis that depicts the mediation tree explaining the type of mediation (Zhou et al., 2010). In the current context, Bootstrapping test also gives the current mediational effect. It was due to the current data being different from the normal distribution. Firstly, the Bootstrapping with 5,000 sample two-tailed analysis was performed. Secondly, the state-of-art mediation analysis was considered for the type of mediation.

Following hypothesis mediation was highlighted, as a result of Bootstrapping:

H4a. Cultural intelligence insignificantly mediates the relationship between knowledge dynamics and multicultural leadership.

H5a. Cultural intelligence significantly mediates the relationship between organizational context and multicultural leadership.

Hypothesis testing based on indirect effects using Specific Indirect Effects by Bootstrapping is shown in Table 9.

Table 9. Indirect Relationships for Hypothesis Testing (Specific Indirect Effects by Bootstrapping).

Hs	Re	SB	SE	*t* statistics	*P* values	Supported	5%BCa	95% BCa
H1	KD → CQ	0.664	0.053	12.456	0.000***	Yes	0.555	0.762
H2	OC → CQ	0.061	0.051	1.186	0.236	No	−0.038	0.162
H3	CQ → ML	0.183	0.043	4.204	0.000***	Yes	0.100	0.269
H4	KD → ML	0.639	0.044	14.480	0.000***	Yes	0.548	0.721
H4a	KD → CQ → ML	0.121	0.032	3.778	0.000***	No	0.064	0.190
H5	OC → ML	0.168	0.041	4.084	0.000***	Yes	0.089	0.250
H5a	OC → CQ → ML	0.011	0.010	1.120	0.263	Yes	−0.007	0.033

Source: Author's own research.

Note: Hs: Hypothesis; Re: Relationship; SB: Standard Beta; SE: Standard Error; BCa: Bias-corrected and accelerated, *P*: Significance Level, ***$P < 0.001$, **$P < 0.01$, *$P < 0.05$.

5.8 Group Differences Analysis (ANOVA)

5.8.1 ANOVA Introduction

According to the precise needs of the analysis, an ANOVA (Analysis of Variance) test is carried out using SPSS. ANOVA examines the means of two or more groups to determine whether there are any appreciable differences between them.

The table first gives each variable's descriptive statistics. The fundamental data collection characteristics are summarized and described using descriptive statistics. In this instance, statistics are produced for each variable to give a thorough knowledge of how scores for each variable are distributed. For instance, the "N" column indicates the number of people in each group and details the sample size. The average score for each variable within each gender group is shown in the "Mean" column. This reveals the data's central tendency and the typical score for each group, providing information about the data. The standard deviation of the scores for each variable within each gender group is shown in the "Std. Deviation" column. This indicates details on the degree of variability or spread of scores around the mean, indicating how much the scores vary from the average. How much the sample mean will likely deviate from the actual population mean is indicated in the "Std. Error" column. The standard error gives us a sense of how much variation we can anticipate if we were to take numerous samples from the same population, which is crucial because sample means can vary by chance. The range of values within which the genuine population mean is predicted to fall with 95% confidence is shown in the "95% Confidence Interval for Mean" column. This clarifies the accuracy of our population mean estimate. The "Minimum" and "Maximum" columns, which show the lowest and highest values recorded, provide information regarding the range of results for each variable within each gender group (Field, 2013, 2017; Gravetter et al., 2020).

The ANOVA table also provides an overview of the ANOVA analysis, a statistical technique that compares the means of two or more groups in order to look for statistically significant variations. It includes a number of significant statistics that aid in the interpretation of the study, including degrees of freedom (df), which are used to compute a number of test statistics, including the sum of squares, mean square, and *F*-statistic. By deducting the number of estimated parameters from the total number of observations, degrees of freedom are calculated (Gravetter et al., 2020; Jaccard & Becker, 2021).

The sum of squares (SS) in an ANOVA is the sum of the squared deviations from the mean for each observation. Total sum of squares (SST), between-group sum of squares (SSB), and within-group sum of squares (SSW) are the three different varieties of sum of squares. SSW is the variability within groups, SSB denotes the variability between groups, and SST denotes the overall variability in the data.

There are two types of mean squares: between-group mean square (MSB) and within-group mean square (MSW). The mean square (MS) is the total of squares divided by the degrees of freedom. While MSW represents variation within each group, MSB represents disparities between the means of several groups. ANOVA assesses if the differences between groups are statistically significant by comparing MSB to MSW.

The *F*-statistic, which measures whether there are statistically significant differences across groups, is the ratio of the MSB to the MSW. If the null hypothesis is true, the *p*-value represents the likelihood of receiving the observed *F*-statistic or a more extreme number. The null hypothesis can be rejected, and it can be determined that there are significant differences between groups if the *p*-value is less than the level of significance (Gravetter et al., 2020).

To summarize, ANOVA uses the mean value to calculate the *F*-statistic, which determines whether there are significant differences between groups. If the between-group variance is much larger than the within-group variance, the *F*-statistic will be large, indicating significant differences between groups. Conversely, a small *F*-statistic suggests no significant differences between groups. The ANOVA table includes these statistics, providing a brief overview of the analysis results and allowing researchers to compare the means of multiple groups and determine whether there are significant differences. Overall, the mean value is a crucial element in ANOVA, as it is used to calculate the MSW, which contributes to the calculation of the *F*-statistic and determines the significance of the differences between groups.

5.8.2 ANOVA Analysis

In Table 10, we have presented, as example, the descriptive analysis based on gender.

After this first step, we have utilized ANOVA for explaining the gender differences among CQ, KD, ML, and OC as reflected in Table 11.

According to the mean value, the nonbinary gender felt more CQ, KD, ML, and OC (M = 104.62, 49.12, 67.12, and 101.62, respectively) than males (M = 102.56, 48.47, 64.83, and 97.34 accordingly) and females (M = 103.01, 48.32, 63.63 and 94.84 accordingly).

The one-way ANOVA revealed that there was a statistically insignificant difference in all levels between gender groups (F (2, 393) = [0.035, 0.028, 0.570, and 1.151 accordingly], $p > 0.05$).

All the other ANOVA test are presented in the Addendum section, with in-detail analysis focused on Education, Continent of work residence, Company sector, Company size (turnover), Company size (number of employees), Functions, Years of experience within the company, Years of experience in total, Number of managed nationalities, Spoken languages, Number of continents with work experience on, Number of countries with work experience on, and Experience in managing virtual teams.

Table 10. Descriptives of Gender.

		N	Mean	Std. Deviation	Std. Error	95% Confidence Interval for Mean		Minimum	Maximum
						Lower Bound	Upper Bound		
Cultural intelligence	Female	188	103.0053	24.61174	1.79500	99.4643	106.5464	24.00	140.00
	Male	200	102.5650	26.22986	1.85473	98.9076	106.2224	21.00	138.00
	Nonbinary	8	104.6250	21.99959	7.77803	86.2329	123.0171	68.00	132.00
	Total	396	102.8157	25.33919	1.27334	100.3123	105.3190	21.00	140.00
Knowledge dynamics	Female	188	48.3298	9.96184	0.72654	46.8965	49.7631	9.00	63.00
	Male	200	48.4700	10.78614	0.76270	46.9660	49.9740	9.00	63.00
	Nonbinary	8	49.1250	6.93722	2.45268	43.3253	54.9247	34.00	56.00
	Total	396	48.4167	10.31801	0.51850	47.3973	49.4360	9.00	63.00
Multicultural leadership	Female	188	63.6383	13.20497	0.96307	61.7384	65.5382	16.00	84.00
	Male	200	64.8300	13.61204	0.96252	62.9320	66.7280	12.00	83.00
	Nonbinary	8	67.1250	5.74301	2.03046	62.3237	71.9263	60.00	74.00
	Total	396	64.3106	13.30392	0.66855	62.9963	65.6250	12.00	84.00
Organizational context	Female	188	94.8404	20.36738	1.48544	91.9100	97.7708	18.00	126.00
	Male	200	97.3450	18.25162	1.29058	94.8000	99.8900	19.00	123.00
	Nonbinary	8	101.6250	6.09303	2.15421	96.5311	106.7189	96.00	113.00
	Total	396	96.2424	19.15749	0.96270	94.3498	98.1351	18.00	126.00

Source: Author's own research.

Table 11. Analysis of Variance (ANOVA) Explaining Gender Differences Among Cultural Intelligence, Knowledge Dynamics, Multicultural Leadership, and Organizational Context.

		Sum of Squares	df	Mean Square	F	Sig.
Cultural intelligence	Between groups	45.518	2	22.759	0.035	0.965
	Within groups	253574.025	393	645.227		
	Total	253619.543	395			
Knowledge dynamics	Between groups	6.002	2	3.001	0.028	0.972
	Within groups	42046.248	393	106.988		
	Total	42052.250	395			
Multicultural leadership	Between groups	202.296	2	101.148	0.570	0.566
	Within groups	69710.499	393	177.380		
	Total	69912.795	395			
Organizational context	Between groups	844.445	2	422.222	1.151	0.317
	Within groups	144124.283	393	366.728		
	Total	144968.727	395			

Source: Author's own research.

5.8.3 Conclusion – ANOVA

Upon analyzing the data for the four categories, it was observed that individuals belonging to different genders, age groups, educational levels, continents affiliations, company sectors, company sizes based on turnover and employee numbers, management levels, years of experience within the company, years of experience in total, number of managed nationalities, spoken languages, number of worked continents, number of worked countries, and experience in managing virtual teams had higher mean scores in CQ compared to OC, KD, and ML.

This implies that individuals possessing certain characteristics, like working in diverse environments, managing virtual teams, and speaking multiple languages, may score higher in CQ. On the other hand, it suggests that individuals may need to focus on improving their skills in the areas of OC, KD, and ML, as reflected in Table 12.

Table 12. Conclusions for ANOVA Tests (Based on Means): Main Demographic Drivers for Researched Variables.

Demographics	CQ - top drivers * from surveys			KD - top drivers * from surveys		
	Leading drivers	Share% from selected demographic	Mean	Leading drivers	Share% from selected demographic	Mean
Gender	female	48%	5.150	males	51%	5.386
Age	>61	9%	5.524	>61	9%	5.822
Education	Ph.D. Graduate	12%	5.460	Ph.D. Graduate	12%	5.632
Continent	Australia	10%	5.458	Europe	33%	5.591
Company sector	Production	22%	5.680	Production	22%	5.771
Turnover	>=50 M. €/year	4%	5.785	>=50 M. €/year	4%	5.987
Employees' number	1000+ employees	5%	5.839	1000+ employees	5%	6.117
Function	Middle Management	37%	5.424	Lower Management	12%	5.594
Years in company	11-15	29%	5.506	6-10	25%	5.684
Total years of experience	21+	8%	5.495	21+	8%	5.904
Number of managed nationalities	16-20	9%	5.811	21-50	11%	5.770
Spoken languages	> 3	16%	5.708	> 3	16%	5.875
Worked countries	> 3	25%	5.711	> 3	25%	5.880
Worked continents	> 3	10%	5.794	> 3	10%	5.925
Experience with virtual teams	5+ years' experience	26%	5.702	5+ years' experience	26%	5.797

Demographics	ML - top drivers * from surveys			OC - top drivers * from surveys		
	Leading drivers	Share% from selected demographic	Mean	Leading drivers	Share% from selected demographic	Mean
Gender	male	51%	5.403	male	51%	5.408
Age	>61	9%	5.819	>61	9%	5.575
Education	Ph.D. Graduate	12%	5.773	Master Graduate	40%	5.417
Continent	Europe	33%	5.543	Europe	33%	5.543
Company sector	Production	22%	5.752	Trade	23%	5.594
Turnover	>=50 M. €/year	4%	5.941	1 M. <=x<5 M. €/year	26%	5.645
Employees' number	1000+ employees	5%	6.037	101-500	29%	5.617
Function	Lower manage	12%	5.569	Middle Manage	37%	5.387
Years in company	16>	7%	5.647	16>	7%	5.585
Total years of experience	21+	8%	5.839	16-20	18%	5.588
Number of managed nationalities	21-50	11%	5.844	4-5	18%	5.638
Spoken languages	> 3	16%	5.924	> 3	16%	5.597
Worked countries	> 3	25%	5.878	3	26%	5.506
Worked continents	> 3	10%	5.956	3	16%	5.398
Experience with virtual teams	5+ years' experience	26%	5.742	5+ years' experience	26%	5.563

Source: Author's own research.

However, it is crucial to keep in mind that mean scores provide only a snapshot of the data, and there may be individual variations within each category. Additionally, there could be other factors that are not captured in the data, which contribute to an individual's CQ, KD, OC, and ML scores. Therefore, it is essential to use this information as a starting point for further exploration and development of CQ, OC, KD, and ML.

Chapter 6

Discussion and Conclusions as per the PLS-SEM Analysis

6.1 Results and Conclusion of the Quantitative Analyzes

This chapter checks if our current findings about cultural intelligence (CQ), knowledge dynamics (KD), organizational context (OC), and multicultural leadership (ML) and their correlations are consistent with past literature and suggests new directional ways. The theoretical basis depicts the current focused variable's relationship with ML. The core discussed hypothesis includes causative and mediational effects that will be presented in consecutive sections of this chapter.

> *H1.* "There is a significant relationship present between Knowledge Dynamics (KD) and Cultural Intelligence (CQ)."

The first hypothesized relationship is between KD and CQ. The current results support this hypothesis. A positive significant causal effect was found between KD and CQ. According to the cross-cultural competence model (Leiba-O'Sullivan, 1999), two competencies lead to CQ. In these competencies (cognitive and affective ones), dynamic competency had KD as the central core because it consistently affects CQ concerning individual differences. By combining knowledge and understanding with emotional awareness and adaptability, individuals with high CQ can navigate unfamiliar cultural situations, build relationships, and effectively communicate in diverse settings (Leiba-O'Sullivan, 1999; Peters et al., 1997). Similarly, literature assessing domains of KD reveals that it is strongly linked with the dynamics of CQ. Such as it strongly links with metacognitive CQ than motivational CQ of students and teachers (Alidoust & Homaei, 2012). Moreover, the literature takes social cognitive theory as a theoretical framework and highlights that KD directly affects metacognitive, cognitive, and motivational CQ. The reason behind this influence is team efficacy in a culturally diverse team. Having higher efficacy results in more knowledge sharing and a more complex KD. Seemingly, it further strengthens the CQ of multicultural teams (Chen & Lin, 2013). According to Earley and Ang (2003) and Thomas et al. (2008), it was considerably suggested that CQ needs internal

Developing Multicultural Leadership using Knowledge Dynamics and Cultural Intelligence, 139–146
Copyright © 2024 Dan Paiuc
Published under exclusive licence by Emerald Publishing Limited
doi:10.1108/978-1-83549-432-520241012

competency and knowledge skills. It is all about excellence in attaining and explaining the dynamics of a multicultural environment. This internal competency results in an enhancement of a person's KD and CQ (Thomas et al., 2008).

> *H2.* "There is a significant relationship present between Organizational Context (OC) and Cultural Intelligence (CQ)."

The second hypothesis concerns the OC and CQ association. Current findings reject this association. An insignificant association was found between OC and CQ. The theoretical and literature results also support this notion. As per the literature review findings it is suggested that the competitiveness framework strengthened CQ. It made international industries accept and focus on CQ to maintain their performance of strategic alliances (Yitmen, 2013). According to social categorization theory, personal characteristics affect CQ more than OC. The organization comprised employees with diverse cultural backgrounds. The personal label of in-group and out-group affect the dynamics of CQ (Ang & Van Dyne, 2008). Furthermore, institutional leadership was found to be an influential factor that signifies CQ as it made true appreciation of each person working in a diverse cultural environment. Thus, it was the leadership style that went forward to make more beneficial cultural interactions and subsequent CQ (Earley & Ang, 2003). Other literature highlighted that globalization-related problems had a causative influence on CQ. It made CQ more critical in cultural interactions between culturally diverse groups (Adler, 2006; Meyer, 2007). Previous experience, complex organizational sectors, and multiple national and international employment rate result in an increase in cognitive and behavioral CQ among employees, according to research results of Crowne (2013). In short, cognitive and behavioral CQ works in engaging the activities of employees in cross-cultural interactions.

> *H3.* "There is a significant relationship present between Cultural Intelligence (CQ) and Multicultural Leadership (ML)."

This section discusses the current findings supporting the significant relationship between CQ and ML. Likewise, the bibliometric analysis explains the causative effect of CQ on ML (Bratianu & Paiuc, 2022). Similarly, according to Javidan and Walker (2012), CQ cultivates ML and makes a global leader. This leadership also pays back CQ. Accepting a diverse cultural background and incorporating culturally diverse workers subsequently enhance CQ. Thus, CQ and ML were found to be bidirectional (Kim & Dyne, 2012). Moreover, Early, Ang, and Tan also suggested the two-tailed effect of CQ (Earley et al., 2006). On the positive side, it enhances the capabilities of multicultural leader, enhances companies' profit, and cultivates a problem-free globalizing environment. Conversely, it causes in- or out-group perception, preference for the same cultural environment, and other problems affecting the organizational environment (Groves & Feyerherm, 2011). Seemingly, CQ and ML directly affect each other among school leaders because a multicultural leader is formed by being culturally intelligent. Similarly, having CQ results in higher management skills of working in a multicultural environment. In the context of school context, literature suggested behavioral and cognitive aspects of CQ as the more influencing ones (K-Keung & Rockinson-Szapkiw, 2013).

H4. "There is a significant relationship present between Knowledge Dynamics (KD) and Multicultural Leadership (ML)."

The fourth supported hypothesis is about the causative association between KD and ML. The theoretical basis of a knowledge-based economy supported this causative effect. Specific to multicultural organizations, it was the KD that made leaders more skillful in the adaptation of ML. As a result, the organization outperforms in its economy (Rigby & Bilodeau, 2011). Similarly, according to the communities of practice (CoP) framework, knowledge sharing and the significance of KD enhanced the ML from senior to junior employees. This, in return, also enhances knowledge sharing or KD among workers (Krishnaveni & Sujatha, 2012; Marouf & Al-Attabi, 2010; Oye et al., 2011). Similarly, literature results dictated that social exchange relationships and KD were increased by multicultural relational leadership. This results in an increase in knowledge sourcing and sharing with subsequent open innovations. Individual reward, skill acquisition, and a sense of reciprocity and drive for group gain further strengthen knowledge and subsequent ML skills (Engelsberger et al., 2022). In the meta-analysis of globalization, KD and resultant ML become more complex as multiple choice in every domain was available. The best fit can only result from having a sharp edge in KD combinations that leads to various management styles. These management styles indirectly plant multicultural skills in a person (Thomas & Inkson, 2004, 2017).

H5. "There is a significant relationship present between Organizational Context (OC) and Multicultural Leadership (ML)."

Partial least squares structural equation modeling results also supported the fifth hypothesis of the current research. It described that OC significantly predicts ML. According to the literature, an organization is comprised of culturally diverse employees. Thus, ML can become a causative or a resultant outcome in the OC. In the context of causation, it made a soothing OC with a multicultural workforce. However, in the context of the result, the organization must be made on more than single-focused culture. Diversity is clearly found in an OC. Thus, this results in the cultivation of ML. That made subsequent workforce in the OC (Cox & Blake, 2021). Similarly, the globalism framework further elaborates on the considered association. According to this framework, globalism results in th e formation of global leaders having ML in the OC. OC has diverse perspectives, workforces, working domains, and core objectives. Thus, ML in this kind of OC enhances the globalization of that organization (Kelly & Chung, 2013). A continuum of changes, community connections, autonomy, higher work self-efficacy, no discrimination, equity policies, and other intrinsic characteristics of OC saves the employees from work dysfunction or turnover intention. This kind of OC can result from the source of ML because it is leadership skills that smoothen the working environment, thus boosting employees' internal competency and organizational competency (Fitzsimmons, 2013).

H4a. "Cultural Intelligence (CQ) significantly mediates the relationship between Knowledge Dynamics (KD) and Multicultural Leadership (ML)."

The current findings unsupported the sixth hypothesis assessing the mediational effect of CQ between KD and ML. Previous literature also suggests no mediational effect of CQ between KD and ML. However, each construct relates independently to the other. As research results of Paiuc (2021c) suggested, CQ is an integral competence for ML. In contrast, KD and sharing can be increased due to CQ. Nevertheless, it did not mediate between KD and ML (Thygesen et al., 2022; Zaman et al., 2021). Other research findings suggested that diversity and inclusion of ML results in CQ and an increase in KD, especially during the COVID-19 period. In other words, ML affected the association between CQ and KD (Bratianu & Paiuc, 2023a). Similarly, the research findings of Bratianu and Leon (2015) and Bratianu and Paiuc (2022) show the strong linkage between KD and ML regardless of the exogenous effects is the diversity and inclusion side of ML. These leadership skills result in the enhancement of KD concerning diversified cultures. Furthermore, in the context of the person–environment (P-E) fit model (Kristof-Brown et al., 2005), it is the characteristics of the person that results in the best fit of the person in a multicultural context. In the current scenario, KD extends to rational, spiritual, and emotional aspects. Thus, it was the KD that cultivated ML. This leadership only influences those having a personal set of KD concerning that position. A stronger leadership skill results in durable position attainment in the context of multicultural teams. Thus, KD and ML go side by side.

H5a. "Cultural Intelligence (CQ) significantly mediates the relationship between Organizational Context (OC) and Multicultural Leadership (ML)."

The last hypothesis relates to the indirect effect of CQ on OC and ML. The current findings supported this hypothesis. Moreover, the theoretical background also provides empirical evidence for this mediational effect. The leadership diversity theory emphasize that CQ strengthens ML, which results in a more effective and multicultural workforce. Similarly, CQ in the OC boosts the generation of ML as it nurtures the organizational culture as a combination of different races, ethnicities, religions, and genders workforce. Thus, it limits misunderstandings concerning particular cultures (Connerley & Pedersen, 2005). In a similar context, a meta-analysis by Rahman (2019) highlighted various cultural differences. It concluded that CQ is an essential competence needed in an OC to foster ML, as the OC always has a complex workforce. Thus, the core of managing OC lies in CQ in the form of ML. In short, CQ strengthened the linkage between OC and subsequent ML (Vinaja, 2003). Other theoretical domains explaining the mediational effects suggest that the organizational environment entails CQ. As well as no discrimination, higher job satisfaction, and executive motivation can enhance ML style. This can result from OC and CQ (Champathes & Swierczek, 2002).

6.2 Theoretical Contribution

This study aimed to shed light on the special relationship between CQ, KD, and ML within an OC. From this perspective, besides a bibliometric study, mixed methods research was carried out based on in-depth interviews (for the qualitative part) as well as questionnaires (for the quantitative section). We conducted 15 interviews with multicultural leaders and asked them about the impact of CQ and KD on their day-to-day leadership and management topics and routines. Based on the obtained results and feedback, we constructed our questionnaires shared with cross-cultural managers from six continents. We have gathered and analyzed 396 answers to our questionnaires related to their practical perspective of ML, CQ, KD, and OC.

This study was motivated by the research topic of how CQ and KD influence ML. According to the findings, four main hypotheses were confirmed, validating in this way our research model:

KD is strongly related to CQ, while CQ, KD, and OC, all, influence ML. We have also demonstrated that CQ mediates the relationship between OC and ML. Our findings enhanced the central role of KD in developing CQ and ML on one side and on the significant contribution of CQ, KD, and OC in developing ML.

6.3 Practical Implications, Recommendations, Limitations, and Future Research Areas

6.3.1 Practical Implications and Recommendations

We live in a world where agility and change reshape the work and labor market. On a recent pole live on LinkedIn during April 2023, Christopher Hummel (2023), the founder of Fitteam Global, asked his 931,250 LinkedIn members (in April 2023) the question "Why did you leave your last job?" and gathered 12,855 answers (Fig. 1). The majority of respondents chose "culture" as their departure reason (41%), followed by "other" (30%) and "money" (29%). This is practically enhancing beyond doubt the importance of the "company culture" and supporting our research findings according to whom the company culture, backed by ML and powered by KD and CQ, has become the main equation to work on in order to ensure both job satisfaction and bottom-line results.

In April and May 2023, two other poles from Christopher Hummel (2023) investigated two new questions "Do you prefer to work from home?" and "Are you currently looking for a job?" From 22,434 answers that received the first pole question – 79% of the respondents stated that they prefer to work from the comfort and

Why did you leave your last job?

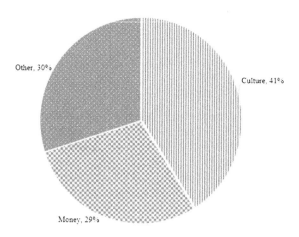

Fig. 1.   Why Did You Leave Your Last Job Pole. *Source:* Adaptation
from LinkedIn/Christopher Hummel (2023).

convenience of their homes. The second pole answers could be regarded as a consequence of a bad "company culture" but also of the lack of work from home options,
and 82% of 21,199 respondents mentioned that they are currently looking for a new
job. Below are the two pole results as extracted from LinkedIn as primary source.

As seen in the above poles and Fig. 2, the *work-from-home* and *work-from-
anywhere* phenomenon puts quite a lot of pressure on ML to manage diverse

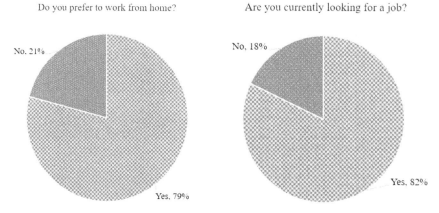

Fig. 2.   Work From Home and Job Searching Poles. *Source:*
Adaptation from LinkedIn/Christopher Hummel (2023).

teams spread worldwide. This is also enhanced by the fact that the biggest perceived gaps noticed among recent university graduates were in communication, flexibility, and leadership (ISACA, 2022), as reflected in Fig. 3.

In this most challenging OC, our research results give managers the perfect tools to develop their multicultural needed leadership based on KD and CQ.

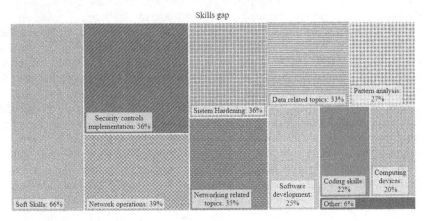

Fig. 3.   Skill Gaps Noticed Among Recent University Graduates; Worldwide Survey; Q4 2021; 2031 Respondents. *Source:* Adaptation from ISACA; LookingGlass; ID 1322398.

6.3.2 Limitations of the Research

During the course of this study, several constraints and restrictions emerged that should be acknowledged when contemplating the findings and their potential applications in various management scenarios.

One significant obstacle that both hindered and fueled the progress of this research but also twisted the entire world of leadership was the emergence of the COVID-19 pandemic, which commenced and concluded within the timeframe of this study, consequently imposing additional limitations, such as work and study from home, and pushed a big part of the research into online.

Due to the qualitative nature of this investigation and the utilization of semi-structured interviews, the outcomes are subject to the perceptions and viewpoints of the individuals involved in the interviews and the researcher's interpretation of such perceptions and viewpoints. Even if practical examples back results, a more significant sample will definitely generate more accurate results.

6.3.3 Future Research Areas

The research demonstrated the influence of CQ and KD on ML within an OC.

To expand on this topic, there are four potential areas for future research backed by our book findings.

The first new study area would be to investigate the impact of CQ training programs in enhancing ML. This research could analyze how such training programs improve leaders' understanding of diverse cultures and ability to navigate multicultural teams effectively while finding best frames for KD.

The second area for future research would be linked to the quantified impact of the diversity and inclusion policies on ML. This may entail assessing the effectiveness of policies like hiring practices, promotion strategies, and mentorship programs in fostering a diverse and inclusive leadership culture.

Technology's role in ML could also be further researched. Investigating the ways in which technology can support and improve ML, such as through virtual communication tools or AI-driven cross-cultural training, may offer insightful information about how to adapt leadership practices and KD for a technologically connected and driven world.

Furthermore, as research and understanding of genetics continue to advance in the fourth future analysis area, there may be potential avenues to explore the relationship between CQ and DNA. These studies could investigate in what percentage of some genetic variations or markers influence an individual's ability to acquire and apply CQ. Researchers could explore how particular genes (for example, the ones related to family tree origins) interact with cultural experiences during development, potentially influencing an individual's ability to navigate and understand different cultural contexts. Additionally, genetic research could investigate the potential role of genes associated with cognitive abilities, such as knowledge processing, empathy, or social cognition, in relation to CQ. These researches could examine whether specific genetic variations are linked to higher levels of CQ, sharing insight into the genetic basis of this trait.

These are a few potential research areas to consider building upon the study of the impact of CQ and KD on ML. By exploring these topics, researchers can contribute to a deeper understanding of how organizations can effectively manage cultural diversity and develop leaders who can navigate and thrive in multicultural environments.

Appendices

Appendix A – My Working Definitions

- *Cultural Intelligence (CQ)* was defined as being the set of skills to relate and work effectively in culturally diverse situations. It is the capability to cross boundaries, prosper in multiple cultures, and impact the bottom-line results.
- *Knowledge Dynamics (KD)* refers to the characteristics of knowledge that transform, change, and evolve as a result of various processes and influences.
- *Multicultural Leadership (ML)* was defined as the process of engaging and leading a workforce comprised of individuals from diverse cultural backgrounds.

Appendices for Qualitative Research

Appendix B – Screening Filtering Questions to Validate Interview Participation

Hello,

In order to test your possible fit for a 30–60 minutes pro-bono interview in a research project that will serve as building support for the thesis/book "Developing multicultural leadership based on knowledge dynamics and cultural intelligence" conducted by PhD candidate Dan Paiuc, from the Department of Management of the National University for Political Studies and Public Administration, Bucharest, Romania – please kindly answer with Yes (Y) or No (N) for the following two questions:

(1) Do you actually manage multicultural teams? Y/N

(2) Are you familiar with the notion of Cultural Intelligence (CQ) as per my working definition: CQ being the set of skills to relate and work effectively in culturally diverse situations? Y/N

Appendix C – Consent to Participate in Research Interviews

Dear Participant,

Thanks for agreeing to participate in the research project that will serve as a building base for the thesis/book "Developing multicultural leadership based on knowledge dynamics and cultural intelligence" conducted by PhD candidate Dan Paiuc, from the Department of Management of the National University for Political Studies and Public Administration, Bucharest, Romania.

With an expected duration of the interview of 30–60 minutes, please agree:

- to voluntarily participate in the interview;
- that all the interviews will be recorded, transcribed, and anonymized by Dan Paiuc;
- all or parts of the anonymized interview may be used in the above thesis/book or related academic articles/conferences.

Appendix D – Interviews' Synthetic Results

Fig. D.1.   Age of Interviewed Managers. *Source:* Author's own research.

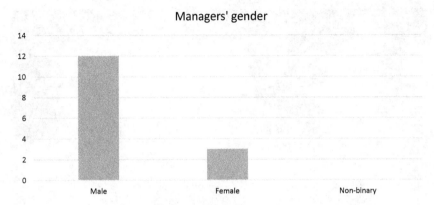

Fig. D.2.   Gender of Interviewed Managers. *Source:* Author's own
research.

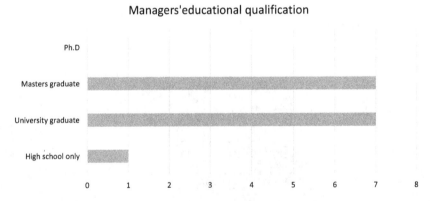

Fig. D.3.   Highest Level of Education Completed by the Interviewed
Managers. *Source:* Author's own research.

Fig. D.4.   Continent-Based Geographical Distribution of Interviewed
Managers. *Source:* Stockphotos.

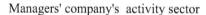

Managers' company's activity sector

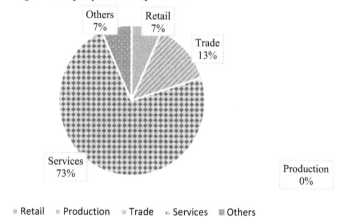

Fig. D.5.   Main Company's Activity Sectors of Interviewed
Managers. *Source:* Author's own research.

The managers' company size (Euro)

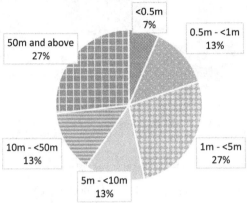

Fig. D.6. Main Sizes of the Companies of Interviewed Managers
(Data in Euro). *Source:* Author's own research.

The managers' company size (nb. of employees)

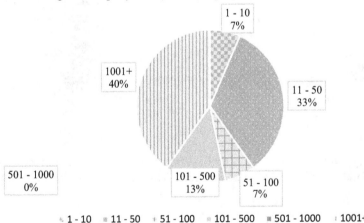

Fig. D.7. Main Sizes of the Companies of Interviewed Managers
(Data in Number of Employees). *Source:* Author's own research.

Managers' hierarchical position

Fig. D.8.   Hierarchical Position of the Interviewed Managers. *Source:* Author's own research.

Managers' working experience in actual company

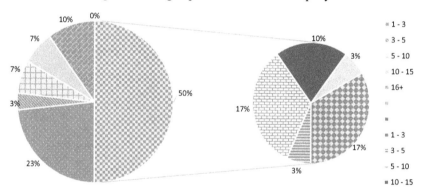

Fig. D.9.   Working Years' Experience in Actual Company and in Total of the Interviewed Managers. *Source:* Author's own research.

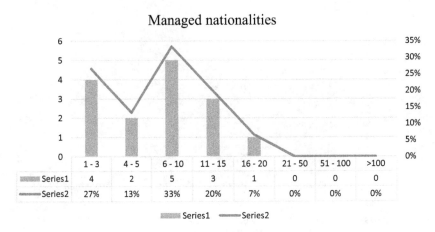

Fig. D.10.   Number of Managed Nationalities of the Interviewed
Managers. *Source:* Author's own research.

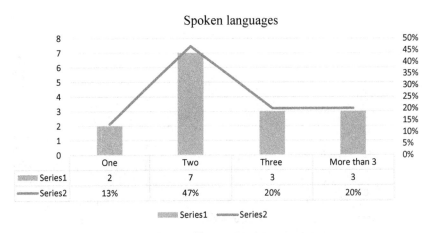

Fig. D.11.   Number of Spoken Languages of the Interviewed
Managers. *Source:* Author's own research.

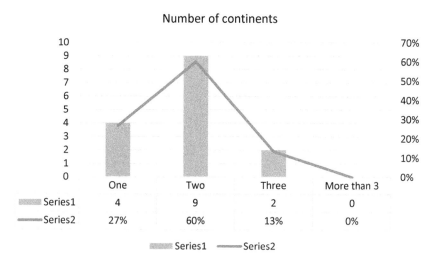

Fig. D.12.   Number of Continents on Which the Interviewed Managers Worked. *Source:* Author's own research.

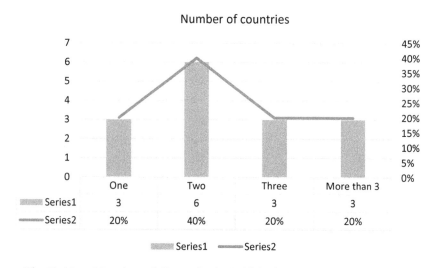

Fig. D.13.   Number of Countries in Which the Interviewed Managers Worked. *Source:* Author's own research.

Appendix E — Sample of One Interview

Table E.1. One Sample Interview.

Description of Variable	Variable	Coding Instructions
Respondent no.	1	
Name or pseudonym	Ahmed AbdelMawla	
Gender	Male (1)	Male = 1, Female = 2, Non-binary = 3
Age	45 years (3)	18–25 = 1, 26–40 = 2, 41–60 = 3, >61 = 4
Education	University graduate (2)	High school only = 1, University graduate = 2, Master graduate = 3, PhD graduate = 4
Geography	Africa (3)	Europe = 1, Asia = 2, Africa = 3, North America = 4, South America = 5, Australia = 6.
Country	Egypt	
Company sector	Services (4)	Retail = 1; Production = 2; Trade = 3; Services = 4; Others = 5
Company size (turnover)	>10M = x < 50M (5)	<0.5M. euro/year as turnover = 1, 0.5 >= x < 1M. euro/year = 2, 1 <= x < 5M. euro = 3, 5 >= x < 10M. euro = 4, >10M = x < 50M = 5, >=50 m euro = 6
Company size (employees' number)	1,001+ employees (6)	1–10/11–50/51–100/ 101–500/501–1,000/1,001+ employees
Function	TOP management (1)	TOP management = 1/ Middle Management = 2/ Lower management = 3
Years of experience within the company	16 years (5)	1–3 = 1/3–5 = 2/5–10 = 3/ 10–15 = 4/>16 = 5

(Continued)

Table E.1. *(Continued)*

Description of Variable	Variable	Coding Instructions
Years of experience in total	21+ years (6)	1–3 = 1/3–5 = 2/5–10 = 3/ 10–15 = 4/16–20 = 5/21+ = 6
Number of nationalities managed	11–15 managed nationalities (4)	1–3 = 1/4–5 = 2/6–10 = 3/ 11–15 = 4/16–20 = 5/ 21–50 = 6/51–100 = 7/ >100 = 8
Number of spoken languages	2 languages (2)	One = 1, Two = 2, Three = 3, more than 3 = 4
Number of continents in which the subject worked	2 continents: Asia, Africa (2)	One = 1, Two = 2, Three = 3, more than 3 = 4
Number of countries in which the subject worked	8 countries (4)	One = 1, Two = 2, Three = 3, more than 3 = 4
CQ	*Questions*	*Answers*
1.	How do you assess the cultural intelligence of your team members?	I used to work with the cultural intelligence scale developed by Yang, but, nowadays, I use a 360' review (developed by Gallup) that helps me assess the cultural and emotional intelligence level of all my team members. Meaning that each employee in our company is assessed by matrix colleagues, direct managers, and subordinates.
2.	How do you leverage your team members' cultural intelligence?	After assessing each team member's cultural and emotional intelligence level, I allocate them the tasks and roles based on their cultural agility, experience, and expertise.

Table E.1. *(Continued)*

Description of Variable	Variable	Coding Instructions
3.	Is there a relationship between the cultural intelligence of your team and your result as a multicultural manager? Please detail.	Yes, if one of the cultural skills is missing within my team – I am trying to develop it; otherwise, my results as a manager – leading 14 nationalities – will be affected and non-performant.
4.	What is your biggest challenge when dealing with cultural intelligence? Why?	My biggest challenge is portrayed by the business etiquette differences between Arab culture and European culture. Leading a team composed mainly of Arabic country members and dealing with European customers – forced me to learn and develop specific European business tactics and approaches. One is the pricing construct, where Europeans prefer a less negotiated option – so my first proposal is close to my target price.
KD	*Questions*	*Answers*
5.	Are your decisions based only on data and rational thinking?	Depending on the situation – my decisions are based on data (rational thinking) or experience. If a situation is urgent and there is no data or no time for getting the data, I rely on my experience and common sense to make the best decision. I cannot lose a contract because I need two days to get the exact numbers.

(Continued)

Table E.1. *(Continued)*

Description of Variable	Variable	Coding Instructions
6.	Do emotions play any role in your decisions?	Emotions do not play any role in my professional decisions. As mentioned before, I believe in data and experience. I am performance-driven, and this is what I am developing within my team. Emotions make you soft and make you lose the big picture and the professional goals.
7.	Do you consider their cultural values when interacting with people from different cultures? I consider their cultural values	When interacting with business people from different cultures, I think that this will show my business partners that I respect their origins and cultures, and this will help the professional partnership between our companies.
8.	Do you consider that it is useful to have a proper balance between rational thinking, emotions, and cultural values when making decisions?	Yes, I really do, but mostly between rational thinking and cultural values. I do not think that emotions are to be involved in the business. Otherwise, the proper balance between rational thinking and cultural values smooths the decision-making process and increases the overall productivity of the teamwork.
ML	*Questions*	*Answers*
9.	What is your leadership style with a multicultural team? Why?	My leadership style is bureaucratic and transactional, and all my employees are strictly advised to follow the

Table E.1. *(Continued)*

Description of Variable	Variable	Coding Instructions
		established rules. This will ensure predictability and uniformity, and these are important characteristics when dealing with multicultural teams.
10.	How do you create trust in your multicultural team?	I create and develop trust within the team by coaching each member. I am also insisting on the company values – as a trust generator.
11.	When assigning tasks, do you consider each team member's cultural background?	I always do because every different cultural team member mostly has a different skill set that I always want to leverage to optimize results.

Source: Author's own research.

Appendix F – The Interviews Codebook and Codes

Table F.1. The Interview Codebook.

Theme	Sub-Theme	Categories	Descriptive Codes
Cultural intelligence	Downplays cultural differences for team culture		* Does not assess cultural intelligence * does not leverage on team members' cultural intelligence * downplays individual cultural intelligence * focusing on assigning tasks to the best hands not based on cultural intelligence * does not deal with cultural intelligence

(Continued)

Table F.1. *(Continued)*

Theme	Sub-Theme	Categories	Descriptive Codes
			because everyone has common understanding of tasks * relationship between cultural intelligence and results is low * results is driven by skills developed and transmitted by the manager to a team member not cultural intelligence * there is no relationship between cultural intelligence and result * unsure of the relationship between cultural intelligence and results as a manager
	Emotional cultural intelligence	Assessing cultural intelligence through emotional intelligence metrics	* Assesses acceptance and adaptability for cultural intelligence * assesses cultural intelligence by reviewing their work in light of applied cultural intelligence "assesses cultural intelligence of team members by analyzing clients' feedback on team members' actions and interactions" * assesses cultural intelligence of team members by having one to one coaching and evaluation sessions every quarter * assesses cultural intelligence through standardized meetings * assesses cultural intelligence using 360 review * assesses team members based on experience * assesses team members skill and experience through communication * assesses the cultural

Table F.1. *(Continued)*

Theme	Sub-Theme	Categories	Descriptive Codes
			intelligence of team members through a report/questionnaire on cultural and emotional intelligence
		Leveraging emotional cultural intelligence for company results	* Leverages on cultural intelligence by assigning team members to task based on their identified cultural expertise * leverage on team members' cultural intelligence through detailed communications * leverage on team members' cultural intelligence by using verbal and nonverbal behavior in cross-cultural encounters * leverages on team members' cultural intelligence through social events * leveraging cultural skill for better result * leveraging emotional cultural intelligence for company result * partner with team members to get the best result
		View emotional intelligence issues as challenges	* The biggest challenge is accepting other opinions * biggest challenge is getting different people to work for a common goal * providing the right feedback based on understanding Canadian feelings * team members having a different attitude to work is a challenge * the biggest challenge is managing diversity * the level of conscious cultural awareness during interactions is a major challenge

(Continued)

Table F.1. *(Continued)*

Theme	Sub-Theme	Categories	Descriptive Codes
	Rational cultural intelligence	Assessing rational cultural intelligence	* Assessing cultural intelligence through knowledge of other cultures * assessing cultural intelligence through staff's prior experience and performance on tasks
		Leveraging rational cultural intelligence for results	*Assigning tasks based on knowledge and experience of culture * leveraging rational cultural intelligence for better results as multicultural manager *
		Views rational cultural intelligence issues as challenges	* generalized beliefs about groups are the biggest challenge when dealing with cultural intelligence * getting team members to be knowledgeable about Canadian practices is a challenge * giving feedback is a challenge because it has the role of driving the adaptation of individual culture to the company's culture "lack of knowledge of different cultures is a challenge when dealing with cultural intelligence" * language is a barrier when dealing with cultural intelligence * managing diversity is a problem because different people understand same task differently
	Spiritual cultural intelligence	Leveraging spiritual cultural intelligence for result	* Leverages on team members' cultural intelligence through a monitored ambience

Table F.1. *(Continued)*

Theme	Sub-Theme	Categories	Descriptive Codes
		View spiritual cultural intelligence issues as challenges	* The biggest challenge in dealing with cultural intelligence is how not to hurt any personal beliefs * the biggest challenge is business etiquette difference * cultural self-awareness * the biggest challenge is not disrespecting the personal belief of others as it might affect productivity
Knowledge dynamics	Combining rational, emotional and cultural values for decision-making		* balancing rational thinking, emotions, and cultural values is a key success factor * considers the balancing of rational thinking, emotions, and cultural values useful in decision-making
	Emotional knowledge		* Emotion plays a role in decision-making
	Rational knowledge		* business should be prioritized when making decisions * data and rational thinking are the main drivers of decision-making
	Spiritual knowledge		* Authentic decision-making * making decisions based on common sense * understanding the values of others is needed for decision-making when interacting with business partners and team members
Multicultural leadership	Conceptual skill		* Identifying practices that lead to productivity * leveraging cultural background for company success * strategic planning
	Interpersonal skill		* Building an environment with a sense of belonging

(Continued)

Table F.1. *(Continued)*

Theme	Sub-Theme	Categories	Descriptive Codes
		Multicultural skill (values)	* coaching and empowerment * collaboration * communication * empathy * friendliness and openness * Equal treatment * finding common ground * respecting cultural differences
		Leaders focus on uniformity and task completion.	* assign tasks based on skillset and not cultural background * focus on uniformity rather than understanding the cultural background

Source: Author's own research.

Table F.2. Interview's Codes.

Themes	Sub-Themes	Files
Cultural Intelligence		
Emotional cultural intelligence		14
	Assessing cultural intelligence through emotional intelligence metrics	11
	Leveraging emotional cultural intelligence for company results	5
	View emotional intelligence issues as challenges	7
Rational cultural intelligence		11
	Assessing cultural intelligence through rational intelligence metrics	6
	Leveraging rational cultural intelligence for results	9
	Views rational cultural intelligence issues as cultural intelligence challenges	6
Spiritual cultural intelligence		4
	Leverages on team members' cultural intelligence through a monitored ambience	1
	View spiritual cultural intelligence issues as challenges	4
Downplays cultural differences for team culture		4

Table F.2. *(Continued)*

Themes	Sub-Themes	Files
Knowledge Dynamics		
Emotional knowledge		6
	Emotion plays a role in decision-making	4
	Emotions play a minimal role in the decision-making process	6
Rational knowledge		14
	Business should be prioritized when making decisions	4
	Does not consider cultural values as the focus when interacting with people of different cultures	2
	Emotions play no role in decision-making	5
	Data and rational thinking are the main drivers in decision-making	13
Spiritual knowledge		11
	Authentic decision-making	1
	Making decisions based on common sense	2
	Understanding the values of others is needed for decision-making when interacting with business partners and team members	10
Combining rational, emotional and cultural values for decision-making		13
	Balancing rational thinking, emotions, and cultural values is a key success factor	3
	Considers the balancing of rational thinking, emotions, and cultural values useful in decision-making	13
Multicultural Leadership		
Conceptual skill		9
	Identifying practices that lead to productivity	4
	Leveraging cultural background for company success	8
	Strategic planning	3
Interpersonal skill		13
	Coaching and empowering team members	7
	Collaboration	3
	Communication	5
	Building an environment with a sense of belonging	2
	Empathy and kindness	3
	Friendliness and openness	4

(Continued)

Table F.2. *(Continued)*

Themes	Sub-Themes	Files
Multicultural skill (Values)		6
Equal treatment		3
Finding common ground		
Respecting cultural differences		3
Leader focuses on uniformity and task completion		7
Assign tasks based on skillset and not cultural background		6
Focus on uniformity rather than understanding the cultural background		2

Source: Author's own research.

Appendix G – Demography and Number of Words Transcribed

Table G.1. Gender and Age Classification – Interviews.

Pseudonym	Number of Words Transcribed	Gender	Age Classification
Ahmed AbdelMawla	616	Male	41–60
Dean Watson	546	Male	41–60
Dusty Wagoner	408	Male	41–60
Khosrow Salour	545	Male	41–60
Kristian Skovrider	380	Male	60+
Pedro Lemos	460	Male	26–40
Rin Senan	465	Male	26–40
Tinatin	413	Female	26–40
Umair Arshad	372	Male	26–40
Yousef Siam	401	Male	41–60
Zeinab Mekawy	486	Female	26–40
Annas Siddiqui	798	Male	26–40
Rana El Maghraby	362	Female	26–40
Saim Ali	537	Male	26–40
Vishal Kumar	263	Male	26–40

Source: Author's own research.

Table G.2. Education, Geography, Country Classification – Interviews.

Pseudonym	Number of Words Transcribed	Education	Geography	Country
Ahmed AbdelMawla	616	University graduate	Africa	Egypt
Dean Watson	546	High school	Europe	England
Dusty Wagoner	408	University graduate	North America	United States of America
Khosrow Salour	545	University graduate	Asia	Iran
Kristian Skovrider	380	Master graduate	Europe	Denmark
Pedro Lemos	460	Master graduate	North America	Canada
Rin Senan	465	Master graduate	North America	Canada
Tinatin	413	University graduate	Europe	Georgia
Umair Arshad	372	Master graduate	Europe	United Kingdom
Yousef Siam	401	University graduate	Asia	Saudi Arabia
Zeinab Mekawy	486	Master graduate	Africa	Egypt
Annas Siddiqui	798	University graduate	Europe	England
Rana El Maghraby	362	University graduate	Africa	Egypt
Saim Ali	537	Master graduate	Europe	England, UK
Vishal Kumar	263	Master graduate	North America	Canada

Source: Author's own research.

Table G.3. Function, Years of Experience Within the Company, Years of Experience in Total Classification – Interviews.

Pseudonym	Number of Words Transcribed	Function	Years of Experience Within the Company	Years of Experience in Total
Ahmed AbdelMawla	616	TOP management	16 years	21+ years
Dean Watson	546	TOP management	5–10 years	21+ years
Dusty Wagoner	408	TOP management	>16	21+ years
Khosrow Salour	545	TOP management	>16	21+ years
Kristian Skovrider	380	TOP management	14 years	21+ years
Pedro Lemos	460	Middle management	10–15 years	10–15 years
Rin Senan	465	Middle management	1–3 years	5–10 years
Tinatin	413	TOP management	2 years	5–10 years
Umair Arshad	372	Middle management	3 years	5–10 years
Yousef Siam	401	TOP management	3–5 years	21+ years
Zeinab Mekawy	486	Middle management	1–3 years	3–5 years
Annas Siddiqui	798	Middle management	1–3 years	5–10 years
Rana El Maghraby	362	TOP management	5–10 years	10–15 years
Saim Ali	537	Middle management	1–3 years	5–10 years
Vishal Kumar	263	Middle management	1–3 years	10–15 years

Source: Author's own research.

Table G.4. Company Sector, Company Size (Turnover, Employee's Number) Classification – Interviews.

Pseudonym	Number of Words Transcribed	Company Sector	Company Size (Turnover)	Company Size (Employees' Number)
Ahmed AbdelMawla	616	Services	$>10M = x < 50M$	1,001+ employees
Dean Watson	546	Other	$0.5>=x<1$	11–50 employees
Dusty Wagoner	408	Services	$5>=x<10M$	51–100 employees
Khosrow Salour	545	Services	$<0.5M$	1–10 employees
Kristian Skovrider	380	Trade	$1<=x<5M$	1–10 employees
Pedro Lemos	460	Services	$>=50$ m	1,001+ employees
Rin Senan	465	Services	$>=50$ m	1,001+ employees
Tinatin	413	Services	$1<=x<5M$	101–500 employees
Umair Arshad	372	Services	$>=50$ m	1,001+ employees
Yousef Siam	401	Retail	$0.5>=x<1$	11–50 employees
Zeinab Mekawy	486	Services	$5>=x<10M$	101–500 employees
Annas Siddiqui	798	Services	$1<=x<5M$	1,001+ employees
Rana El Maghraby	362	Services	$0.5>=x<1$	11–50 employees
Saim Ali	537	Trade	20 million	11–50 employees
Vishal Kumar	263	Services	$>=50$ m	1,001+ employees

Source: Author's own research.

Table G.5. Number of Words Transcribed, Number of Nationalities Managed, Number of Spoken Languages, Number of Countries in Which Subject Worked – Interviews.

Pseudonym	Number of Words Transcribed	Number of Nationalities Managed	Number of Spoken Languages	Number of Continents in Which the Subject Worked	Number of Countries in Which the Subject Worked
Ahmed AbdelMawla	616	11–15 nationalities	2 languages	2 continents	8 countries
Dean Watson	546	1–3 nationalities	1 language	1 continent	1 country
Dusty Wagoner	408	1–3 nationalities	1 language	1 continent	1 country
Khosrow Salour	545	6–10 nationalities	3 languages	3 continents	3 countries
Kristian Skovrider	380	6–10 nationalities	3 languages	2 continents	3 countries
Pedro Lemos	460	16–20 nationalities	2 languages	3 continents	More than 3 countries
Rin Senan	465	11–15 nationalities	2 languages	2 continents	2 countries
Tinatin	413	6–10 nationalities	5 languages	2 continents	2 countries
Umair Arshad	372	4 nationalities	2 languages	2 continents	2 countries
Yousef Siam	401	4–5 nationalities	2 languages	2 continents	2 countries
Zeinab Mekawy	486	1–3 nationalities	2 languages	2 continents	2 countries
Annas Siddiqui	798	11–15 nationalities	2 languages	2 continents	2 countries
Rana El Maghraby	362	1–3 nationalities	3 languages	1 continent	1 country
Saim Ali	537	6–10 nationalities	5 languages	2 continents	More than 3 countries
Vishal Kumar	263	6–10 nationalities	More than 3 languages	1 continent	3 countries

Source: Author's own research.

Appendix H – Transcribed Words and Participants per Variable

Table H.1. Gender Classification – Transcribed Words per Participant for Interview Section.

No.	Pseudonym	Transcribed Words	Transcribed Total Words
	Gender: Male		
1	Ahmed AbdelMawla	616	616
2	Dean Watson	546	1,162
3	Dusty Wagoner	408	1,570
4	Khosrow Salour	545	2,115
5	Kristian Skovrider	380	2,495
6	Pedro Lemos	460	2,955
7	Rin Senan	465	3,420
8	Umair Arshad	372	3,792
9	Yousef Siam	401	4,193
10	Annas Siddiqui	798	4,991
11	Saim Ali	537	5,528
12	Vishal Kumar	263	5,791
	Gender: Female		
13	Tinatin	413	6,204
14	Zeinab Mekawy	486	6,690
15	Rana El Maghraby	362	7,052

Source: Author's own research.

Table H.2. Age Classification – Transcribed Words per Participant for Interview Section.

No.	Pseudonym	Transcribed Words	Transcribed Total Words
	Age classification 60+ years		
1	Kristian Skovrider	380	2,896
	Age classification 41–60 years		
2	Ahmed AbdelMawla	616	616

(Continued)

Table H.2. *(Continued)*

No.	Pseudonym	Transcribed Words	Transcribed Total Words
3	Dean Watson	546	1,162
4	Dusty Wagoner	408	1,570
5	Khosrow Salour	545	2,115
6	Yousef Siam	401	2,516
	Age classification *26–40 years*		
7	Pedro Lemos	460	3,356
8	Rin Senan	465	3,821
9	Tinatin	413	4,234
10	Umair Arshad	372	4,606
11	Zeinab Mekawy	486	5,092
12	Annas Siddiqui	798	5,890
13	Rana El Maghraby	362	6,252
14	Saim Ali	537	6,789
15	Vishal Kumar	263	7,052

Source: Author's own research.

Table H.3. Education Classification – Transcribed Words per Participant for Interview Section.

No	Pseudonym	Transcribed Words	Transcribed Total Words
	Education: High School		
1	Dean Watson	546	546
	Education: University Graduate		
2	Ahmed AbdelMawla	616	1,162
3	Dusty Wagoner	408	1,150
4	Khosrow Salour	545	2,115
5	Tinatin	413	2,528
6	Yousef Siam	401	2,929
7	Annas Siddiqui	798	3,727
8	Rana El Maghraby	362	4,089
	Education: Master Graduate		
9	Kristian Skovrider	380	4,469
10	Pedro Lemos	460	4,929

Table H.3. *(Continued)*

No	Pseudonym	Transcribed Words	Transcribed Total Words
11	Rin Senan	465	5,394
12	Umair Arshad	372	5,766
13	Zeinab Mekawy	486	6,252
14	Saim Ali	537	6,789
15	Vishal Kumar	263	7,052

Source: Author's own research.

Table H.4. Geography Classification – Transcribed Words per Participant for Interview Section.

No	Pseudonym	Transcribed Total	Transcribed Total Words
	Geography Africa		
1	Ahmed AbdelMawla	616	616
2	Zeinab Mekawy	486	1,102
3	Rana El Maghraby	362	1,464
	Geography Europe		
4	Dean Watson	546	2,010
5	Kristian Skovrider	380	2,390
6	Tinatin	413	2,809
7	Umair Arshad	372	3,175
8	Annas Siddiqui	798	3,973
9	Saim Ali	537	4,510
	Geography North America		
10	Dusty Wagoner	408	4,918
11	Pedro Lemos	460	5,378
12	Rin Senan	465	5,843
13	Vishal Kumar	263	6,106
	Geography Asia		
14	Khosrow Salour	545	6,651
15	Yousef Siam	401	7,052

Source: Author's own research.

Table H.5. Country Classification – Transcribed Words per Participant for Interview Section.

No	Pseudonym	Transcribed Words	Transcribed Total Words
	Country: Egypt		
1	Ahmed AbdelMawla	616	616
2	Zeinab Mekawy	486	1,102
3	Rana El Maghraby	362	1,464
	Country: England		
4	Dean Watson	546	2,010
5	Annas Siddiqui	798	2,808
6	Umair Arshad	372	3,180
7	Saim Ali	537	3,717
	Country: Canada		
8	Pedro Lemos	460	4,177
9	Rin Senan	465	4,642
10	Vishal Kumar	263	4,905
	Country: Denmark		
11	Kristian Skovrider	380	5,283
	Country: Saudi Arabia		
12	Yousef Siam	401	5,686
	Country: Iran		
13	Khosrow Salour	545	6,231
	Country: Georgia		
14	Tinatin	413	6,644
	Country: The United States		
15	Dusty Wagoner	408	7,052

Source: Author's own research.

Table H.6. Function Classification – Transcribed Words per Participant for Interview Section.

No	Pseudonym	Transcribed Words	Transcribed Total Words
	Function: TOP Management		
1	Ahmed AbdelMawla	616	616
2	Dean Watson	546	1,162
3	Dusty Wagoner	408	1,570

Table H.6. *(Continued)*

No	Pseudonym	Transcribed Words	Transcribed Total Words
4	Khosrow Salour	545	2,115
5	Kristian Skovrider	380	2,495
6	Tinatin	413	2,908
7	Yousef Siam	401	3,309
8	Rana El Maghraby	362	3,671
	Function: Middle Management		
9	Pedro Lemos	460	4,131
10	Rin Senan	465	4,596
11	Umair Arshad	372	4,968
12	Zeinab Mekawy	486	5,454
13	Saim Ali	537	5,991
14	Vishal Kumar	263	6,254
15	Annas Siddiqui	798	7,052

Source: Author's own research.

Table H.7. Years of Experience Within the Company Classification – Transcribed Words per Participant for Interview Section.

No	Pseudonym	Transcribed Total	Transcribed Total Words
	Years of Experince: 1–5 Years		
1	Rin Senan	465	465
2	Zeinab Mekawy	486	951
3	Annas Siddiqui	798	1,749
4	Saim Ali	537	2,286
5	Vishal Kumar	263	2,549
6	Umair Arshad	372	2,921
7	Tinatin	413	3,334
8	Yousef Siam	401	3,735
	Years of Experience: 5–10 Years		
9	Dean Watson	546	4,281
10	Rana El Maghraby	362	4,643
	Years of Experience: 10–15 Years		
11	Pedro Lemos	460	5,103
12	Kristian Skovrider	380	5,483

(Continued)

Table H.7. *(Continued)*

No	Pseudonym	Transcribed Total	Transcribed Total Words
	Years of Experience: 16+ Years		
13	Ahmed AbdelMawla	616	6,099
14	Dusty Wagoner	408	6,507
15	Khosrow Salour	545	7,052

Source: Author's own research.

Table H.8. Years of Experience in Total Classification – Transcribed Words per Participant for Interview Section.

No	Pseudonym	Transcribed Total	Transcribed Total Words
	Years of Experience in Total 21+ Years		
1	Ahmed AbdelMawla	616	616
2	Dean Watson	546	1,162
3	Dusty Wagoner	408	1,570
4	Khosrow Salour	545	2,115
5	Kristian Skovrider	380	2,495
6	Yousef Siam	401	2,896
	Years of Experience 10–15 Years		
7	Pedro Lemos	460	3,356
8	Rana El Maghraby	362	3,718
9	Vishal Kumar	263	3,981
	Years of Experience in Total 5–10 Years		
10	Rin Senan	465	4,446
11	Tinatin	413	4,859
12	Umair Arshad	372	5,231
13	Annas Siddiqui	798	6,029
14	Saim Ali	537	6,566
	Years of Experience in Total 3–5 Years		
15	Zeinab Mekawy	486	7,052

Source: Author's own research.

Table H.9. Company Sector Classification – Transcribed Words per
Participant for Interview Section.

No	Pseudonym	Transcribed Total	Transcribed Total Words
	Company Sector Services		
1	Ahmed Abdel	616	616
2	Dusty Wagoner	408	1,024
3	Khosrow Salour	545	1,569
4	Pedro Lemos	460	2,029
5	Rin Senan	465	2,494
6	Tinatin	413	2,907
7	Umair Arshad	372	3,279
8	Zeinab Mekawy	486	3,765
9	Annas Siddiqui	798	4,563
10	Rana El Maghraby	362	4,925
11	Vishal Kumar	263	5,188
	Company Trade		
12	Kristian Skovrider	380	5,568
13	Saim Ali	537	6,105
	Company Retail		
14	Yousef Siam	401	6,506
	Company Other		
15	Dean Watson	546	7,052

Source: Author's own research.

Table H.10. Company Size (Turnover) Classification – Transcribed Words
per Participant for Interview Section.

No	Pseudonym	Transcribed Words	Transcribed Total Words
	Company Size (Turnover): 0.5M to <1M Euro		
1	Khosrow Salour	545	545
2	Rana El Maghraby	362	907
3	Dean Watson	546	1,453
4	Yousef Siam	401	1,854

(Continued)

Table H.10. *(Continued)*

No	Pseudonym	Transcribed Words	Transcribed Total Words
	Company Size (Turnover): 1M to <5M Euro		
5	Kristian Skovrider	380	2,234
6	Tinatin	413	2,647
7	Annas Siddiqui	798	3,445
	Company Size (Turnover): 5M to >10M Euro		
8	Dusty Wagoner	408	3,853
9	Zeinab Mekawy	486	4,339
	Company Size (Turnover): 10M to >50M		
10	Ahmed Abdel	616	4,955
11	Saim Ali	537	5,492
	Company Size (Turnover): 50M+		
12	Pedro Lemos	460	5,952
13	Rin Senan	465	6,417
14	Umair Arshad	372	6,789
15	Vishal Kumar	263	7,052

Source: Author's own research.

Table H.11. Company Size (Employees) Classification – Transcribed Words per Participant for Interview Section.

No	Pseudonym	Transcribed Total	Transcribed Total Words
	Company Size Employee 1,001+ Employees		
1	Ahmed AbdelMawla	616	616
2	Pedro Lemos	460	1,076
3	Rin Senan	465	1,541
4	Umair Arshad	372	1,913
5	Annas Siddiqui	798	2,711
6	Vishal Kumar	263	2,974
	Company Size 101–500 Employees		
7	Tinatin	413	3,387
8	Zeinab Mkawy	486	3,873

Table H.11. *(Continued)*

No	Pseudonym	Transcribed Total	Transcribed Total Words
	Company Size		
	51–100		
9	Dusty Wagoner	408	4,281
	Company Size Employee		
	11–50 Employees		
10	Dean Watson	546	4,827
11	Yousef Siam	401	5,228
12	Rana El Maghraby	362	5,590
13	Saim Ali	537	6,127
	Company Size		
	1–10 Employees		
14	Kristian Skovrider	380	6,507
14	Khosrow Salour	545	7,052

Source: Author's own research.

Table H.12. Number of Nationalities Managed Classification – Transcribed Words per Participant for Interview Section.

No	Pseudonym	Transcribed Words	Transcribed Total Words
	Number of Nationalities Managed: 1–3		
1	Dean Watson	546	546
2	Dusty Wagoner	408	954
3	Zeinab Mekawy	486	1,440
4	Rana El Maghraby	362	1,802
	Number of Nationalities Managed: 4–5		
5	Umair Arshad	372	2,174
6	Yousef Siam	401	2,575
	Number of Nationalities Managed: 6–10		
7	Khosrow Salour	545	3,120
8	Kristian Skovrider	380	3,500
9	Tinatin	413	3,913
10	Saim	537	4,450

(Continued)

Table H.12. *(Continued)*

No	Pseudonym	Transcribed Words	Transcribed Total Words
11	Vishal Kumar	263	4,713
	Number of Nationalities Managed: 11–15		
12	Ahmed AbdelMawla	616	5,329
13	Rin Senan	465	5,794
14	Annas Siddiqui	798	6,592
	Number of Nationalities Managed: 16–20		
15	Pedro Lemos	460	7,052

Source: Author's own research.

Table H.13. Number of Languages Spoken Classification – Transcribed Words per Participant for Interview Section.

No	Pseudonym	Transcribed Words	Transcribed Total Words
	Number of Languages Spoken: 1 Language		
1	Dean Watson	546	546
2	Dusty Wagoner	408	954
	Number of Languages Spoken: 2 Languages		
3	Ahmed AbdelMawla	616	1,570
4	Pedro Lemos	460	2,030
5	Rin Senan	465	2,495
6	Umair Arshad	372	2,867
7	Yousef Siam	401	3,268
8	Zeinab Mekawy	486	3,754
9	Annas Siddiqui	798	4,552
	Number of Languages Spoken: 3 Languages		
10	Khosrow Salour	545	5,097
11	Kristian Skovrider	380	5,477
12	Rana El Maghraby	362	5,839
	Number of Languages Spoken: More than 3 Languages		
13	Vishal Kumar	263	6,102
14	Saim Ali	537	6,639
15	Tinatin	413	7,052

Source: Author's own research.

Table H.14. Number of Continents in Which the Subject Worked
Classification – Transcribed Words per Participant for Interview Section.

No	Pseudonym	Transcribed Total	Transcribed Total Words
	No of Continents *3 Continents*		
1	Khosrow Salour	545	545
2	Pedro Lemos	460	1,005
	No of Continents *2 Continents*		
3	Ahmed AbdelMawla	616	1,621
4	Kristian Skovrider	380	2,001
5	Rin Senan	465	2,466
6	Tinatin	413	2,879
7	Umair Arshad	372	3,251
8	Yousef Siam	401	3,652
9	Zeinab Mekawy	486	4,138
10	Annas Siddiqui	798	4,936
11	Saim	537	5,473
	No of Continents *1 Continent*		
12	Dean Watson	546	6,019
13	Dusty Wagoner	408	6,429
14	Rana El Maghraby	362	6,789
15	Vishal Kumar	263	7,052

Source: Author's own research.

Table H.15. Number of Countries in Which the Subject Worked
Classification – Transcribed Words per Participant for Interview Section.

No	Pseudonym	Transcribed Words	Transcribed Total Words
	Number of Countries in Which the Subject Worked: 1		
1	Dean Watson	546	546
2	Dusty Wagoner	408	954
3	Rana El Maghraby	362	1,316
	Number of Countries in Which the Subject Worked: 2		
4	Rin Senan	465	1,781
5	Tinatin	413	2,194
6	Umair Arshad	372	2,566

(Continued)

Table H.15. *(Continued)*

No	Pseudonym	Transcribed Words	Transcribed Total Words
7	Yousef Siam	401	2,967
8	Zeinab Mekawy	486	3,453
9	Annas Siddiqui	798	4,251
	Number of Countries in Which the Subject Worked: 3		
10	Khosrow Salour	545	4,796
11	Kristian Skovrider	380	5,176
12	Vishal Kumar	263	5,439
	Number of Countries in Which the Subject Worked: More than 3		
13	Ahmed AbdelMawla	616	6,055
14	Pedro Lemos	460	6,515
15	Saim	537	7,052

Source: Author's own research.

Appendix I – Total Transcribed Words per Variable

Table I.1. Gender Classification – Total Transcribed Words for Interview Section.

Total Interviews	Total Words Transcribed	Total Male	Total Female
15	7,052	12	3

Source: Author's own research.

Table I.2. Age Classification – Total Transcribed Words for Interview Section.

Total Interviews	Total Words Transcribed	26–40	41–60	60+
15	7,052	9	5	1

Source: Author's own research.

Table I.3. Education Classification – Total Transcribed Words for Interview Section.

Total Interviews	Total Words Transcribed	High School	University Graduate	Masters
15	7,052	1	7	7

Source: Author's own research.

Table I.4. Geography Classification – Total Transcribed Words for Interview Section.

Total Interviews	Total Words Transcribed	Africa	Europe	North America	Asia
15	7,052	3	6	4	2

Source: Author's own research.

Table I.5. Countries Classification – Total Transcribed Words for Interview Section.

Total Interviews	Total Words Transcribed	Egypt	England	Canada	Denmark	Saudi Arabia	Iran	Georgia	US
15	7,052	3	4	3	1	1	1	1	1

Source: Author's own research.

Table I.6. Company Sector Classification – Total Transcribed Words for Interview Section.

Total Interviews	Total Words Transcribed	Services	Trade	Other	Retail
15	7,052	11	2	1	1

Source: Author's own research.

Table I.7. Company size (Turnover) Classification – Total Transcribed Words for Interview Section.

Total Interviews	Total Words Transcribed	<0.5M.euro/	0.5>=x< 1M euro/	1<=x < 5M	5<=x < 10M	10M = x < 50M	50M +
15	7,052	1	3	3	2	2	4

Source: Author's own research.

Table I.8. Company Size (Employees) Classification – Total Transcribed Words for Interview Section.

Total Interviewed	Total Words Transcribed	1,001+	11–50	51–50	1–10	101–500
15	7,052	6	4	1	2	2

Source: Author's own research.

Table I.9. Function Classification – Total Transcribed Words for Interview Section.

Total Interviewed	Total Words Transcribed	Top Management	Middle Management
15	7,052	8	7

Source: Author's own research.

Table I.10. Years of Experience Within the Company Classification – Total Transcribed Words for Interview Section.

Total Interviewed	Total Words Transcribed	1–5	5–10	10–15	16+
15	7,052	8	2	2	3

Source: Author's own research.

Table I.11. Years of Experience in Total Classification – Total Transcribed Words for Interview Section.

Total Interviewed	Total Words Transcribed	3–5	5–10	10–15	21+
15	7,052	1	5	3	6

Source: Author's own research.

Table I.12. Number of Nationalities Managed Classification – Total Transcribed Words for Interview Section.

Total Interviewed	Total Words Transcribed	1–3	4–5	6–10	11–15	16–20
15	7,052	4	2	5	3	1

Source: Author's own research.

Table I.13. Number of Spoken Languages Classification – Total Transcribed Words for Interview Section.

Total Interviewed	Total Words Transcribed	One	Two	Three	More than 3
15	7,052	2	7	3	3

Source: Author's own research.

Table I.14. Number of Continents in Which the Subject Worked Classification – Total Transcribed Words for Interview Section.

Total Interviewed	Total Words Transcribed	One	Two	Three
15	7,052	4	9	2

Source: Author's own research.

Table I.15. Number of Countries in Which Subjects Work Classification – Total Transcribed Words for Interview Section.

Total Interviewed	Total Words Transcribed	One	Two	Three	More than 3
15	7,052	3	6	3	3

Source: Author's own research.

Appendices for Quantitative Research

Appendix J – Introduction Section for Questionnaire

Dear participant,

My name is Dan Paiuc and I am a PhD student at SNSPA Bucharest, Romania. The purpose of my questionnaire is to find out the impact of cultural intelligence and knowledge dynamics on multinational leadership, within organizational context, and I need your co-operation to help me answer this survey questions. I assure you that your responses are just for academic purposes and will be used only for statistical purposes.

It is estimated that this questionnaire will take 10–12 minutes, and I really appreciate your help in fulfilling this research endeavor that will benefit both academic and business-related areas.

Your participation in this survey is completely voluntary and you won't be compensated for it. However, you have the freedom to decline participating in the research or exit the survey at any time without any consequences. It is preferred that you answer all the questions but you are not obligated to. Your survey responses will be stored in a secure electronic format by Google Forms, and any identifying information such as your name, email address, or IP address won't be collected. Hence, your responses will be completely anonymous and in compliance with GDPR policy. It is assured that no one will be able to identify you by your responses, and no one will know if you participated in the study or not. Answering the questionnaire will represent your consent in regards all the above mentions.

Thank you very much for your time, effort, and participation! It is much appreciated.

Appendix K – Descriptive Statistics (Quantitative Research)

Table K.1. Descriptive Statistics for Quantitative Research: Frequencies and Percentages.

Variables	Group	Category	Frequency	Percentage (%)
MCQ1	1	Strongly disagree	12	3.0
	2	Disagree	22	5.6
	3	Somewhat disagree	36	9.1
	4	Neutral	50	12.6
	5	Somewhat agree	72	18.2
	6	Agree	103	26.0
	7	Strongly agree	101	25.5
MCQ2	1	Strongly disagree	17	4.3
	2	Disagree	21	5.3
	3	Somewhat disagree	24	6.1
	4	Neutral	54	13.6
	5	Somewhat agree	97	24.5
	6	Agree	77	19.4
	7	Strongly agree	106	26.8
MCQ3	1	Strongly disagree	10	2.5
	2	Disagree	12	3.0
	3	Somewhat disagree	36	9.1
	4	Neutral	63	15.9
	5	Somewhat agree	82	20.7
	6	Agree	74	18.7
	7	Strongly agree	119	30.1
MCQ4	1	Strongly disagree	10	2.5
	2	Disagree	17	4.3
	3	Somewhat disagree	36	9.1
	4	Neutral	54	13.6
	5	Somewhat agree	84	21.2
	6	Agree	78	19.7
	7	Strongly agree	117	29.5
COCQ1	1	Strongly disagree	13	3.3
	2	Disagree	22	5.6
	3	Somewhat disagree	38	9.6
	4	Neutral	70	17.7
	5	Somewhat agree	74	18.7

Table K.1. *(Continued)*

Variables	Group	Category	Frequency	Percentage (%)
	6	Agree	94	23.7
	7	Strongly agree	85	21.5
COCQ2	1	Strongly disagree	7	1.8
	2	Disagree	20	5.1
	3	Somewhat disagree	42	10.6
	4	Neutral	61	15.4
	5	Somewhat agree	91	23.0
	6	Agree	79	19.9
	7	Strongly agree	96	24.2
COCQ3	1	Strongly disagree	7	1.8
	2	Disagree	30	7.6
	3	Somewhat disagree	42	10.6
	4	Neutral	61	15.4
	5	Somewhat agree	78	19.7
	6	Agree	63	15.9
	7	Strongly agree	115	29.0
COCQ4	1	Strongly disagree	13	3.3
	2	Disagree	26	6.6
	3	Somewhat disagree	32	8.1
	4	Neutral	53	13.4
	5	Somewhat agree	106	26.8
	6	Agree	85	21.5
	7	Strongly agree	81	20.5
COCQ5	1	Strongly disagree	16	4.0
	2	Disagree	26	6.6
	3	Somewhat disagree	25	6.3
	4	Neutral	65	16.4
	5	Somewhat agree	70	17.7
	6	Agree	86	21.7
	7	Strongly agree	108	27.3
COCQ6	1	Strongly disagree	14	3.5
	2	Disagree	25	6.3
	3	Somewhat disagree	46	11.6
	4	Neutral	63	15.9
	5	Somewhat agree	77	19.4

(Continued)

Table K.1. *(Continued)*

Variables	Group	Category	Frequency	Percentage (%)
	6	Agree	81	20.5
	7	Strongly agree	90	22.7
MOTCQ1	1	Strongly disagree	0.290	0.523
	2	Disagree	13	3.3
	3	Somewhat disagree	26	6.6
	4	Neutral	36	9.1
	5	Somewhat agree	69	17.4
	6	Agree	76	19.2
	7	Strongly agree	68	17.2
MOTCQ2	1	Strongly disagree	10	2.5
	2	Disagree	18	4.5
	3	Somewhat disagree	46	11.6
	4	Neutral	56	14.1
	5	Somewhat agree	61	15.4
	6	Agree	82	20.7
	7	Strongly agree	123	31.1
MOTCQ3	1	Strongly disagree	13	3.3
	2	Disagree	22	5.6
	3	Somewhat disagree	33	8.3
	4	Neutral	56	14.1
	5	Somewhat agree	79	19.9
	6	Agree	72	18.2
	7	Strongly agree	121	30.6
MOTCQ4	1	Strongly disagree	9	2.3
	2	Disagree	18	4.5
	3	Somewhat disagree	41	10.4
	4	Neutral	60	15.2
	5	Somewhat agree	62	15.7
	6	Agree	84	21.2
	7	Strongly agree	122	30.8
MOTCQ5	1	Strongly disagree	16	4.0
	2	Disagree	20	5.1
	3	Somewhat disagree	33	8.3
	4	Neutral	51	12.9
	5	Somewhat agree	78	19.7

Table K.1. *(Continued)*

Variables	Group	Category	Frequency	Percentage (%)
	6	Agree	83	21.0
	7	Strongly agree	115	29.0
BEHCQ1	1	Strongly disagree	18	4.5
	2	Disagree	20	5.1
	3	Somewhat disagree	36	9.1
	4	Neutral	59	14.9
	5	Somewhat agree	84	21.2
	6	Agree	93	23.5
	7	Strongly agree	86	21.7
BEHCQ2	1	Strongly disagree	9	2.3
	2	Disagree	21	5.3
	3	Somewhat disagree	41	10.4
	4	Neutral	57	14.4
	5	Somewhat agree	68	17.2
	6	Agree	76	19.2
	7	Strongly agree	124	31.3
BEHCQ3	1	Strongly disagree	9	2.3
	2	Disagree	22	5.6
	3	Somewhat disagree	43	10.9
	4	Neutral	51	12.9
	5	Somewhat agree	80	20.2
	6	Agree	70	17.7
	7	Strongly agree	121	30.6
BEHCQ4	1	Strongly disagree	11	2.8
	2	Disagree	23	5.8
	3	Somewhat disagree	38	9.6
	4	Neutral	52	13.1
	5	Somewhat agree	70	17.7
	6	Agree	85	21.5
	7	Strongly agree	117	29.5
BEHCQ5	1	Strongly disagree	9	2.3
	2	Disagree	19	4.8
	3	Somewhat disagree	28	7.1
	4	Neutral	48	12.1
	5	Somewhat agree	84	21.2

(Continued)

Table K.1. *(Continued)*

Variables	Group	Category	Frequency	Percentage (%)
	6	Agree	93	23.5
	7	Strongly agree	115	29.0
RKD1	1	Strongly disagree	5	1.3
	2	Disagree	22	5.6
	3	Somewhat disagree	35	8.8
	4	Neutral	60	15.2
	5	Somewhat agree	93	23.5
	6	Agree	103	26.0
	7	Strongly agree	78	19.7
RKD2	1	Strongly disagree	4	1.0
	2	Disagree	19	4.8
	3	Somewhat disagree	24	6.1
	4	Neutral	50	12.6
	5	Somewhat agree	79	19.9
	6	Agree	82	20.7
	7	Strongly agree	138	34.8
RKD3	1	Strongly disagree	10	2.5
	2	Disagree	17	4.3
	3	Somewhat disagree	15	3.8
	4	Neutral	67	16.9
	5	Somewhat agree	91	23.0
	6	Agree	100	25.3
	7	Strongly agree	96	24.2
SKD1	1	Strongly disagree	8	2.0
	2	Disagree	17	4.3
	3	Somewhat disagree	26	6.6
	4	Neutral	78	19.7
	5	Somewhat agree	93	23.5
	6	Agree	80	20.2
	7	Strongly agree	94	23.7
SKD2	1	Strongly disagree	6	1.5
	2	Disagree	15	3.8
	3	Somewhat disagree	26	6.6
	4	Neutral	48	12.1
	5	Somewhat agree	98	24.7

Table K.1. *(Continued)*

Variables	Group	Category	Frequency	Percentage (%)
	6	Agree	93	23.5
	7	Strongly agree	110	27.8
SKD3	1	Strongly disagree	0.472	0.461
	2	Disagree	5	1.3
	3	Somewhat disagree	10	2.5
	4	Neutral	26	6.6
	5	Somewhat agree	52	13.1
	6	Agree	75	18.9
	7	Strongly agree	100	25.3
EKD1	1	Strongly disagree	10	2.5
	2	Disagree	9	2.3
	3	Somewhat disagree	20	5.1
	4	Neutral	39	9.8
	5	Somewhat agree	52	13.1
	6	Agree	111	28.0
	7	Strongly agree	155	39.1
EKD2	1	Strongly disagree	9	2.3
	2	Disagree	23	5.8
	3	Somewhat disagree	28	7.1
	4	Neutral	46	11.6
	5	Somewhat agree	83	21.0
	6	Agree	83	21.0
	7	Strongly agree	124	31.3
EKD3	1	Strongly disagree	8	2.0
	2	Disagree	8	2.0
	3	Somewhat disagree	38	9.6
	4	Neutral	38	9.6
	5	Somewhat agree	66	16.7
	6	Agree	87	22.0
	7	Strongly agree	151	38.1
AS_ML1	1	Strongly disagree	6	1.5
	2	Disagree	15	3.8
	3	Somewhat disagree	26	6.6
	4	Neutral	54	13.6
	5	Somewhat agree	82	20.7

(Continued)

Table K.1. *(Continued)*

Variables	Group	Category	Frequency	Percentage (%)
	6	Agree	80	20.2
	7	Strongly agree	133	33.6
AS_ML2	1	Strongly disagree	9	2.3
	2	Disagree	11	2.8
	3	Somewhat disagree	26	6.6
	4	Neutral	53	13.4
	5	Somewhat agree	83	21.0
	6	Agree	83	21.0
	7	Strongly agree	131	33.1
AS_ML3	1	Strongly disagree	11	2.8
	2	Disagree	8	2.0
	3	Somewhat disagree	21	5.3
	4	Neutral	47	11.9
	5	Somewhat agree	107	27.0
	6	Agree	86	21.7
	7	Strongly agree	116	29.3
IS_ML1	1	Strongly disagree	11	2.8
	2	Disagree	14	3.5
	3	Somewhat disagree	32	8.1
	4	Neutral	67	16.9
	5	Somewhat agree	84	21.2
	6	Agree	90	22.7
	7	Strongly agree	98	24.7
IS_ML2	1	Strongly disagree	4	1.0
	2	Disagree	14	3.5
	3	Somewhat disagree	18	4.5
	4	Neutral	53	13.4
	5	Somewhat agree	78	19.7
	6	Agree	85	21.5
	7	Strongly agree	144	36.4
IS_ML3	1	Strongly disagree	7	1.8
	2	Disagree	8	2.0
	3	Somewhat disagree	27	6.8
	4	Neutral	52	13.1
	5	Somewhat agree	69	17.4

Table K.1. *(Continued)*

Variables	Group	Category	Frequency	Percentage (%)
	6	Agree	102	25.8
	7	Strongly agree	131	33.1
CS_ML1	1	Strongly disagree	4	1.0
	2	Disagree	14	3.5
	3	Somewhat disagree	20	5.1
	4	Neutral	26	6.6
	5	Somewhat agree	63	15.9
	6	Agree	127	32.1
	7	Strongly agree	142	35.9
CS_ML2	1	Strongly disagree	12	3.0
	2	Disagree	9	2.3
	3	Somewhat disagree	28	7.1
	4	Neutral	45	11.4
	5	Somewhat agree	85	21.5
	6	Agree	95	24.0
	7	Strongly agree	122	30.8
CS_ML3	1	Strongly disagree	9	2.3
	2	Disagree	33	8.3
	3	Somewhat disagree	34	8.6
	4	Neutral	50	12.6
	5	Somewhat agree	95	24.0
	6	Agree	78	19.7
	7	Strongly agree	97	24.5
MLS_ML1	1	Strongly disagree	4	1.0
	2	Disagree	15	3.8
	3	Somewhat disagree	46	11.6
	4	Neutral	74	18.7
	5	Somewhat agree	78	19.7
	6	Agree	89	22.5
	7	Strongly agree	90	22.7
MLS_ML2	1	Strongly disagree	9	2.3
	2	Disagree	10	2.5
	3	Somewhat disagree	44	11.1
	4	Neutral	53	13.4
	5	Somewhat agree	70	17.7

(Continued)

Table K.1. *(Continued)*

Variables	Group	Category	Frequency	Percentage (%)
	6	Agree	108	27.3
	7	Strongly agree	102	25.8
MLS_ML3	1	Strongly disagree	12	3.0
	2	Disagree	12	3.0
	3	Somewhat disagree	29	7.3
	4	Neutral	60	15.2
	5	Somewhat agree	93	23.5
	6	Agree	91	23.0
	7	Strongly agree	99	25.0
ACL_OC1	1	Strongly disagree	7	1.8
	2	Disagree	13	3.3
	3	Somewhat disagree	41	10.4
	4	Neutral	66	16.7
	5	Somewhat agree	85	21.5
	6	Agree	93	23.5
	7	Strongly agree	91	23.0
ACL_OC2	1	Strongly disagree	5	1.3
	2	Disagree	17	4.3
	3	Somewhat disagree	23	5.8
	4	Neutral	46	11.6
	5	Somewhat agree	82	20.7
	6	Agree	98	24.7
	7	Strongly agree	125	31.6
ACL_OC3	1	Strongly disagree	7	1.8
	2	Disagree	10	2.5
	3	Somewhat disagree	25	6.3
	4	Neutral	55	13.9
	5	Somewhat agree	97	24.5
	6	Agree	77	19.4
	7	Strongly agree	125	31.6
CCL_OC1	1	Strongly disagree	9	2.3
	2	Disagree	15	3.8
	3	Somewhat disagree	30	7.6
	4	Neutral	62	15.7
	5	Somewhat agree	99	25.0

Table K.1. *(Continued)*

Variables	Group	Category	Frequency	Percentage (%)
	6	Agree	96	24.2
	7	Strongly agree	85	21.5
CCL_OC2	1	Strongly disagree	8	2.0
	2	Disagree	5	1.3
	3	Somewhat disagree	26	6.6
	4	Neutral	36	9.1
	5	Somewhat agree	77	19.4
	6	Agree	104	26.3
	7	Strongly agree	140	35.4
CCL_OC3	1	Strongly disagree	6	1.5
	2	Disagree	13	3.3
	3	Somewhat disagree	23	5.8
	4	Neutral	46	11.6
	5	Somewhat agree	95	24.0
	6	Agree	79	19.9
	7	Strongly agree	134	33.8
DEIL_OC1	1	Strongly disagree	9	2.3
	2	Disagree	15	3.8
	3	Somewhat disagree	42	10.6
	4	Neutral	65	16.4
	5	Somewhat agree	85	21.5
	6	Agree	84	21.2
	7	Strongly agree	96	24.2
DEIL_OC2	1	Strongly disagree	7	1.8
	2	Disagree	10	2.5
	3	Somewhat disagree	33	8.3
	4	Neutral	68	17.2
	5	Somewhat agree	76	19.2
	6	Agree	89	22.5
	7	Strongly agree	113	28.5
DEIL_OC3	1	Strongly disagree	6	1.5
	2	Disagree	9	2.3
	3	Somewhat disagree	33	8.3
	4	Neutral	53	13.4
	5	Somewhat agree	76	19.2

(Continued)

Table K.1. *(Continued)*

Variables	Group	Category	Frequency	Percentage (%)
	6	Agree	80	20.2
	7	Strongly agree	139	35.1
EAIL_OC1	1	Strongly disagree	5	1.3
	2	Disagree	10	2.5
	3	Somewhat disagree	24	6.1
	4	Neutral	51	12.9
	5	Somewhat agree	87	22.0
	6	Agree	98	24.7
	7	Strongly agree	121	30.6
EAIL_OC2	1	Strongly disagree	7	1.8
	2	Disagree	15	3.8
	3	Somewhat disagree	34	8.6
	4	Neutral	52	13.1
	5	Somewhat agree	72	18.2
	6	Agree	81	20.5
	7	Strongly agree	135	34.1
EAIL_OC3	1	Strongly disagree	6	1.5
	2	Disagree	9	2.3
	3	Somewhat disagree	30	7.6
	4	Neutral	45	11.4
	5	Somewhat agree	102	25.8
	6	Agree	88	22.2
	7	Strongly agree	116	29.3
FTL_OC1	1	Strongly disagree	7	1.8
	2	Disagree	12	3.0
	3	Somewhat disagree	35	8.8
	4	Neutral	58	14.6
	5	Somewhat agree	94	23.7
	6	Agree	96	24.2
	7	Strongly agree	94	23.7
FTL_OC2	1	Strongly disagree	7	1.8
	2	Disagree	12	3.0
	3	Somewhat disagree	26	6.6
	4	Neutral	55	13.9
	5	Somewhat agree	68	17.2

Table K.1. *(Continued)*

Variables	Group	Category	Frequency	Percentage (%)
	6	Agree	90	22.7
	7	Strongly agree	138	34.8
FTL_OC3	1	Strongly disagree	12	3.0
	2	Disagree	7	1.8
	3	Somewhat disagree	30	7.6
	4	Neutral	67	16.9
	5	Somewhat agree	80	20.2
	6	Agree	84	21.2
	7	Strongly agree	116	29.3
SL_OC1	1	Strongly disagree	8	2.0
	2	Disagree	20	5.1
	3	Somewhat disagree	38	9.6
	4	Neutral	50	12.6
	5	Somewhat agree	105	26.5
	6	Agree	101	25.5
	7	Strongly agree	74	18.7
SL_OC2	1	Strongly disagree	10	2.5
	2	Disagree	15	3.8
	3	Somewhat disagree	27	6.8
	4	Neutral	55	13.9
	5	Somewhat agree	71	17.9
	6	Agree	91	23.0
	7	Strongly agree	127	32.1
SL_OC3	1	Strongly disagree	13	3.3
	2	Disagree	18	4.5
	3	Somewhat disagree	29	7.3
	4	Neutral	48	12.1
	5	Somewhat agree	76	19.2
	6	Agree	112	28.3
	7	Strongly agree	100	25.3

Source: Author's own research.

Note: MCQ: Metacognitive Cultural Intelligence, COCQ: Cognitive Cultural Intelligence, MOTCQ: Motivational Cultural Intelligence, BEHCQ: Behavioral Cultural Intelligence, RKD: Rational Knowledge Dynamics, SKD: Spiritual Knowledge Dynamics, EKD: Emotional Rational Knowledge Dynamics, AS_ML Administrative Skills, IS_ML: Interpersonal Skills, CS_ML Conceptual Skills, MLS_ML: Multicultural Leadership Skills, ACL_OC: Agility and Change Level, CCL_OC: Community and Connection Level, DIEL_OC: Diversity, Equity, and Inclusion Level, EAIL_OC: Entrepreneurship, Autonomy, and Innovation Level, FTL_OC: Flexibility and Transparency Level, SL_OC: Strength Level of the Company's Culture.

Appendix L – Assessing Normality (Quantitative Research) – Mean Based

Table L.1. Assessing Normality for Quantitative Research – Mean Based.

Indicators	Minimum	Maximum	Mean	Median	Std. Deviation	Skewness	Kurtosis
MCQ1	1	7	mai.17	6	1.653	−0.764	−0.285
MCQ2	1	7	mai.14	5	1.672	−0.787	−0.079
MCQ3	1	7	mai.26	5	1.591	−0.670	−0.276
MCQ4	1	7	mai.24	5	1.618	−0.707	−0.290
COCQ1	1	7	5.00	5	1.640	−0.592	−0.448
COCQ2	1	7	05.oct	5	1.575	−0.534	−0.511
COCQ3	1	7	05.aug	5	1.693	−0.488	−0.800
COCQ4	1	7	5.00	5	1.616	−0.669	−0.244
COCQ5	1	7	05.nov	5	1.719	−0.721	−0.363
COCQ6	1	7	apr.94	5	1.695	−0.515	−0.642
MOTCQ1	1	7	05.mar	5	1.710	−0.546	−0.614
MOTCQ2	1	7	mai.22	6	1.682	−0.650	−0.582
MOTCQ3	1	7	mai.19	5	1.696	−0.702	−0.392
MOTCQ4	1	7	mai.24	6	1.653	−0.665	−0.515
MOTCQ5	1	7	mai.18	6	1.705	−0.772	−0.263
BEHCQ1	1	7	05.ian	5	1.675	−0.690	−0.293
BEHCQ2	1	7	mai.22	6	1.674	−0.643	−0.572
BEHCQ3	1	7	mai.18	5	1.673	−0.620	−0.580
BEHCQ4	1	7	mai.20	6	1.687	−0.703	−0.461
BEHCQ5	1	7	mai.32	6	1.581	−0.839	−0.012
RKD1	1	7	05.nov	5	1.500	−0.616	−0.317
RKD2	1	7	mai.47	6	1.532	−0.835	−0.102
RKD3	1	7	mai.26	5	1.507	−0.842	0.317
EKD1	1	7	mai.69	6	1.509	−1.286	1.122
EKD2	1	7	mai.31	6	1.630	−0.817	−0.164
.EKD3	1	7	mai.55	6	1.559	−0.964	0.120
SKD1	1	7	mai.14	5	1.519	−0.585	−0.201
SKD2	1	7	mai.36	6	1.479	−0.813	0.138
SKD3	1	7	mai.51	6	1.454	−0.875	0.159
MLS_ML1	1	7	05.nov	5	1.511	−0.429	−0.672
MLS_ML2	1	7	mai.27	6	1.552	−0.743	−0.201
MLS_ML3	1	7	mai.22	5	1.546	−0.777	0.110
CS_ML1	1	7	mai.72	6	1.408	−1.286	1.173
CS_ML2	1	7	mai.41	6	1.547	−0.964	0.420
CS_ML3	1	7	05.mai	5	1.663	−0.605	−0.536
IS_ML1	1	7	mai.17	5	1.565	−0.690	−0.135

Table L.1. *(Continued)*

Indicators	Minimum	Maximum	Mean	Median	Std. Deviation	Skewness	Kurtosis
IS_ML2	1	7	mai.57	6	1.464	−0.906	0.187
IS_ML3	1	7	mai.52	6	1.478	−0.933	0.293
AS_ML1	1	7	mai.43	6	1.532	−0.807	−0.062
AS_ML2	1	7	mai.43	6	1.537	−0.872	0.170
AS_ML3	1	7	mai.41	6	1.479	−0.945	0.674
SL_OC1	1	7	05.aug	5	1.513	−0.680	−0.147
SL_OC2	1	7	mai.38	6	1.591	−0.869	0.029
SL_OC3	1	7	mai.25	6	1.608	−0.898	0.094
CCL_OC1	1	7	mai.16	5	1.499	−0.705	0.023
CCL_OC2	1	7	mai.63	6	1.441	−1.116	0.876
CCL_OC3	1	7	mai.48	6	1.487	−0.874	0.220
EAIL_OC1	1	7	mai.48	6	1.429	−0.853	0.242
EAIL_OC2	1	7	mai.40	6	1.586	−0.785	−0.237
EAIL_OC3	1	7	mai.41	6	1.446	−0.800	0.178
FTL_OC1	1	7	mai.23	5	1.483	−0.681	−0.094
FTL_OC2	1	7	mai.49	6	1.530	−0.891	0.087
FTL_OC3	1	7	mai.30	6	1.554	−0.766	0.049
ACL_OC1	1	7	mai.15	5	1.515	−0.575	−0.357
ACL_OC2	1	7	mai.47	6	1.495	−0.905	0.177
ACL_OC3	1	7	mai.41	6	1.481	−0.784	0.125
DEIL_OC1	1	7	05.dec	5	1.571	−0.571	−0.405
DEIL_OC2	1	7	mai.31	6	1.513	−0.669	−0.230
DEIL_OC3	1	7	mai.47	6	1.517	−0.794	−0.125

Source: Author's own research.

Appendix M – Assessing Normality (Quantitative Research): Kolmogorov-Smirnov and Shapiro-Wilk Test

Table M.1. Assessing Normality for Quantitative Research: Kolmogorov-Smirnov and Shapiro-Wilk Test.

	Kolmogorov-Smirnov			Shapiro-Wilk		
	Statistic	df	Sig.	Statistic	df	Sig.
MCQ1	0.206	396	0.000	0.886	396	0.000
MCQ2	0.173	396	0.000	0.886	396	0.000
MCQ3	0.168	396	0.000	0.889	396	0.000

(Continued)

Table M.1. *(Continued)*

	Kolmogorov-Smirnov			Shapiro-Wilk		
	Statistic	df	Sig.	Statistic	df	Sig.
MCQ4	0.173	396	0.000	0.887	396	0.000
COCQ1	0.181	396	0.000	0.910	396	0.000
COCQ2	0.159	396	0.000	0.910	396	0.000
COCQ3	0.163	396	0.000	0.896	396	0.000
COCQ4	0.187	396	0.000	0.907	396	0.000
COCQ5	0.187	396	0.000	0.886	396	0.000
COCQ6	0.167	396	0.000	0.912	396	0.000
MOTCQ1	0.159	396	0.000	0.900	396	0.000
MOTCQ2	0.197	396	0.000	0.880	396	0.000
MOTCQ3	0.172	396	0.000	0.883	396	0.000
MOTCQ4	0.197	396	0.000	0.881	396	0.000
MOTCQ5	0.184	396	0.000	0.880	396	0.000
BEHCQ1	0.176	396	0.000	0.902	396	0.000
BEHCQ2	0.185	396	0.000	0.882	396	0.000
BEHCQ3	0.169	396	0.000	0.887	396	0.000
BEHCQ4	0.193	396	0.000	0.882	396	0.000
BEHCQ5	0.192	396	0.000	0.878	396	0.000
RKD1	0.181	396	0.000	0.911	396	0.000
RKD2	0.190	396	0.000	0.862	396	0.000
RKD3	0.183	396	0.000	0.889	396	0.000
EKD1	0.252	396	0.000	0.808	396	0.000
EKD2	0.186	396	0.000	0.872	396	0.000
EKD3	0.214	396	0.000	0.840	396	0.000
SKD1	0.154	396	0.000	0.909	396	0.000
SKD2	0.179	396	0.000	0.885	396	0.000
SKD3	0.208	396	0.000	0.868	396	0.000
MLS_ML1	0.175	396	0.000	0.914	396	0.000
MLS_ML2	0.212	396	0.000	0.888	396	0.000
MLS_ML3	0.173	396	0.000	0.895	396	0.000
CS_ML1	0.257	396	0.000	0.815	396	0.000
CS_ML2	0.196	396	0.000	0.865	396	0.000
CS_ML3	0.170	396	0.000	0.900	396	0.000
IS_ML1	0.176	396	0.000	0.901	396	0.000

Table M.1. *(Continued)*

	Kolmogorov-Smirnov			Shapiro-Wilk		
	Statistic	df	Sig.	Statistic	df	Sig.
IS_ML2	0.199	396	0.000	0.855	396	0.000
IS_ML3	0.216	396	0.000	0.861	396	0.000
AS_ML1	0.183	396	0.000	0.871	396	0.000
AS_ML2	0.185	396	0.000	0.868	396	0.000
AS_ML3	0.172	396	0.000	0.872	396	0.000
SL_OC1	0.186	396	0.000	0.909	396	0.000
SL_OC2	0.202	396	0.000	0.868	396	0.000
SL_OC3	0.214	396	0.000	0.877	396	0.000
CCL_OC1	0.170	396	0.000	0.906	396	0.000
CCL_OC2	0.218	396	0.000	0.841	396	0.000
CCL_OC3	0.184	396	0.000	0.866	396	0.000
EAIL_OC1	0.194	396	0.000	0.876	396	0.000
EAIL_OC2	0.193	396	0.000	0.868	396	0.000
EAIL_OC3	0.172	396	0.000	0.883	396	0.000
FTL_OC1	0.177	396	0.000	0.903	396	0.000
FTL_OC2	0.206	396	0.000	0.859	396	0.000
FTL_OC3	0.178	396	0.000	0.884	396	0.000
ACL_OC1	0.177	396	0.000	0.910	396	0.000
ACL_OC2	0.202	396	0.000	0.867	396	0.000
ACL_OC3	0.174	396	0.000	0.879	396	0.000
DEIL_OC1	0.168	396	0.000	0.908	396	0.000
DEIL_OC2	0.186	396	0.000	0.891	396	0.000
DEIL_OC3	0.194	396	0.000	0.866	396	0.000

Source: Author's own research.

Appendix N – ANOVA Tests

Based on the mean values, participants aged between 41 and 60 exhibited higher levels of cultural Intelligence ($M = 107.28$), while those aged 18–25 demonstrated lower levels of cultural Intelligence ($M = 87.507$). Furthermore, participants over the age of 61 scored higher in Knowledge Dynamics, Multicultural Leadership, and Organizational Context ($M = 52.40$, 69.82, and 100.34, respectively) compared to other age groups. A one-way ANOVA indicated a statistically significant difference in all levels of Cultural

Table N.1. Descriptives of Age.

		N	Mean	Std. Deviation	Std. Error	95% Confidence Interval for Mean		Minimum	Maximum
						Lower Bound	Upper Bound		
Cultural Intelligence	18–25	65	87.5077	31.30950	3.88347	79.7496	95.2658	21.00	135.00
	26–40	136	102.9044	26.08160	2.23648	98.4813	107.3275	22.00	140.00
	41–60	160	107.2813	19.66166	1.55439	104.2113	110.3512	27.00	136.00
	>61	35	110.4857	22.42553	3.79061	102.7823	118.1892	41.00	135.00
	Total	396	102.8157	25.33919	1.27334	100.3123	105.3190	21.00	140.00
Knowledge Dynamics	18–25	65	41.8615	14.18282	1.75916	38.3472	45.3759	9.00	62.00
	26–40	136	48.6324	10.49360	0.89982	46.8528	50.4119	18.00	63.00
	41–60	160	50.0250	7.69624	0.60844	48.8233	51.2267	9.00	63.00
	>61	35	52.4000	5.75582	0.97291	50.4228	54.3772	35.00	63.00
	Total	396	48.4167	10.31801	0.51850	47.3973	49.4360	9.00	63.00
Multicultural Leadership	18–25	65	55.5385	18.92838	2.34778	50.8482	60.2287	12.00	80.00
	26–40	136	64.7426	12.72501	1.09116	62.5847	66.9006	26.00	82.00
	41–60	160	66.3000	9.82027	0.77636	64.7667	67.8333	16.00	84.00
	>61	35	69.8286	9.49144	1.60435	66.5681	73.0890	28.00	83.00
	Total	396	64.3106	13.30392	0.66855	62.9963	65.6250	12.00	84.00
Organizational Context	18–25	65	85.9692	28.54874	3.54103	78.8952	93.0433	19.00	124.00
	26–40	136	97.7941	17.48020	1.49891	94.8297	100.7585	51.00	126.00
	41–60	160	98.2000	15.56758	1.23073	95.7693	100.6307	18.00	125.00
	>61	35	100.3429	11.67436	1.97333	96.3326	104.3531	71.00	117.00
	Total	396	96.2424	19.15749	0.96270	94.3498	98.1351	18.00	126.00

Source: Author's own research.

Table N.2. Analysis of Variance (ANOVA) Explaining Age Differences Among Cultural Intelligence, Knowledge Dynamics, Multicultural Leadership, and Organizational Context.

		Sum of Squares	df	Mean Square	F	Sig.
		ANOVA				
Cultural Intelligence	Between groups	20482.453	3	6827.484	11.480	0.000
	Within groups	233137.090	392	594.737		
	Total	253619.543	395			
Knowledge Dynamics	Between groups	3768.579	3	1256.193	12.863	0.000
	Within groups	38283.671	392	97.662		
	Total	42052.250	395			
Multicultural Leadership	Between groups	6726.078	3	2242.026	13.909	0.000
	Within groups	63186.718	392	161.191		
	Total	69912.795	395			
Organizational Context	Between groups	8389.068	3	2796.356	8.026	0.000
	Within groups	136579.659	392	348.417		
	Total	144968.727	395			

Source: Author's own research.

Intelligence, Knowledge Dynamics, Multicultural Leadership, and Organizational Context across at least three age groups (F (3, 392) = [11.480, 12.863, 13.909, and 8.026, respectively], p = 0.000).

The table shows descriptive statistics for our four variables across different levels of education. The table provides data on the number of participants, the mean score for each level of education. It can be observed that as the level of education increases, the mean score for all variables also tends to increase.

The significant values in the ANOVA table (i.e., those with a Sig. value less than 0.05) indicate that there are statistically significant differences between the groups for each variable. Specifically, for Cultural Intelligence, there are significant differences between the groups of different education

Table N.3. Descriptives of Education.

Education Descriptives

		N	Mean	Std. Deviation	Std. Error	95% Confidence Interval for Mean		Minimum	Maximum
						Lower Bound	Upper Bound		
Cultural Intelligence	High school only	27	88.3333	34.50195	6.63990	74.6848	101.9819	21.00	135.00
	University graduate	164	100.6402	24.80869	1.93723	96.8149	104.4656	32.00	134.00
	Master graduate	157	105.6242	24.29451	1.93891	101.7943	109.4541	22.00	140.00
	PhD graduate	48	109.2083	20.95279	3.02428	103.1243	115.2924	45.00	137.00
	Total	396	102.8157	25.33919	1.27334	100.3123	105.3190	21.00	140.00
Knowledge Dynamics	High school only	27	42.5185	14.95216	2.87754	36.6036	48.4334	9.00	63.00
	University graduate	164	47.3110	10.73642	0.83837	45.6555	48.9664	12.00	62.00
	Master graduate	157	49.8917	9.00682	0.71882	48.4718	51.3116	9.00	63.00
	PhD graduate	48	50.6875	8.07717	1.16584	48.3421	53.0329	19.00	62.00
	Total	396	48.4167	10.31801	0.51850	47.3973	49.4360	9.00	63.00
Multicultural Leadership	High school only	27	58.0370	21.00821	4.04303	49.7265	66.3476	12.00	81.00
	University graduate	164	62.7866	13.47197	1.05198	60.7093	64.8639	16.00	84.00
	Master graduate	157	65.4650	11.68087	0.93223	63.6235	67.3064	16.00	83.00

		N	Mean	Std. Dev	Std. Error	Lower	Upper	Min	Max
	PhD graduate	48	69.2708	10.03767	1.44881	66.3562	72.1855	31.00	81.00
	Total	396	64.3106	13.30392	0.66855	62.9963	65.6250	12.00	84.00
Organizational Context	High school only	27	85.8148	29.54662	5.68625	74.1266	97.5031	19.00	122.00
	University graduate	164	96.3963	19.47521	1.52076	93.3934	99.3993	26.00	125.00
	Master graduate	157	97.5032	16.99910	1.35668	94.8234	100.1830	18.00	126.00
	PhD graduate	48	97.4583	16.05040	2.31668	92.7978	102.1189	48.00	120.00
	Total	396	96.2424	19.15749	0.96270	94.3498	98.1351	18.00	126.00

Source: Author's own research.

Table N.4. Analysis of Variance (ANOVA) Explaining Educational Differences Among Cultural Intelligence, Knowledge Dynamics, Multicultural Leadership, and Organizational Context.

		ANOVA				
		Sum of Squares	**df**	**Mean Square**	***F***	**Sig.**
Cultural Intelligence	Between groups	9639.024	3	3213.008	5.162	0.002
	Within groups	243980.519	392	622.399		
	Total	253619.543	395			
Knowledge Dynamics	Between groups	1728.897	3	576.299	5.602	0.001
	Within groups	40323.353	392	102.866		
	Total	42052.250	395			
Multicultural Leadership	Between groups	2833.766	3	944.589	5.520	0.001
	Within groups	67079.030	392	171.120		
	Total	69912.795	395			
Organizational Context	Between groups	3260.250	3	1086.750	3.006	0.030
	Within groups	141708.477	392	361.501		
	Total	144968.727	395			

Source: Author's own research.

levels (high school only, university graduate, master graduate, and PhD graduate). Similarly, there are significant differences between the education groups for Knowledge Dynamics and Multicultural Leadership.

For Organizational Context, there is a significant difference between the groups, but the significance level is nearer (0.030) than to the typical cut-off of 0.05, indicating a weaker level of significance.

The average scores for Cultural Intelligence vary from 98.30 (Africa) to 109.16 (Australia), and for Knowledge Dynamics, they range from 46.67 (North America) to 50.32 (Europe). The average scores for Multicultural Leadership range from 62.22 (North America) to 66.52 (Europe), and for Organizational Context range from 92.71 (North America) to 99.77 (Europe).

Table N.5. Descriptives of Continent Affiliation.

		N	Mean	Std. Deviation	Std. Error	95% Confidence Interval for Mean		Minimum	Maximum
						Lower Bound	Upper Bound		
Cultural Intelligence	Africa	47	98.2979	29.15246	4.25232	89.7384	106.8574	22.00	135.00
	Asia	79	97.7089	30.45221	3.42614	90.8879	104.5298	21.00	140.00
	Australia	38	109.1579	16.37818	2.65689	103.7745	114.5413	48.00	138.00
	Europe	130	108.8615	15.23804	1.33646	106.2173	111.5058	37.00	135.00
	North America	73	98.9041	30.10960	3.52406	91.8790	105.9292	27.00	136.00
	South America	29	98.4828	30.51887	5.66721	86.8740	110.0915	24.00	135.00
	Total	396	102.8157	25.33919	1.27334	100.3123	105.3190	21.00	140.00
Knowledge Dynamics	Africa	47	47.6596	10.80514	1.57609	44.4871	50.8321	21.00	63.00
	Asia	79	47.1899	12.49315	1.40559	44.3916	49.9882	9.00	63.00
	Australia	38	49.7632	9.41946	1.52804	46.6671	52.8593	12.00	62.00
	Europe	130	50.3231	5.56598	0.48817	49.3572	51.2889	15.00	62.00
	North America	73	46.6712	13.01714	1.52354	43.6341	49.7084	9.00	61.00
	South America	29	47.0690	12.05028	2.23768	42.4853	51.6526	18.00	60.00
	Total	396	48.4167	10.31801	0.51850	47.3973	49.4360	9.00	63.00
	Africa	47	63.1489	14.51832	2.11771	58.8862	67.4117	26.00	84.00

(*Continued*)

Table N.5. *(Continued)*

		N	Mean	Std. Deviation	Std. Error	95% Confidence Interval for Mean		Minimum	Maximum
						Lower Bound	Upper Bound		
Multicultural Leadership	Asia	79	62.6709	16.43848	1.84947	58.9889	66.3529	12.00	82.00
	Australia	38	65.9474	11.77480	1.91012	62.0771	69.8176	16.00	80.00
	Europe	130	66.5154	7.79707	0.68385	65.1624	67.8684	23.00	81.00
	North America	73	62.2192	15.93062	1.86454	58.5023	65.9361	16.00	83.00
	South America	29	63.8966	15.30720	2.84248	58.0740	69.7191	16.00	81.00
	Total	396	64.3106	13.30392	0.66855	62.9963	65.6250	12.00	84.00
Organizational Context	Africa	47	98.0638	17.91575	2.61328	92.8036	103.3241	51.00	121.00
	Asia	79	94.1013	23.53045	2.64738	88.8307	99.3718	19.00	126.00
	Australia	38	93.9474	18.23265	2.95773	87.9544	99.9403	27.00	117.00
	Europe	130	99.7692	13.14177	1.15261	97.4888	102.0497	32.00	125.00
	North America	73	92.7123	21.47833	2.51385	87.7011	97.7236	18.00	125.00
	South America	29	95.2069	23.86477	4.43158	86.1292	104.2846	26.00	122.00
	Total	396	96.2424	19.15749	0.96270	94.3498	98.1351	18.00	126.00

Source: Author's own research.

Table N.6. Analysis of Variance (ANOVA) Explaining Continent Affiliation Differences Among Cultural Intelligence, Knowledge Dynamics, Multicultural Leadership, and Organizational Context.

		Sum of Squares	df	Mean Square	F	Sig.
		ANOVA				
Cultural Intelligence	Between groups	10961.279	5	2192.256	3.523	0.004
	Within groups	242658.264	390	622.201		
	Total	253619.543	395			
Knowledge Dynamics	Between groups	962.274	5	192.455	1.827	0.107
	Within groups	41089.976	390	105.359		
	Total	42052.250	395			
Multicultural Leadership	Between groups	1333.848	5	266.770	1.517	0.183
	Within groups	68578.947	390	175.843		
	Total	69912.795	395			
Organizational Context	Between groups	3276.040	5	655.208	1.803	0.111
	Within groups	141692.688	390	363.315		
	Total	144968.727	395			

Source: Author's own research.

According to the ANOVA table, the differences in mean scores for Cultural Intelligence across the continents are statistically significant ($F = 3.523$, $p = 0.004$). However, the mean differences in scores for Knowledge Dynamics, Multicultural Leadership, and Organizational Context are insignificant as the p-value is greater than 0.05.

Based on the mean values, participants from the production sector exhibited higher levels of Cultural Intelligence, Knowledge Dynamics, and Multicultural Leadership ($M = 113.59$, 51.94, and 69.02 accordingly), while the organizational context level was high among those who were from trade sector ($M = 100.69$) compared to other sectors. A one-way ANOVA indicated a statistically significant difference in all levels of Cultural Intelligence,

Table N.7. Descriptives of Company Sector.

		N	Mean	Std. Deviation	Std. Error	95% Confidence Interval for Mean		Minimum	Maximum
						Lower Bound	Upper Bound		
Cultural Intelligence	Production	87	113.5977	17.27914	1.85252	109.9150	117.2804	41.00	136.00
	Retail	95	82.8000	29.34338	3.01057	76.8224	88.7776	21.00	138.00
	Services	115	106.4696	21.00013	1.95827	102.5902	110.3489	27.00	135.00
	Trade	92	107.9348	20.86682	2.17552	103.6134	112.2562	24.00	136.00
	Other	7	113.1429	26.58589	10.04852	88.5550	137.7307	57.00	140.00
	Total	396	102.8157	25.33919	1.27334	100.3123	105.3190	21.00	140.00
Knowledge Dynamics	Production	87	51.9425	6.23448	0.66841	50.6138	53.2713	27.00	63.00
	Retail	95	40.1895	13.34748	1.36942	37.4705	42.9085	9.00	62.00
	Services	115	50.1478	7.82623	0.72980	48.7021	51.5936	9.00	62.00
	Trade	92	51.6522	7.62793	0.79527	50.0725	53.2319	20.00	63.00
	Other	7	45.2857	11.52843	4.35734	34.6237	55.9477	23.00	54.00
	Total	396	48.4167	10.31801	0.51850	47.3973	49.4360	9.00	63.00
Multicultural Leadership	Production	87	69.0230	9.60859	1.03015	66.9751	71.0709	20.00	83.00
	Retail	95	54.5474	16.94344	1.73836	51.0958	57.9989	12.00	80.00
	Services	115	65.5391	11.33717	1.05720	63.4448	67.6334	16.00	84.00
	Trade	92	68.3261	8.57560	0.89407	66.5501	70.1020	36.00	81.00

Company Sector Descriptives

Other	7	65.2857	12.85450	4.85854	53.3973	77.1741	40.00	79.00
Total	396	64.3106	13.30392	0.66855	62.9963	65.6250	12.00	84.00
Organizational Context Production	87	98.3563	17.09343	1.83261	94.7132	101.9994	32.00	125.00
Retail	95	87.2737	24.66647	2.53073	82.2489	92.2985	19.00	124.00
Services	115	98.0957	17.44514	1.62677	94.8730	101.3183	18.00	125.00
Trade	92	100.6957	12.97651	1.35289	98.0083	103.3830	58.00	123.00
Other	7	102.7143	18.65221	7.04987	85.4639	119.9647	69.00	126.00
Total	396	96.2424	19.15749	0.96270	94.3498	98.1351	18.00	126.00

Source: Author's own research.

Table N.8. Analysis of Variance (ANOVA) Explaining Company Sector Differences Among Cultural Intelligence, Knowledge Dynamics, Multicultural Leadership, and Organizational Context.

		Sum of Squares	df	Mean Square	F	Sig.
		ANOVA				
Cultural Intelligence	Between groups	52866.314	4	13216.579	25.741	0.000
	Within groups	200753.229	391	513.435		
	Total	253619.543	395			
Knowledge Dynamics	Between groups	8888.163	4	2222.041	26.198	0.000
	Within groups	33164.087	391	84.819		
	Total	42052.250	395			
Multicultural Leadership	Between groups	12651.085	4	3162.771	21.596	0.000
	Within groups	57261.711	391	146.449		
	Total	69912.795	395			
Organizational Context	Between groups	10543.034	4	2635.759	7.667	0.000
	Within groups	134425.693	391	343.800		
	Total	144968.727	395			

Source: Author's own research.

Knowledge Dynamics, Multicultural Leadership, and Organizational Context across at least four sectors ($F (4, 391)$ = [25.74, 26.198, 21.596, and 7.667, respectively], p = 0.000).

The company size is divided into the described six groups, which are based on their annual turnover.

The table provides insights into the relationship between company size and the four variables measured in the study. For instance, in the Cultural Intelligence category, there are 50 companies with a turnover of less than 0.5M. €/year, and the mean turnover for these companies is 77.42M. €/year, with a standard deviation of 32.07M. €/year. Similarly, for the Knowledge Dynamics category, there are 72 companies with a turnover between 0.5M.

Table N.9. Descriptives of Company's Size (Company's Yearly Turnover in Millions €).

| | | | | | | 95% Confidence Interval for Mean | | | |
| | | | Std. Deviation | Std. Error | | Lower Bound | Upper Bound | Minimum | Maximum |
		N	Mean						
Cultural Intelligence	<0.5M. €/year as turnover	50	77.4200	32.06695	4.53495	68.3067	86.5333	21.00	137.00
	0.5>=x<1M. €/year	72	90.5139	29.25796	3.44808	83.6386	97.3892	22.00	135.00
	1M. <=x < 5M. €/year	102	108.8431	16.60833	1.64447	105.5810	112.1053	54.00	140.00
	5M.>=x < 10M. €/year	107	111.0093	18.54698	1.79300	107.4545	114.5642	37.00	136.00
	>10M = x < 50M €/year	48	112.0833	13.88989	2.00483	108.0501	116.1165	73.00	138.00
	>=50M. €/year	17	115.7059	22.47989	5.45217	104.1478	127.2640	67.00	136.00
	Total	396	102.8157	25.33919	1.27334	100.3123	105.3190	21.00	140.00
Knowledge Dynamics	<0.5M. €/year as turnover	50	40.6200	14.16937	2.00385	36.5931	44.6469	9.00	62.00
	0.5>=x < 1M. €/year	72	42.8611	13.55978	1.59804	39.6747	46.0475	9.00	61.00
	1M. <=x < 5M. €/year	102	50.8333	6.89825	0.68303	49.4784	52.1883	20.00	62.00

(Continued)

Table N.9. (*Continued*)

Size by Turnover Descriptives

		N	Mean	Std. Deviation	Std. Error	95% Confidence Interval for Mean		Minimum	Maximum
						Lower Bound	Upper Bound		
	5M.>=x < 10M. €/year	107	50.9813	7.04029	0.68061	49.6319	52.3307	23.00	63.00
	>10M. = x < 50M €/year	48	52.0833	4.59803	0.66367	50.7482	53.4185	41.00	63.00
	>=50M. €/year	17	53.8824	4.94826	1.20013	51.3382	56.4265	43.00	60.00
	Total	396	48.4167	10.31801	0.51850	47.3973	49.4360	9.00	63.00
Multicultural Leadership	<0.5M. €/year as turnover	50	54.5400	18.11439	2.56176	49.3919	59.6881	12.00	80.00
	0.5>=x < 1M. €/year	72	57.2361	17.61041	2.07541	53.0979	61.3744	16.00	82.00
	1M. <=x < 5M. €/year	102	67.3627	8.62392	0.85390	65.6688	69.0566	35.00	81.00
	5M.>=x < 10M. €/year	107	67.5888	8.85092	0.85565	65.8924	69.2852	36.00	84.00
	>10M = x < 50M €/year	48	68.8333	7.56626	1.09209	66.6363	71.0303	46.00	83.00
	>=50M. €/year	17	71.2941	7.99034	1.93794	67.1859	75.4024	50.00	82.00
	Total	396	64.3106	13.30392	0.66855	62.9963	65.6250	12.00	84.00

Organizational Context								
<0.5M. €/year as turnover	50	89.8800	25.75524	3.64234	82.5604	97.1996	19.00	124.00
0.5>=x < 1M. €/year	72	89.5000	25.82771	3.04382	83.4308	95.5692	18.00	123.00
1M. <=x < 5M. €/year	102	101.6176	13.28965	1.31587	99.0073	104.2280	58.00	126.00
5M.>=x < 10M. €/year	107	99.0187	12.87163	1.24435	96.5517	101.4857	54.00	118.00
>10M = x < 50M €/year	48	97.1458	15.53718	2.24260	92.6343	101.6574	61.00	120.00
>=50M. €/year	17	91.2353	23.48278	5.69541	79.1616	103.3090	40.00	125.00
Total	396	96.2424	19.15749	0.96270	94.3498	98.1351	18.00	126.00

Source: Author's own research.

Table N.10. Analysis of Variance (ANOVA) Explaining Company's Size (Company's Yearly Turnover in Millions €) Differences Among Cultural Intelligence, Knowledge Dynamics, Multicultural Leadership, and Organizational Context.

		ANOVA				
		Sum of Squares	df	Mean Square	*F*	Sig.
Cultural Intelligence	Between groups	60979.700	5	12195.940	24.691	0.000
	Within groups	192639.843	390	493.948		
	Total	253619.543	395			
Knowledge Dynamics	Between groups	7714.298	5	1542.860	17.523	0.000
	Within groups	34337.952	390	88.046		
	Total	42052.250	395			
Multicultural Leadership	Between groups	12287.708	5	2457.542	16.632	0.000
	Within groups	57625.087	390	147.757		
	Total	69912.795	395			
Organizational Context	Between groups	9534.358	5	1906.872	5.491	0.000
	Within groups	135434.369	390	347.268		
	Total	144968.727	395			

Source: Author's own research.

€/year and 1M. €/year, and the mean turnover for these companies is 42.86M. €/year, with a standard deviation of 13.56M. €/year. The results suggest that there are significant differences between groups for all four factors, as indicated by the low p-values (all <0.05) for the F-tests.

For Cultural Intelligence, the mean score increases with an increase in the number of employees. The mean score is the lowest for the group with 1–10 employees (75.55) and the highest for the group with over 1,000 employees (116.77). For Knowledge Dynamics, the mean score also increases with an increase in the number of employees. The mean score is the lowest for the group with 1–10 employees (38.74) and the highest for the group with over 1,000 employees (55.06). For Multicultural Leadership, the mean score also increases with an increase in the number of employees. The mean score is the lowest for the

Table N.11. Descriptives of Company's Size (Employees' Number).

		N	Mean	Std. Deviation	Std. Error	95% Confidence Interval for Mean		Minimum	Maximum
						Lower Bound	Upper Bound		
Cultural Intelligence	1–10	53	75.5472	30.65099	4.21024	67.0987	83.9956	21.00	137.00
	11–50	65	90.8308	29.50030	3.65906	83.5210	98.1406	22.00	135.00
	51–100	84	107.3810	19.04016	2.07745	103.2490	111.5129	37.00	135.00
	101–500	116	112.3448	15.99680	1.48527	109.4028	115.2869	41.00	140.00
	501–1,000	60	110.8833	15.57169	2.01030	106.8607	114.9059	67.00	138.00
	1,000+ employees	18	116.7778	20.00163	4.71443	106.8312	126.7244	69.00	136.00
	Total	396	102.8157	25.33919	1.27334	100.3123	105.3190	21.00	140.00
Knowledge Dynamics	1–10	53	38.7358	13.75213	1.88900	34.9453	42.5264	9.00	62.00
	11–50	65	44.2923	13.72580	1.70248	40.8912	47.6934	9.00	62.00
	51–100	84	49.9881	7.77003	0.84778	48.3019	51.6743	20.00	62.00
	101–500	116	51.3879	6.52723	0.60604	50.1875	52.5884	23.00	63.00
	501–1,000	60	51.5000	4.86600	0.62820	50.2430	52.7570	41.00	63.00
	1,000+ employees	18	55.0556	3.29835	0.77743	53.4153	56.6958	50.00	60.00
	Total	396	48.4167	10.31801	0.51850	47.3973	49.4360	9.00	63.00

(Continued)

Table N.11. (*Continued*)

Company's Size (Employees' Number) Descriptives

		N	Mean	Std. Deviation	Std. Error	95% Confidence Interval for Mean		Minimum	Maximum
						Lower Bound	Upper Bound		
Multicultural Leadership	1–10	53	52.8113	17.32057	2.37916	48.0372	57.5855	12.00	80.00
	11–50	65	58.1692	17.65429	2.18975	53.7947	62.5438	16.00	82.00
	51–100	84	66.5476	10.37189	1.13167	64.2968	68.7985	20.00	80.00
	101–500	116	67.6207	8.42837	0.78255	66.0706	69.1708	36.00	84.00
	501–1,000	60	69.1500	6.95707	0.89815	67.3528	70.9472	50.00	81.00
	1,000+ employees	18	72.4444	6.25180	1.47356	69.3355	75.5534	60.00	83.00
	Total	396	64.3106	13.30392	0.66855	62.9963	65.6250	12.00	84.00
Organizational Context	1–10	53	86.5094	25.95604	3.56534	79.3551	93.6638	19.00	124.00
	11–50	65	92.0615	24.61762	3.05344	85.9616	98.1615	18.00	123.00
	51–100	84	99.8452	16.41003	1.79048	96.2840	103.4064	32.00	123.00
	101–500	116	101.1121	11.48138	1.06602	99.0005	103.2236	61.00	126.00
	501–1,000	60	95.6167	15.43064	1.99209	91.6305	99.6028	58.00	120.00
	1,000+ employees	18	93.8889	23.60182	5.56300	82.1520	105.6258	40.00	125.00
	Total	396	96.2424	19.15749	0.96270	94.3498	98.1351	18.00	126.00

Source: Author's own research.

Table N.12. Analysis of Variance (ANOVA) Explaining Company's Size (Employees' Number) Differences Among Cultural Intelligence, Knowledge Dynamics, Multicultural Leadership, and Organizational Context.

		ANOVA				
		Sum of Squares	**df**	**Mean Square**	***F***	**Sig.**
Cultural Intelligence	Between groups	68443.962	5	13688.792	28.830	0.000
	Within groups	185175.581	390	474.809		
	Total	253619.543	395			
Knowledge Dynamics	Between groups	8668.026	5	1733.605	20.252	0.000
	Within groups	33384.224	390	85.601		
	Total	42052.250	395			
Multicultural Leadership	Between groups	13747.329	5	2749.466	19.092	0.000
	Within groups	56165.466	390	144.014		
	Total	69912.795	395			
Organizational Context	Between groups	10121.236	5	2024.247	5.854	0.000
	Within groups	134847.491	390	345.763		
	Total	144968.727	395			

Source: Author's own research.

group with 1–10 employees (52.81) and the highest for the group with over 1,000 employees (72.44). For Organizational Context, the mean score also increases with an increase in the number of employees. The mean score is the lowest for the group with 1–10 employees (86.51) and the highest for the group with over 1,000 employees (93.89).

Based on the ANOVA table, we can see that all four groups show a significant difference between groups, as indicated by their F-statistics and p-values (all p-values are less than 0.05). This suggests that there are meaningful differences between the groups on the variables being measured. Additionally, the p-values for each group are very low (all less than 0.001), suggesting that the differences between the groups are highly significant.

Table N.13. Descriptives of Function (From a Management Level Point of View).

Function (From a Management Level Point of View) Descriptives						95% Confidence Interval for Mean			
		N	Mean	Std. Deviation	Std. Error	Lower Bound	Upper Bound	Minimum	Maximum
Cultural Intelligence	Lower management	46	103.2609	23.65346	3.48751	96.2367	110.2851	41.00	138.00
	Middle management	145	108.4897	20.76626	1.72454	105.0810	111.8983	32.00	137.00
	TOP management	205	98.7024	27.84752	1.94496	94.8676	102.5372	21.00	140.00
	Total	396	102.8157	25.33919	1.27334	100.3123	105.3190	21.00	140.00
Knowledge Dynamics	Lower management	46	50.3478	8.54327	1.25964	47.8108	52.8849	26.00	63.00
	Middle management	145	50.0207	8.55819	0.71072	48.6159	51.4255	19.00	63.00
	TOP management	205	46.8488	11.54113	0.80607	45.2595	48.4381	9.00	63.00
	Total	396	48.4167	10.31801	0.51850	47.3973	49.4360	9.00	63.00
Multicultural Leadership	Lower management	46	66.8261	12.15512	1.79217	63.2165	70.4357	28.00	81.00
	Middle management	145	66.1241	10.60129	0.88039	64.3840	67.8643	16.00	83.00

	TOP management	205	62.4634	14.95303	1.04436	60.4043	64.5225	12.00	84.00
	Total	396	64.3106	13.30392	0.66855	62.9963	65.6250	12.00	84.00
Organizational Context	Lower management	46	92.7609	19.83060	2.92386	86.8719	98.6498	33.00	117.00
	Middle management	145	96.9724	18.02427	1.49683	94.0138	99.9310	26.00	123.00
	TOP management	205	96.5073	19.78329	1.38173	93.7830	99.2316	18.00	126.00
	Total	396	96.2424	19.15749	0.96270	94.3498	98.1351	18.00	126.00

Source: Author's own research.

Table N.14. Analysis of Variance (ANOVA) Explaining Function (From a Management Level Point of View) Differences Among Cultural Intelligence, Knowledge Dynamics, Multicultural Leadership, and Organizational Context.

	ANOVA					
		Sum of Squares	**df**	**Mean Square**	**F**	**Sig.**
Cultural Intelligence	Between groups	8145.590	2	4072.795	6.520	0.002
	Within groups	245473.953	393	624.616		
	Total	253619.543	395			
Knowledge Dynamics	Between groups	1048.565	2	524.283	5.025	0.007
	Within groups	41003.685	393	104.335		
	Total	42052.250	395			
Multicultural Leadership	Between groups	1467.446	2	733.723	4.213	0.015
	Within groups	68445.350	393	174.161		
	Total	69912.795	395			
Organizational Context	Between groups	649.229	2	324.615	0.884	0.414
	Within groups	144319.498	393	367.225		
	Total	144968.727	395			

Source: Author's own research.

For Cultural Intelligence, the mean scores are 103.26 for lower management, 108.49 for middle management, and 98.70 for TOP management. The mean scores are significantly different between groups ($p = 0.002$). For Knowledge Dynamics, the mean scores are 50.35 for lower management, 50.02 for middle management, and 46.85 for TOP management. The differences between groups are statistically significant ($p < 0.05$ and $= 0.007$). For Multicultural Leadership, the mean scores are 66.83 for lower management, 66.12 for middle management, and 62.46 for TOP management. The differences between groups are statistically significant ($p < 0.05$). For Organizational Context, the mean scores are 92.76 for lower management, 96.97 for

Table N.15. Descriptives of Years of Experience Within the Company.

| | | | Years of Experience within the Company Descriptives | | | | | |
| | | | | | 95% Confidence Interval for Mean | | | |
		N	Mean	Std. Deviation	Std. Error	Lower Bound	Upper Bound	Minimum	Maximum
Cultural Intelligence	1–3	72	92.0694	30.44151	3.58757	84.9160	99.2228	21.00	137.00
	4–5	82	96.5488	29.14296	3.21830	90.1454	102.9522	22.00	136.00
	6–10	100	107.2700	23.64931	2.36493	102.5775	111.9625	27.00	140.00
	11–15	116	110.1121	15.45078	1.43457	107.2705	112.9537	45.00	136.00
	16>	26	102.6538	25.69972	5.04013	92.2735	113.0342	37.00	135.00
	Total	396	102.8157	25.33919	1.27334	100.3123	105.3190	21.00	140.00
Knowledge Dynamics	1–3	72	42.5139	13.47611	1.58817	39.3472	45.6806	9.00	62.00
	4–5	82	46.7439	11.64051	1.28548	44.1862	49.3016	21.00	62.00
	6–10	100	51.1600	9.22636	0.92264	49.3293	52.9907	9.00	63.00
	11–15	116	50.5345	5.90126	0.54792	49.4492	51.6198	19.00	61.00
	16>	26	50.0385	8.17548	1.60334	46.7363	53.3406	21.00	62.00
	Total	396	48.4167	10.31801	0.51850	47.3973	49.4360	9.00	63.00
Multicultural Leadership	1–3	72	57.4861	17.53387	2.06639	53.3659	61.6064	12.00	80.00
	4–5	82	62.1707	16.24337	1.79378	58.6017	65.7398	20.00	82.00
	6–10	100	66.5300	10.37134	1.03713	64.4721	68.5879	16.00	81.00
	11–15	116	67.3707	8.27414	0.76823	65.8490	68.8924	31.00	84.00

(Continued)

Table N.15. (*Continued*)

Years of Experience within the Company Descriptives

	N	Mean	Std. Deviation	Std. Error	95% Confidence Interval for Mean		Minimum	Maximum
					Lower Bound	Upper Bound		
16>	26	67.7692	10.14419	1.98944	63.6719	71.8666	34.00	79.00
Total	396	64.3106	13.30392	0.66855	62.9963	65.6250	12.00	84.00
Organizational Context 1–3	72	89.9167	25.59145	3.01598	83.9030	95.9304	19.00	124.00
4–5	82	93.9146	21.97653	2.42690	89.0859	98.7434	32.00	125.00
6–10	100	98.9900	17.83453	1.78345	95.4512	102.5288	18.00	126.00
11–15	116	98.4828	12.32141	1.14401	96.2167	100.7488	54.00	121.00
16>	26	100.5385	14.50305	2.84428	94.6806	106.3964	47.00	123.00
Total	396	96.2424	19.15749	0.96270	94.3498	98.1351	18.00	126.00

Source: Author's own research.

Table N.16. Analysis of Variance (ANOVA) Explaining the Differences of Years of Experience Within the Company Among Cultural Intelligence, Knowledge Dynamics, Multicultural Leadership, and Organizational Context.

		ANOVA				
		Sum of Squares	df	Mean Square	*F*	Sig.
Cultural Intelligence	Between groups	19695.448	4	4923.862	8.230	0.000
	Within groups	233924.095	391	598.271		
	Total	253619.543	395			
Knowledge Dynamics	Between groups	4079.378	4	1019.845	10.501	0.000
	Within groups	37972.872	391	97.117		
	Total	42052.250	395			
Multicultural Leadership	Between groups	5618.614	4	1404.653	8.542	0.000
	Within groups	64294.182	391	164.435		
	Total	69912.795	395			
Organizational Context	Between groups	5142.408	4	1285.602	3.595	0.007
	Within groups	139826.319	391	357.612		
	Total	144968.727	395			

Source: Author's own research.

middle management, and 96.51 for TOP management. However, the difference between groups is not significant ($p > 0.05$). Overall, the differences between groups are statistically significant for all dimensions except for Cultural Intelligence. The significance values are very low ($p < 0.01$), indicating that the differences between the groups are highly significant.

For Cultural Intelligence, the mean score increases with years of experience, from 92.0694 for those with 1–3 years of experience to 102.6538 for those with more than 16 years of experience. The difference between the groups is statistically significant, as evidenced by the 95% confidence intervals for the mean not overlapping. Similarly, for Knowledge Dynamics, the mean score also increases with years of experience, from 42.5139 for those with 1–3 years of experience to 50.0385 for those with more than 16 years of experience. Again, the difference

Table N.17. Descriptives of Years of Experience in Total.

					95% Confidence Interval for Mean			
Years of Experience in Total Descriptives		N	Mean	Std. Deviation	Std. Error	Lower Bound	Upper Bound	Minimum	Maximum

		N	Mean	Std. Deviation	Std. Error	Lower Bound	Upper Bound	Minimum	Maximum
Cultural Intelligence	1–3	33	89.7879	33.46804	5.82604	77.9206	101.6551	21.00	135.00
	4–5	63	86.3333	28.16942	3.54901	79.2390	93.4277	22.00	137.00
	6–10	88	106.3409	21.90622	2.33521	101.6994	110.9824	24.00	140.00
	11–15	110	107.7273	20.54840	1.95921	103.8442	111.6104	38.00	138.00
	16–20	72	108.4444	21.18655	2.49686	103.4658	113.4230	27.00	136.00
	21+	30	109.9000	25.38307	4.63429	100.4218	119.3782	37.00	135.00
	Total	396	102.8157	25.33919	1.27334	100.3123	105.3190	21.00	140.00
Knowledge Dynamics	1–3	33	42.9091	14.57816	2.53773	37.7399	48.0783	9.00	62.00
	4–5	63	41.3810	12.49829	1.57464	38.2333	44.5286	12.00	62.00
	6–10	88	49.4886	9.32059	0.99358	47.5138	51.4635	25.00	63.00
	11–15	110	50.5545	7.55965	0.72078	49.1260	51.9831	18.00	63.00
	16–20	72	50.5556	8.80283	1.03742	48.4870	52.6241	9.00	62.00
	21+	30	53.1333	4.38440	0.80048	51.4962	54.7705	46.00	63.00
	Total	396	48.4167	10.31801	0.51850	47.3973	49.4360	9.00	63.00
Multicultural Leadership	1–3	33	57.4545	19.92030	3.46768	50.3911	64.5180	12.00	80.00
	4–5	63	55.7460	16.57531	2.08829	51.5716	59.9205	16.00	81.00

6–10	88	64.4091	12.18878	1.29933	61.8265	66.9916	32.00	82.00
11–15	110	67.4818	8.56998	0.81712	65.8623	69.1013	27.00	80.00
16–20	72	67.5833	11.10989	1.30931	64.9726	70.1940	16.00	84.00
21+	30	70.0667	7.05121	1.28737	67.4337	72.6996	57.00	81.00
Total	396	64.3106	13.30392	0.66855	62.9963	65.6250	12.00	84.00
Organizational Context								
1–3	33	86.4545	28.44522	4.95168	76.3683	96.5408	19.00	117.00
4–5	63	87.3968	24.44978	3.08038	81.2392	93.5544	27.00	123.00
6–10	88	98.3523	17.71423	1.88834	94.5990	102.1056	54.00	126.00
11–15	110	98.7273	13.81855	1.31755	96.1159	101.3386	48.00	121.00
16–20	72	100.5833	15.93804	1.87832	96.8381	104.3286	18.00	123.00
21+	30	99.8667	13.06676	2.38565	94.9875	104.7459	61.00	117.00
Total	396	96.2424	19.15749	0.96270	94.3498	98.1351	18.00	126.00

Source: Author's own research.

Table N.18. Analysis of Variance (ANOVA) Explaining Years of Experience in Total Differences Among Cultural Intelligence, Knowledge Dynamics, Multicultural Leadership, and Organizational Context.

		Sum of Squares	df	Mean Square	F	Sig.
		ANOVA				
Cultural Intelligence	Between groups	30249.959	5	6049.992	10.563	0.000
	Within groups	223369.584	390	572.743		
	Total	253619.543	395			
Knowledge Dynamics	Between groups	5720.260	5	1144.052	12.281	0.000
	Within groups	36331.990	390	93.159		
	Total	42052.250	395			
Multicultural Leadership	Between groups	9044.574	5	1808.915	11.590	0.000
	Within groups	60868.221	390	156.072		
	Total	69912.795	395			
Organizational Context	Between groups	10912.602	5	2182.520	6.349	0.000
	Within groups	134056.126	390	343.734		
	Total	144968.727	395			

Source: Author's own research.

between the groups is statistically significant. For Multicultural Leadership, the mean score also increases with years of experience, from 57.4861 for those with 1–3 years of experience to 67.7692 for those with more than 16 years of experience. Once again, the difference between the groups is statistically significant. For Organizational Context, the mean score also increases with years of experience, from 89.9167 for those with 1–3 years of experience to 100.5385 for those with more than 16 years of experience. The difference between the groups is statistically significant. Overall, the results suggest that as employees gain more years of experience within the company, they tend to score higher on measures of Cultural Intelligence, Knowledge Dynamics, Multicultural Leadership, and Organizational Context.

For Cultural Intelligence, the mean values increase as the years of experience increase, with the highest mean of 109.9 for those with 21+ years of experience. The lowest mean is for those with 1–3 years of experience, with a mean of 89.8. Similarly, for Knowledge Dynamics, the mean values increase as the years of experience increase, with the highest mean of 53.1 for those with 21+ years of experience. The lowest mean is for those with 1–3 years of experience, with a mean of 42.9. For Multicultural Leadership, the mean values also increase as the years of experience increase, with the highest mean of 67.5 for those with 11–15 years of experience. The lowest mean is for those with 1–3 years of experience, with a mean of 57.5. Finally, for Organizational Context, the mean values increase as the years of experience increase, with the highest mean of 100.6 for those with 16–20 years of experience. The lowest mean is for those with 1–3 years of experience, with a mean of 86.5. Overall, it is clear that the mean values significantly generally increase with more years of experience in all four areas, with some variation between the different categories as $p < 0.001$.

The ranges of managed nationalities are divided into eight categories: 1–3, 4–5, 6–10, 11–15, 16–20, 21–50, 51–100, and greater than 100. The mean values show the central tendency of the data in each group. For example, the mean Cultural Intelligence score for the category of 1–3 managed nationalities is 82.6196, while the mean score for the category of greater than 100 managed nationalities is 115.0000. This indicates that as the number of managed nationalities increases, the mean Cultural Intelligence score also increases. Similarly, the mean Knowledge Dynamics score increases as the number of managed nationalities increases, from 39.4674 for the 1–3 category to 48.8750 for the >100 category. The Multicultural Leadership scores show a steady increase as the number of managed nationalities increases, with the highest mean score of 70.1333 for the 21–50 category. Finally, the Organizational Context scores also increase as the number of managed nationalities increases, with a mean score of 87.7935 for the 1–3 category and a mean score of 111.4828 for the >100 category. In general, the results suggest that there are significant differences between the groups for all four variables ($p = 0.000$).

For the construct of Cultural Intelligence, the mean score increases as the number of spoken languages increases. The group that speaks more than three languages has the highest mean score (114.1538), followed by the group that speaks three languages (108.2878), the group that speaks two languages (100.6667), and the group that speaks one language (76.5556). The differences between the means are statistically significant, as the 95% confidence intervals for the means do not overlap and $p < 0.001$. For the construct of Knowledge Dynamics, the mean score also increases as the number of spoken languages increases. The group that speaks more than three languages has the highest mean score (52.8769), followed by the group that speaks three languages (50.2302), the group that speaks two languages (47.5374), and the group that

Table N.19. Descriptives of Number of Managed Nationalities.

		N	Mean	Std. Deviation	Std. Error	95% Confidence Interval for Mean		Minimum	Maximum
						Lower Bound	Upper Bound		
Cultural Intelligence	1–3	92	82.6196	30.59298	3.18954	76.2839	88.9552	21.00	140.00
	4–5	72	108.3472	23.09269	2.72150	102.9207	113.7737	45.00	137.00
	6–10	54	105.0000	20.03488	2.72640	99.5315	110.4685	24.00	135.00
	11–15	66	109.7121	17.18923	2.11585	105.4865	113.9378	41.00	134.00
	16–20	35	116.2286	14.50778	2.45226	111.2450	121.2122	60.00	135.00
	21–50	45	110.2889	20.06197	2.99066	104.2616	116.3162	32.00	138.00
	51–100	24	102.1250	21.16871	4.32104	93.1862	111.0638	37.00	126.00
	>100	8	115.0000	16.04458	5.67262	101.5864	128.4136	98.00	136.00
	Total	396	102.8157	25.33919	1.27334	100.3123	105.3190	21.00	140.00
Knowledge Dynamics	1–3	92	39.4674	13.68841	1.42712	36.6326	42.3022	9.00	62.00
	4–5	72	51.2639	8.93638	1.05316	49.1639	53.3638	19.00	63.00
	6–10	54	51.1296	7.19026	0.97847	49.1671	53.0922	24.00	62.00
	11–15	66	50.6818	6.12726	0.75421	49.1755	52.1881	21.00	63.00
	16–20	35	51.5143	7.08092	1.19689	49.0819	53.9467	26.00	63.00
	21–50	45	51.9333	4.42822	0.66012	50.6030	53.2637	39.00	60.00
	51–100	24	50.5833	7.37750	1.50593	47.4681	53.6986	23.00	59.00
	>100	8	48.8750	9.53846	3.37235	40.9007	56.8493	27.00	56.00
	Total	396	48.4167	10.31801	0.51850	47.3973	49.4360	9.00	63.00

Number of Managed Nationalities Descriptives

Multicultural Leadership								
1–3	92	54.3261	17.35290	1.80917	50.7324	57.9198	12.00	81.00
4–5	72	66.1111	13.26072	1.56279	62.9950	69.2272	16.00	82.00
6–10	54	66.8889	9.92741	1.35095	64.1792	69.5986	36.00	83.00
11–15	66	67.1818	8.39580	1.03345	65.1179	69.2458	26.00	81.00
16–20	35	68.1429	8.86879	1.49910	65.0963	71.1894	36.00	84.00
21–50	45	70.1333	7.09225	1.05725	68.0026	72.2641	54.00	82.00
51–100	24	66.4583	8.34568	1.70355	62.9343	69.9824	49.00	79.00
>100	8	65.8750	13.37842	4.72999	54.6904	77.0596	36.00	79.00
Total	396	64.3106	13.30392	0.66855	62.9963	65.6250	12.00	84.00
Organizational Context								
1–3	92	87.7935	25.80763	2.69063	82.4489	93.1381	18.00	126.00
4–5	72	101.4861	18.67513	2.20088	97.0977	105.8746	26.00	123.00
6–10	54	99.8333	16.09729	2.19056	95.4396	104.2270	40.00	125.00
11–15	66	98.2273	14.85809	1.82890	94.5747	101.8798	48.00	123.00
16–20	35	97.8857	12.07275	2.04067	93.7386	102.0328	63.00	117.00
21–50	45	96.9333	13.72523	2.04604	92.8098	101.0568	66.00	125.00
51–100	24	94.6250	15.87126	3.23971	87.9232	101.3268	58.00	117.00
>100	8	99.3750	19.69726	6.96403	82.9077	115.8423	54.00	115.00
Total	396	96.2424	19.15749	0.96270	94.3498	98.1351	18.00	126.00

Source: Author's own research.

Table N.20. Analysis of Variance (ANOVA) Explaining Number of Managed Nationalities Differences Among Cultural Intelligence, Knowledge Dynamics, Multicultural Leadership, and Organizational Context.

		ANOVA				
		Sum of Squares	**df**	**Mean Square**	**F**	**Sig.**
Cultural Intelligence	Between groups	53133.968	7	7590.567	14.690	0.000
	Within groups	200485.575	388	516.715		
	Total	253619.543	395			
Knowledge Dynamics	Between groups	9694.700	7	1384.957	16.607	0.000
	Within groups	32357.550	388	83.396		
	Total	42052.250	395			
Multicultural Leadership	Between groups	12477.996	7	1782.571	12.042	0.000
	Within groups	57434.799	388	148.028		
	Total	69912.795	395			
Organizational Context	Between groups	9760.731	7	1,394.390	4.001	0.000
	Within groups	135207.996	388	348.474		
	Total	144968.727	395			

Source: Author's own research.

speaks one language (39.2444). The differences between the means are statistically significant, as $p < 0.001$. For the construct of Multicultural Leadership, the mean score also increases as the number of spoken languages increases. The group that speaks more than three languages has the highest mean score (71.0923), followed by the group that speaks three languages (66.5540), the group that speaks two languages (62.3537), and the group that speaks one language (53.9778). The differences between the means are statistically significant, as the 95% confidence intervals for the means do not overlap and $p < 0.001$. Finally, for the construct of Organizational Context, the mean score also increases as the number of spoken languages increases. The group that speaks more than three languages has the highest mean score

Table N.21. Descriptives of Spoken Languages.

Spoken Languages Descriptives

		N	Mean	Std. Deviation	Std. Error	95% Confidence Interval for Mean		Minimum	Maximum
						Lower Bound	Upper Bound		
Cultural Intelligence	One	45	76.5556	32.24237	4.80641	66.8689	86.2422	21.00	134.00
	Two	147	100.6667	25.33754	2.08980	96.5365	104.7968	24.00	140.00
	Three	139	108.2878	19.42815	1.64787	105.0294	111.5461	32.00	136.00
	More than Three	65	114.1538	16.69134	2.07031	110.0179	118.2898	54.00	138.00
	Total	396	102.8157	25.33919	1.27334	100.3123	105.3190	21.00	140.00
Knowledge Dynamics	One	45	39.2444	14.03106	2.09163	35.0290	43.4598	9.00	59.00
	Two	147	47.5374	10.41158	0.85873	45.8403	49.2346	18.00	63.00
	Three	139	50.2302	8.09841	0.68690	48.8720	51.5884	12.00	62.00
	More than Three	65	52.8769	6.68839	0.82959	51.2196	54.5342	20.00	63.00
	Total	396	48.4167	10.31801	0.51850	47.3973	49.4360	9.00	63.00
Multicultural Leadership	One	45	53.9778	17.49609	2.60816	48.7214	59.2342	12.00	81.00
	Two	147	62.3537	14.27125	1.17707	60.0274	64.6800	16.00	84.00
	Three	139	66.5540	9.97255	0.84586	64.8814	68.2265	16.00	82.00

(Continued)

Table N.21. (*Continued*)

Spoken Languages Descriptives

		N	Mean	Std. Deviation	Std. Error	95% Confidence Interval for Mean		Minimum	Maximum
						Lower Bound	Upper Bound		
	More than Three	65	71.0923	7.83367	0.97165	69.1512	73.0334	36.00	83.00
	Total	396	64.3106	13.30392	0.66855	62.9963	65.6250	12.00	84.00
Organizational Context	One	45	86.4000	25.66072	3.82527	78.6907	94.1093	18.00	123.00
	Two	147	95.0680	20.82532	1.71764	91.6734	98.4627	26.00	126.00
	Three	139	98.5683	15.15000	1.28501	96.0275	101.1092	27.00	125.00
	More than Three	65	100.7385	14.98674	1.85888	97.0249	104.4520	54.00	121.00
	Total	396	96.2424	19.15749	0.96270	94.3498	98.1351	18.00	126.00

Source: Author's own research.

Table N.22. Analysis of Variance (ANOVA) Explaining Spoken Languages Differences Among Cultural Intelligence, Knowledge Dynamics, Multicultural Leadership, and Organizational Context.

		Sum of Squares	df	Mean Square	F	Sig.
		ANOVA				
Cultural Intelligence	Between groups	44228.814	3	14742.938	27.600	0.000
	Within groups	209390.729	392	534.160		
	Total	253619.543	395			
Knowledge Dynamics	Between groups	5649.746	3	1883.249	20.280	0.000
	Within groups	36402.504	392	92.864		
	Total	42052.250	395			
Multicultural Leadership	Between groups	9056.421	3	3018.807	19.445	0.000
	Within groups	60856.375	392	155.246		
	Total	69912.795	395			
Organizational Context	Between groups	6627.953	3	2209.318	6.260	0.000
	Within groups	138340.774	392	352.910		
	Total	144968.727	395			

Source: Author's own research.

(100.7385), followed by the group that speaks three languages (98.5683), the group that speaks two languages (95.0680), and the group that speaks one language (86.4000). There is a statistically significant difference ($p = 0.000$) between the means, as the 95% confidence intervals for the means do not intersect.

Cultural Intelligence scores generally increase as the number of worked continents increases, with the "More than Three" group having the highest mean score of 115.8750 and the "One" group having the lowest mean score of 93.6506. Similarly, Knowledge Dynamics scores also generally increase as the number of worked continents increases, with the "More than Three" group

Table N.23. Descriptives of Number of Worked Continents.

						95% Confidence Interval for Mean			
		N	Mean	Std. Deviation	Std. Error	Lower Bound	Upper Bound	Minimum	Maximum
Cultural Intelligence	One	166	93.6506	30.61370	2.37608	88.9592	98.3421	21.00	140.00
	Two	128	108.5234	19.20874	1.69783	105.1637	111.8831	39.00	137.00
	Three	62	107.1452	17.13863	2.17661	102.7928	111.4976	37.00	135.00
	More than Three	40	115.8750	14.41720	2.27956	111.2642	120.4858	80.00	138.00
	Total	396	102.8157	25.33919	1.27334	100.3123	105.3190	21.00	140.00
Knowledge Dynamics	One	166	45.3976	12.44960	0.96628	43.4897	47.3055	9.00	63.00
	Two	128	50.1797	9.10432	0.80472	48.5873	51.7721	12.00	63.00
	Three	62	49.6935	6.08570	0.77288	48.1481	51.2390	24.00	61.00
	More than Three	40	53.3250	4.28706	0.67784	51.9539	54.6961	46.00	61.00
	Total	396	48.4167	10.31801	0.51850	47.3973	49.4360	9.00	63.00
Multicultural Leadership	One	166	61.0663	15.95947	1.23870	58.6205	63.5120	12.00	84.00
	Two	128	65.7188	12.07453	1.06725	63.6069	67.8306	16.00	83.00
	Three	62	65.4677	7.99942	1.01593	63.4363	67.4992	36.00	79.00

More than Three	40	71.4750	5.83969	0.92334	69.6074	73.3426	55.00	81.00
Total	396	64.3106	13.30392	0.66855	62.9963	65.6250	12.00	84.00
One	166	95.5723	21.91618	1.70103	92.2137	98.9309	18.00	126.00
Two	128	96.5391	18.99312	1.67877	93.2171	99.8610	26.00	125.00
Three	62	97.1613	14.07147	1.78708	93.5878	100.7348	48.00	121.00
More than Three	40	96.6500	14.03211	2.21867	92.1623	101.1377	58.00	115.00
Total	396	96.2424	19.15749	0.96270	94.3498	98.1351	18.00	126.00

Organizational Context

Source: Author's own research.

Table N.24. Analysis of Variance (ANOVA) Explaining Number of Worked Continents Differences Among Cultural Intelligence, Knowledge Dynamics, Multicultural Leadership, and Organizational Context.

		Sum of Squares	df	Mean Square	*F*	Sig.
		ANOVA				
Cultural Intelligence	Between groups	26097.810	3	8699.270	14.988	0.000
	Within groups	227521.733	392	580.413		
	Total	253619.543	395			
Knowledge Dynamics	Between groups	2975.671	3	991.890	9.950	0.000
	Within groups	39076.579	392	99.685		
	Total	42052.250	395			
Multicultural Leadership	Between groups	4137.239	3	1379.080	8.219	0.000
	Within groups	65775.557	392	167.795		
	Total	69912.795	395			
Organizational Context	Between groups	144.803	3	48.268	0.131	0.942
	Within groups	144823.924	392	369.449		
	Total	144968.727	395			

Source: Author's own research.

having the highest mean score of 53.3250 and the "One" group having the lowest mean score of 45.3976.

Meanwhile, Multicultural Leadership scores show a similar trend, with the "More than Three" group having the highest mean score of 71.4750 and the "One" group having the lowest mean score of 61.0663. On the other hand, Organizational Context scores do not show a clear trend based on the number of worked continents. The mean scores for all four groups are relatively close, with the "Three" group having the highest mean score of 97.1613 and the "One" group having the lowest mean score of 95.5723. The significance values provided in the ANOVA table indicate that for Cultural Intelligence, Knowledge Dynamics, and Multicultural Leadership, the significance values

Table N.25. Descriptives of Number of Worked Countries.

| | | | | | | 95% Confidence Interval for Mean | | | |
		N	Mean	Std. Deviation	Std. Error	Lower Bound	Upper Bound	Minimum	Maximum
Cultural Intelligence	One	93	81.0430	29.98547	3.10935	74.8676	87.2184	21.00	140.00
	Two	99	106.9697	19.70106	1.98003	103.0404	110.8990	24.00	135.00
	Three	104	107.3750	20.52571	2.01271	103.3833	111.3667	37.00	137.00
	More than Three	100	114.2100	16.97550	1.69755	110.8417	117.5783	61.00	138.00
	Total	396	102.8157	25.33919	1.27334	100.3123	105.3190	21.00	140.00
Knowledge Dynamics	One	93	41.1290	12.87923	1.33551	38.4766	43.7815	9.00	63.00
	Two	99	49.2828	9.24391	0.92905	47.4392	51.1265	19.00	63.00
	Three	104	49.7788	8.53884	0.83730	48.1183	51.4394	12.00	63.00
	More than Three	100	52.9200	6.09136	0.60914	51.7113	54.1287	21.00	62.00
	Total	396	48.4167	10.31801	0.51850	47.3973	49.4360	9.00	63.00
Multicultural Leadership	One	93	55.9247	16.37153	1.69765	52.5531	59.2964	12.00	81.00
	Two	99	64.9394	12.08120	1.21421	62.5298	67.3489	16.00	81.00
	Three	104	65.2212	11.84361	1.16136	62.9179	67.5244	16.00	84.00

(Continued)

Table N.25. (*Continued*)

		N	Mean	Std. Deviation	Std. Error	95% Confidence Interval for Mean		Minimum	Maximum
						Lower Bound	Upper Bound		
	More than Three	100	70.5400	7.75694	0.77569	69.0009	72.0791	26.00	83.00
	Total	396	64.3106	13.30392	0.66855	62.9963	65.6250	12.00	84.00
Organizational Context	One	93	89.6989	23.12198	2.39764	84.9370	94.4608	18.00	126.00
	Two	99	98.8384	18.36407	1.84566	95.1757	102.5010	26.00	124.00
	Three	104	99.1154	17.34533	1.70085	95.7422	102.4886	27.00	125.00
	More than Three	100	96.7700	16.27097	1.62710	93.5415	99.9985	48.00	121.00
	Total	396	96.2424	19.15749	0.96270	94.3498	98.1351	18.00	126.00

Source: Author's own research.

Table N.26. Analysis of Variance (ANOVA) Explaining Number of Worked Countries Differences Among Cultural Intelligence, Knowledge Dynamics, Multicultural Leadership, and Organizational Context.

		ANOVA				
		Sum of Squares	df	Mean Square	*F*	Sig.
Cultural Intelligence	Between groups	60939.841	3	20313.280	41.327	0.000
	Within groups	192679.702	392	491.530		
	Total	253619.543	395			
Knowledge Dynamics	Between groups	7234.444	3	2411.481	27.150	0.000
	Within groups	34817.806	392	88.821		
	Total	42052.250	395			
Multicultural Leadership	Between groups	10545.933	3	3515.311	23.212	0.000
	Within groups	59366.863	392	151.446		
	Total	69912.795	395			
Organizational Context	Between groups	5535.418	3	1845.139	5.187	0.002
	Within groups	139433.309	392	355.697		
	Total	144968.727	395			

Source: Author's own research.

are all less than 0.05, which means that there are significant differences between the means of the groups. However, for Organizational Context, the significance value is 0.942, which is greater than 0.05, indicating that there is not enough evidence to suggest that the means of the groups are significantly different.

The ANOVA results indicate that all four variables have significant differences between the groups. For Cultural Intelligence, the mean difference is highest for those who worked in more than three countries. For Knowledge Dynamics, the mean difference is also highest for those who worked in more than three countries. For Multicultural Leadership, the mean difference is highest for those who worked in more than three countries. For

Table N.27. Descriptives of Experience in Managing Virtual Teams.

						95% Confidence Interval for Mean			
Experience in Managing Virtual Teams Descriptives									
		N	Mean	Std. Deviation	Std. Error	Lower Bound	Upper Bound	Minimum	Maximum
Cultural Intelligence	No experience	51	68.7255	28.45774	3.98488	60.7216	76.7294	21.00	131.00
	1–2 years experience	99	99.4141	26.73071	2.68654	94.0828	104.7455	22.00	140.00
	3–4 years experience	142	109.2113	17.05387	1.43113	106.3820	112.0405	37.00	136.00
	5+ years' experience	104	114.0385	14.86961	1.45809	111.1467	116.9302	61.00	136.00
	Total	396	102.8157	25.33919	1.27334	100.3123	105.3190	21.00	140.00
Knowledge Dynamics	No experience	51	39.7843	16.24969	2.27541	35.2140	44.3546	9.00	63.00
	1–2 years experience	99	46.2626	11.04313	1.10988	44.0601	48.4651	20.00	62.00
	3–4 years experience	142	50.2676	7.50784	0.63004	49.0221	51.5132	19.00	63.00
	5+ years' experience	104	52.1731	5.15477	0.50547	51.1706	53.1756	34.00	63.00
	Total	396	48.4167	10.31801	0.51850	47.3973	49.4360	9.00	63.00

		N						Min	Max
Multicultural Leadership	No experience	51	51.2549	19.46982	2.72632	45.7789	56.7309	12.00	78.00
	1–2 years experience	99	63.1010	13.91629	1.39864	60.3255	65.8766	30.00	84.00
	3–4 years experience	142	66.4789	10.63696	0.89263	64.7142	68.2435	16.00	81.00
	5+ years' experience	104	68.9038	6.48152	0.63557	67.6434	70.1643	48.00	83.00
	Total	396	64.3106	13.30392	0.66855	62.9963	65.6250	12.00	84.00
Organizational Context	No experience	51	84.0588	29.80162	4.17306	75.6770	92.4407	18.00	125.00
	1–2 years experience	99	95.2727	19.69037	1.97896	91.3456	99.1999	40.00	126.00
	3–4 years experience	142	98.4507	16.58187	1.39152	95.6998	101.2016	26.00	123.00
	5+ years' experience	104	100.1250	11.60573	1.13804	97.8680	102.3820	48.00	125.00
	Total	396	96.2424	19.15749	0.96270	94.3498	98.1351	18.00	126.00

Source: Author's own research.

Table N.28. Analysis of Variance (ANOVA) Explaining Experience in Managing Virtual Teams Differences Among Cultural Intelligence, Knowledge Dynamics, Multicultural Leadership, and Organizational Context.

		ANOVA				
		Sum of Squares	**df**	**Mean Square**	**F**	**Sig.**
Cultural Intelligence	Between groups	79321.858	3	26440.619	59.466	0.000
	Within groups	174297.685	392	444.637		
	Total	253619.543	395			
Knowledge Dynamics	Between groups	6213.735	3	2071.245	22.655	0.000
	Within groups	35838.515	392	91.425		
	Total	42052.250	395			
Multicultural Leadership	Between groups	11699.644	3	3899.881	26.261	0.000
	Within groups	58213.151	392	148.503		
	Total	69912.795	395			
Organizational Context	Between groups	9923.737	3	3307.912	9.602	0.000
	Within groups	135044.990	392	344.503		
	Total	144968.727	395			

Source: Author's own research.

Organizational Context, the mean difference is highest for those who worked in three countries.

For instance, for Cultural Intelligence: the group with 5+ years of experience in managing virtual teams has the highest mean score of 114.04, followed by the group with 3–4 years of experience (109.21), the group with 1–2 years of experience (99.41), and the group with no experience (68.73). That is statistically significant at 0.001 level. For Knowledge Dynamics, the group with 5+ years of experience in managing virtual teams has the highest mean score of 52.17, followed by the group with 3–4 years of experience (50.27), the group with 1–2 years of experience (46.26), and the group with no experience

(39.78). The overall mean score for all groups is 48.42. For Multicultural Leadership, the group with 5+ years of experience in managing virtual teams has the highest mean score of 68.90, followed by the group with 3–4 years of experience (66.48), the group with 1–2 years of experience (63.10), and the group with no experience (51.25). The overall mean score for all groups is 64.31. For Organizational Context, the group with 5+ years of experience in managing virtual teams has the highest mean score of 100.13, followed by the group with 3–4 years of experience (98.45), the group with 1–2 years of experience (95.27), and the group with no experience (84.06). The overall mean score for all groups is 96.24. The ANOVA table shows that Cultural Intelligence, Knowledge Dynamics, Multicultural Leadership, and Organizational Context all have significant F values and p-values, indicating significant differences between the mean scores of their experience in managing virtual teams.

References

Aamir, A., Jan, S. U., Qadus, A., Nassani, A. A., & Haffar, M. (2021). Impact of knowledge sharing on sustainable performance: Mediating role of employee's ambidexterity. *Sustainability, 13*(22), 12788. https://doi.org/10.3390/su132212788

Abaker, M.-O. S. M., Al-Titi, O. A. K., & Al-Nasr, N. S. (2019). Organizational policies and diversity management in Saudi Arabia. *Employee Relations: The International Journal, 41*(3), 454–474. https://doi.org/10.1108/er-05-2017-0104

Accenture. (2021). *Global demographic data.* https://www.accenture.com/us-en/about/inclusion-diversity/gender-equality

Adesina, A. O., & Ocholla, D. N. (2019). The SECI model in knowledge management practices: Past, present and future. *Mousaion: South African Journal of Information Studies, 37*(3). https://doi.org/10.25159/2663-659x/6557

Adler, N. J. (2006). The arts & leadership: Now that we can do anything, what will we do? *The Academy of Management Learning and Education, 5*(4), 486–499. https://doi.org/10.5465/amle.2006.23473209

Afsar, B., Al-Ghazali, B. M., Cheema, S., & Javed, F. (2021). Cultural intelligence and innovative work behavior: The role of work engagement and interpersonal trust. *European Journal of Innovation Management, 24*(4), 1082–1109. https://doi.org/10.1108/ejim-01-2020-0008

Ahmad, U. Q., Ghani, M. B. A., Parveen, T., Lodhi, F. A. K., Khan, M. W. J., & Gillani, S. F. (2021). How to improve organizational performance during Coronavirus: A serial mediation analysis of organizational learning culture with knowledge creation. *Knowledge and Process Management, 28*(2), 141–152. https://doi.org/10.1002/kpm.1663

Akanmu, M. D., Hassan, M. G., Mohamad, B., & Nordin, N. (2021). Sustainability through TQM practices in the food and beverages industry. *International Journal of Quality & Reliability Management, 40*(2), 335–364. https://doi.org/10.1108/ijqrm-05-2021-0143

Akdere, M., Acheson, K., & Jiang, Y. (2021). An examination of the effectiveness of virtual reality technology for intercultural competence development. *International Journal of Intercultural Relations, 82*, 109–120. https://doi.org/10.1016/j.ijintrel.2021.03.009

Al Shraah, A., Abu-Rumman, A., Al Madi, F., Alhammad, F. A. F., & AlJboor, A. A. (2021). The impact of quality management practices on knowledge management processes: A study of a social security corporation in Jordan. *The TQM Journal, 34*(4), 605–626. https://doi.org/10.1108/tqm-08-2020-0183

Alidoust, A. R., & Homaei, M. H. (2012). Analysis the effects of cultural intelligence on knowledge management practice (Case study: Higher Education Institutions). *Interdisciplinary Journal of Contemporary Research in Business, 3*(10), 633–649. https://journal-archieves15.webs.com/633-649.pdf

Aminullah, A. A., Yusuf, A., Azizan, F. L., Salisu, I., & Bin Mansor, Z. (2022). Linking academic self-initiated expatriate's cultural intelligence to specific job outcomes: The enabling role of psychological capital. *Cogent Business & Management, 9*(1), 2017546. https://doi.org/10.1080/23311975.2021.2017546

Ang, S., & Van Dyne, L. (2008). Conceptualization of cultural intelligence: Definition, distinctiveness, and nomological network. In S. Ang & L. Van Dyne (Eds.), *Handbook on cultural intelligence: Theory, measurement and applications* (pp. 3–15). Routledge.

Ang, S., & Van Dyne, L. (2015). *Handbook of cultural intelligence: Theory, measurement, and applications.* Routledge.

Ang, S., Van Dyne, L., & Koh, C. (2006). Personality correlates of the four-factor model of cultural intelligence. *Group & Organization Management, 31*(1), 100–123. https://doi.org/10.1177/1059601105275267

Ang, S., Van Dyne, L., & Tan, M. L. (2011). Cultural intelligence. In *Cambridge handbook on intelligence* (pp. 582–602). Cambridge University Press. https://doi.org/10.1017/CBO9780511977244.030

Aristotle. (2020). *The nicomachean ethics.* Penguin Publishing Group.

Ashok, M., Al Badi Al Dhaheri, M. S. M., Madan, R., & Dzandu, M. D. (2021). How to counter organisational inertia to enable knowledge management practices adoption in public sector organisations. *Journal of Knowledge Management, 25*(9), 2245–2273. https://doi.org/10.1108/jkm-09-2020-0700

Atif, A., Richards, D., & Bilgin, A. (2013). A student retention model: Empirical, theoretical and pragmatic considerations. In *Proceedings of the 24th Australasian Conference on Information Systems.* https://aisel.aisnet.org/acis2013/141

Avdimiotis, S., Kilipiris, F., & Tragouda, A. (2022). SECI model questionnaire validation for hospitality establishments. *International Journal of Technology Marketing, 16*(4), 370–385. https://doi.org/10.1504/ijtmkt.2022.126274

Bach-Mortensen, A. M., & Montgomery, P. (2018). What are the barriers and facilitators for third sector organisations (non-profits) to evaluate their services? A systematic review. *Systematic Reviews, 7*(1), 13–31. https://doi.org/10.1186/s13643-018-0681-1

Barak, M. E. M. (2017). *Managing diversity: Toward a globally inclusive workplace.* Sage Publications.

Barron, D., & Hurley, J. (2011). Emotional intelligence and leadership. In J. Hurley & P. Linsley (Eds.), *Emotional intelligence in health and social care: A guide for improving human relationships* (pp. 75–87). Routledge.

Batsa, E. T., Abadir, S., & Neubert, M. (2020). Bicultural managers leading multicultural teams: A conceptual case study. *International Journal of Teaching and Case Studies, 11*(1), 71–93. https://doi.org/10.1504/ijtcs.2020.108178

Becker, B. (2021). The 8 most common leadership styles & how to find your own. *HubSpot.* https://blog.hubspot.com/marketing/leadership-styles

Benitez, J., Henseler, J., Castillo, A., & Schuberth, F. (2020). How to perform and report an impactful analysis using partial least squares: Guidelines for confirmatory and explanatory IS research. *Information & Management, 57*(2), 103168. https://doi.org/10.1016/j.im.2019.05.003

Berraies, S. (2019). Effect of middle managers' cultural intelligence on firms' innovation performance: Knowledge sharing as mediator and collaborative climate as moderator. *Personnel Review, 49*(4), 1015–1038. https://doi.org/10.1108/pr-10-2018-0426

Bratianu, C., & Bejinaru, R. (2019). Knowledge dynamics: A thermodynamics approach. *Kybernetes, 49*(1), 6–21. https://doi.org/10.1108/k-02-2019-0122

Bratianu, C., Iliescu, A., & Paiuc, D. (2021). Self-management and cultural intelligence as the new competencies for knowmads. In *Conference: European Conference on Management, Leadership and Governance.* University of Malta.

Bratianu, C., & Leon, R. D. (2015). Strategies to enhance intergenerational learning and reducing knowledge loss: An empirical study of universities. *VINE Journal of Information and Knowledge Management Systems, 45*(4), 551–567. https://doi.org/10.1108/vine-01-2015-0007

Bratianu, C., & Paiuc, D. (2022). A bibliometric analysis of cultural intelligence and multicultural leadership. *Revista de Management Comparat International, 23*(3), 319–337. https://www.ceeol.com/search/article-detail?id=1060034

Bratianu, C., & Paiuc, D. (2023a). Diversity and inclusion within multicultural leadership in the Covid years: A bibliometric study 2019–2022. *Oradea Journal of Business and Economics, 8*(1), 40–51. https://doi.org/10.47535/1991ojbe163

Bratianu, C., & Paiuc, D. (2023b). Emotional and cultural intelligences: A comparative analysis between the United States of America and Romania. *Management & Marketing, 18*(2), 91112. https://doi.org/10.2478/mmcks-2023-0006

Burgess, C., Fricker, A., & Weuffen, S. (2022). Lessons to learn, discourses to change, relationships to build: How Decolonising Race Theory can articulate the interface between school leadership and Aboriginal students' schooling experiences. *Australian Educational Researcher, 50*(1), 111–129. https://doi.org/10.1007/s13384-022-00546-z

Canonico, P., De Nito, E., Esposito, V., Pezzillo Iacono, M., & Consiglio, S. (2020). Knowledge creation in the automotive industry: Analysing obeya-oriented practices using the SECI model. *Journal of Business Research, 112,* 450–457. https://doi.org/10.1016/j.jbusres.2019.11.047

Caputo, A., Ayoko, O. B., & Amoo, N. (2018). The moderating role of cultural intelligence in the relationship between cultural orientations and conflict management styles. *Journal of Business Research, 89*(1), 10–20. https://doi.org/10.1016/j.jbusres.2018.03.042

Cardoni, A., Zanin, F., Corazza, G., & Paradisi, A. (2020). Knowledge management and performance measurement systems for SMEs' economic sustainability. *Sustainability, 12*(7), 2594. https://doi.org/10.3390/su12072594

Cavazotte, F., Mello, S. F., & Oliveira, L. B. (2021). Expatriate's engagement and burnout: The role of purpose-oriented leadership and cultural intelligence. *Journal of Global Mobility: The Home of Expatriate Management Research, 9*(1), 90–106. https://doi.org/10.1108/jgm-05-2020-0031

Center for Creative Leadership. (2021). *Diversity and inclusion: Building a culture that works.* https://www.ccl.org/articles/white-papers/diversity-and-inclusion-building-a-culture-that-works/

Champathes Rodsutti, M., & Swierczek, F. W. (2002). Leadership and organizational effectiveness in multinational enterprises in southeast Asia. *The Leadership & Organization Development Journal, 23*(5), 250–259. https://doi.org/10.1108/01437730210435965

Charoensukmongkol, P. (2020). The efficacy of cultural intelligence for adaptive selling behaviors in cross-cultural selling: The moderating effect of trait mindfulness. *Journal of Global Marketing*, *33*(3), 141–157. https://doi.org/10.1080/08911762.2019.1654586

Charoensukmongkol, P. (2021). How Chinese expatriates' cultural intelligence promotes supervisor-subordinate Guanxi with Thai Employees: The mediating effect of expatriates' benevolence. *International Journal of Cross Cultural Management*, *21*(1), 9–30. https://doi.org/10.1177/1470595821996735

Chen, M. (2019). The impact of expatriates' cross-cultural adjustment on work stress and job involvement in the high-tech industry. *Frontiers in Psychology*, *10*. https://doi.org/10.3389/fpsyg.2019.02228

Chen, A. S., Bian, M., Nguyen, T. K., & Chang, C.-H. (2022). From curiosity to innovativeness: The mediating mechanisms of cultural intelligence and knowledge sharing behaviour. *European Journal of Innovation Management*. https://doi.org/10.1108/ejim-01-2022-0055

Chen, M.-L., & Lin, C.-P. (2013). Assessing the effects of cultural intelligence on team knowledge sharing from a socio-cognitive perspective. *Human Resource Management*, *52*(5), 675–695. https://doi.org/10.1002/hrm.21558

Cheung, C., Tung, V., & Goopio, J. (2021). Maximizing study abroad learning outcomes through cultural intelligence and emotional intelligence development. *Journal of Hospitality, Leisure, Sports and Tourism Education*, *30*, 100359. https://doi.org/10.1016/j.jhlste.2021.100359

Chin, W. W. (1998). The partial least squares approach to structural equation modeling. In G. A. Marcoulides (Ed.), *Modern methods for business research* (pp. 295–358). Taylor and Francis Group.

Chowdhury, S., Budhwar, P., Dey, P. K., Joel-Edgar, S., & Abadie, A. (2022). AI-employee collaboration and business performance: Integrating knowledge-based view, socio-technical systems and organisational socialisation framework. *Journal of Business Research*, *144*, 31–49. https://doi.org/10.1016/j.jbusres.2022.01.069

Christensen, J., Aarøe, L., Baekgaard, M., Herd, P., & Moynihan, D. P. (2019). Human capital and administrative burden: The role of cognitive resources in citizen-state interactions. *Public Administration Review*, *80*(1), 127–136. https://doi.org/10.1111/puar.13134

Christopher Hummel. (2023). Linkedin poles. https://www.linkedin.com/in/christopherhummel/recent-activity/all/

Cohen, J. (1988). *Statistical power analysis for the behavioral sciences*. Lawrence Erlbaum.

Cohendet, P., Grandadam, D., & Suire, R. (2021). Reconsidering the dynamics of local knowledge creation: Middlegrounds and local innovation commons in the case of FabLabs. *Zeitschrift für Wirtschaftsgeographie*, *65*(1), 1–11. https://doi.org/10.1515/zfw-2020-0042

Colina, A. V., Espinoza-Mina, M., López Alvarez, D., & Navarro Espinosa, J. (2022). Bibliometric software: The most commonly used in research. In *ICAIW 2022: Workshops at the 5th International Conference on Applied Informatics*, Arequipa, Peru (pp. 47–65). Ecotec University, Samborondon, Ecuador. https://ceur-ws.org/Vol-3282/icaiw_aiesd_1.pdf

Connerley, M. L., & Pedersen, P. B. (2005). *Leadership in a diverse and multicultural environment: Developing awareness, knowledge, and skills.* SAGE Publications.

Cooke, F. L., Schuler, R., & Varma, A. (2020). Human resource management research and practice in Asia: Past, present and future. *Human Resource Management Review, 30*(4), 100778. https://doi.org/10.1016/j.hrmr.2020.100778

Cornell, B. (2015). *Annual report 2015—Target.* Target. https://corporate.target.com/_media/TargetCorp/annualreports/2015/pdfs/Target-2015-Annual-Report.pdf

Cortes, A. F., & Herrmann, P. (2020). CEO transformational leadership and SME innovation: The mediating role of social capital and employee participation. *International Journal of Innovation Management, 24*(3), 2050024. https://doi.org/10.1142/s1363919620500243

Cox, T., & Blake, S. (2021). *Multicultural organizations* (2nd ed.). John Wiley & Sons.

Crowne, K. A. (2013). Cultural exposure, emotional intelligence, and cultural intelligence. *International Journal of Cross Cultural Management, 13*(1), 5–22. https://doi.org/10.1177/1470595812452633

Czerwionka, L., Artamonova, T., & Barbosa, M. (2015). Intercultural knowledge development: Evidence from student interviews during short-term study abroad. *International Journal of Intercultural Relations, 49*, 80–99. https://doi.org/10.1016/j.ijintrel.2015.06.012

Davey, J., & Holton, K. (2013, April 17). *Tesco quits U.S. and takes £2.3 billion global write down.* Reuters. https://www.reuters.com/article/uk-tesco-results-id UKBRE93G06P20130417

Davidavičienė, V., Al Majzoub, K., & Meidute-Kavaliauskiene, I. (2020). Factors affecting knowledge sharing in virtual teams. *Sustainability, 12*(17), 6917. https://doi.org/10.3390/su12176917

Deepu, T. S., & Ravi, V. (2021). Supply chain digitalization: An integrated MCDM approach for inter-organizational information systems selection in an electronic supply chain. *International Journal of Information Management Data Insights, 1*(2), 100038. https://doi.org/10.1016/j.jjimei.2021.100038

Diamantopoulos, A., & Winklhofer, H. M. (2001). Index construction with formative indicators: An alternative to scale development. *Journal of Marketing Research, 38*(2), 269–277. https://doi.org/10.1509/jmkr.38.2.269.18845

Dudek, B., Koniarek, J., & Szymczak, W. (2007). Work-related stress and the Conservation of Resources Theory by Stevan Hobfoll. *Medycyna Pracy, 58*(4), 317–324. https://www.proquest.com/openview/172f14e87ac92188e75713bd817576 d2/1?pq-origsite=gscholar&cbl=45820

Du, J., Lin, X., & Zhang, M. (2022). Does cultural intelligence matter within cross-cultural teams in hospitality industry? Understanding the role of team dissimilarity climate. *Current Psychology*, 1–14. https://doi.org/10.1007/s12144-022-04073-z

E Souza, B. de M., Martini, A. C., & Amelia, P. T. (2021). A bibliometric study on cultural intelligence in business research. *Organizational Cultures: An International Journal, 21*(1), 51–74. https://doi.org/10.18848/2327-8013/cgp/v21i01/51-74

Earley, P. C., & Ang, S. (2003). *Cultural intelligence: Individual interactions across cultures.* Stanford University Press.

Earley, P. C., Ang, S., & Tan, J. (2006). *Developing cultural intelligence at work.* Stanford Business Book.

Engelsberger, A., Cavanagh, J., Bartram, T., & Halvorsen, B. (2022). Multicultural skills in open innovation: Relational leadership enabling knowledge sourcing and sharing. *Personnel Review, 51*(3), 980–1002. https://doi.org/10.1108/pr-10-2019-0539

Falk, R. F., & Miller, N. B. (1992). *A primer for soft modeling.* University of Akron Press.

Farzaneh, M., Ghasemzadeh, P., Nazari, J. A., & Mehralian, G. (2021). Contributory role of dynamic capabilities in the relationship between organizational learning and innovation performance. *European Journal of Innovation Management, 24*(3), 655–673. https://doi.org/10.1108/ejim-12-2019-0355

Fayyaz, A., Chaudhry, B. N., & Fiaz, M. (2021). Upholding knowledge sharing for organization innovation efficiency in Pakistan. *Journal of Open Innovation: Technology, Market, and Complexity, 7*(1), 4. https://doi.org/10.3390/joitmc7010004

Feitosa, J., Hagenbuch, S., Patel, B., & Davis, A. (2022). Performing in diverse settings: A diversity, equity, and inclusion approach to culture. *International Journal of Cross Cultural Management, 22*(3), 433–457. https://doi.org/10.1177/14705958221136707

Fermín, N.-N., Clavel-San Emeterio, M., Fernández Ortiz, R., & Arias Oliva, M. (2020). The strategic influence of school principal leadership in the digital transformation of schools. *Computers in Human Behavior, 112*, 106481. https://doi.org/10.1016/j.chb.2020.106481

Ferreira, J., Cardim, S., & Coelho, A. (2020). Dynamic capabilities and mediating effects of innovation on the competitive advantage and firm's performance: The moderating role of organizational learning capability. *Journal of the Knowledge Economy, 12*, 620–644. https://doi.org/10.1007/s13132-020-00655-z

Field, A. (2013). *Discovering statistics using IBM SPSS statistics.* Sage Publications.

Field, A. (2017). *Discovering statistics using IBM SPSS statistics* (5th ed.). SAGE Publications.

Fitzsimmons, S. R. (2013). Multicultural employees: A framework for understanding how they contribute to organizations. *Academy of Management Review, 38*(4), 525–549. https://doi.org/10.5465/amr.2011.0234

Fornell, C., & Larcker, D. F. (1981). Evaluating structural equation models with unobservable variables and measurement error. *Journal of Marketing Research, 18*(1), 39–50. https://doi.org/10.1177/002224378101800104

Franke, G., & Sarstedt, M. (2019). Heuristics versus statistics in discriminant validity testing: A comparison of four procedures. *Internet Research, 29*(3), 430–447. https://doi.org/10.1108/intr-12-2017-0515

Fu, L., & Charoensukmongkol, P. (2021). Effect of cultural intelligence on burnout of Chinese expatriates in Thailand: The mediating role of host country national coworker support. *Current Psychology, 42*(5), 4041–4052. https://doi.org/10.1007/s12144-021-01728-1

Gabel-Shemueli, R., Westman, M., Chen, S., & Bahamonde, D. (2019). Does cultural intelligence increase work engagement? The role of idiocentrism-allocentrism and organizational culture in MNCs. *Cross Cultural & Strategic Management, 26*(1), 46–66. https://doi.org/10.1108/ccsm-10-2017-0126

Galetto, M., Weber, S., Larsson, B., Bechter, B., & Prosser, T. (2023). "You see similarities more than differences after a while". Communities of Practice in

European industrial relations. The case of the hospital European Sectoral Social Dialogue. *Industrial Relations Journal, 54*(2), 167–185. https://doi.org/10.1111/irj.12396

Goleman, D. (1996). *Emotional intelligence: Why it can matter more than IQ.* Bloomsbury Publishing Plc.

Goleman, D. (2000, March). Leadership that gets results. *Harvard Business Review.* https://hbr.org/2000/03/leadership-that-gets-results

Goleman, D. (2021). *Leadership: The power of emotional intelligence.* More Than Sound LLC.

Goodhue, D., Lewis, W., & Thompson, R. (2012). Does PLS have advantages for small sample size or non-normal data? *MIS Quarterly, 36*(3), 981–1001. https://doi.org/10.2307/41703490

Grapin, S. L., & Pereiras, M. I. (2019). Supporting diverse students and faculty in higher education through multicultural organizational development. *Training and Education in Professional Psychology, 13*(4), 307. https://doi.org/10.1037/tep0000226

Gravetter, F. J., Wallnau, L. B., Forzano, L. A.-B., & Witnauer, J. E. (2020). *Essentials of statistics for the behavioral sciences.* Cengage Learning.

Grosz, A. S., Jozsa, L., & Maung, S. (2023). Cross-cultural negotiation conflicts: The Myanmar case. *International Review of Management and Marketing, 13*(3), 1–8.

Groves, K. S., & Feyerherm, A. E. (2011). Leader cultural intelligence in context: Testing the moderating effects of team cultural diversity on leader and team performance. *Group & Organization Management, 36*(5), 535–566. https://doi.org/10.1177/1059601111415664

Guan, Y., Deng, H., & Zhou, X. (2020). Understanding the impact of the COVID-19 pandemic on career development: Insights from cultural psychology. *Journal of Vocational Behavior, 119*, 103438. https://doi.org/10.1016/j.jvb.2020.103438

Guest, G., Bunce, A., & Johnson, L. (2006). How many interviews are enough? An experiment with data saturation and variability. *Field Methods, 18*(1), 59–82. https://doi.org/10.1177/1525822X05279903

Habibi Soola, A., Ajri-Khameslou, M., Mirzaei, A., & Bahari, Z. (2022). Predictors of patient safety competency among emergency nurses in Iran: A cross-sectional correlational study. *BMC Health Services Research, 22*(1), 547. https://doi.org/10.1186/s12913-022-07962-y

Hagaman, A. (2014). 'Qualitative interview saturation' across four cultural settings: How many interviews are really enough? In *142nd APHA Annual Meeting and Exposition 2014,* APHA. New Orleans, LA. https://aphanew.confex.com/apha/142am/webprogram/Paper300912.html

Hair, J., Hollingsworth, C. L., Randolph, A. B., & Chong, A. Y. L. (2017). An updated and expanded assessment of PLS-SEM in information systems research. *Industrial Management & Data Systems, 117*(3), 442–458. https://doi.org/10.1108/imds-04-2016-0130

Hair, J. F., Hult, J. T. M., Ringle, C. M., & Sarstedt, M. (2017). *A primer on partial least squares structural equation modeling (PLS-SEM)* (2nd ed.). Sage Publications.

Hair, J. F., Hult, G. T. M., Ringle, C. M., Sarstedt, M., Danks, N. P., & Ray, S. (2021). Partial least squares structural equation modeling (PLS-SEM) using R. In

254

Classroom companion: Business. Springer International Publishing. https://doi.org/10.1007/978-3-030-80519-7

Hair, J. F., Ringle, C. M., & Sarstedt, M. (2011). PLS-SEM: Indeed a silver bullet. *Journal of Marketing Theory and Practice, 19*(2), 139–152. https://doi.org/10.2753/MTP1069-6679190202

Hair, J. F., Risher, J. J., Sarstedt, M., & Ringle, C. M. (2019). When to use and how to report the results of PLS-SEM. *European Business Review, 31*(1), 2–24. https://doi.org/10.1108/EBR-11-2018-0203

Hair, J. F., Sarstedt, M., & Ringle, C. M. (2019). Rethinking some of the rethinking of partial least squares. *European Journal of Marketing, 53*(4), 566–584. https://doi.org/10.1108/ejm-10-2018-0665

Hair, J. F., Sarstedt, M., Ringle, C. M., & Gudergan, S. P. (2018). *Advanced issues in partial least squares structural equation modeling (PLS-SEM).* Sage Publications.

Hanelt, A., Bohnsack, R., Marz, D., & Antunes, C. (2021). A systematic review of the literature on digital transformation: Insights and implications for strategy and organizational change. *Journal of Management Studies, 58*(5), 1159–1197. https://doi.org/10.1111/joms.12639

Hattangadi, V. P. (2021). Edgar Schein's three levels of organizational culture. *Linkedin.* https://www.linkedin.com/pulse/edgar-scheins-three-levels-organizational-culture-hattangadi/

Hennink, M. M., Kaiser, B. N., & Marconi, V. C. (2016). Code saturation versus meaning saturation: How many interviews are enough? *Qualitative Health Research, 27*(4), 591–608. https://doi.org/10.1177/1049732316665344

Henseler, J., Ringle, C. M., & Sarstedt, M. (2015). A new criterion for assessing discriminant validity in variance-based structural equation modeling. *Journal of the Academy of Marketing Science, 43*(1), 115–135. https://doi.org/10.1007/s11747-014-0403-8

Hoelzle, J. B., & Meyer, G. J. (2013). Exploratory factor analysis: Basics and beyond. In I. B. Weiner, J. A. Schinka, & W. F. Velicer (Eds.), *Handbook of psychology: Research methods in psychology* (pp. 164–188). John and Wiley.

Hofstede, G. (2010). *Cultures and organizations: Software of the mind—Intercultural cooperation and its importance for survival* (3rd ed.). McGraw Hill.

Hunt, V., Layton, D., & Prince, S. (2015, February 1). *Why diversity matters.* McKinsey & Company. https://www.mckinsey.com/business-functions/organization/our-insights/why-diversity-matters

Ikea Group. (2021). *Diversity and inclusion report FY21.* https://www.ikea.com/global/en/pdf/reports-downloads/ikea-group-diversity-and-inclusion-report-fy21.pd

ILO. (2021). *World employment and social outlook: Trends 2021.* International Labour Organization. https://www.ilo.org/wcmsp5/groups/public/—dgreports/—dcomm/—publ/documents/publication/wcms_795453.pdf

Intel. (2020). *Intel's 2020 diversity and inclusion report.* https://www.intel.com/content/dam/www/public/us/en/documents/corporate-information/intel-2020-diversity-inclusion-report.pdf

ISACA. (2022, March 17). *Which of the following skills gaps have you noticed among recent university graduates? [Graph].* Statista. https://www.statista.com/statistics/1322398/cybersecurity-university-graduates-skills-gap-worldwide/. Accessed on May 13, 2023.

Iskhakova, M., Bradly, A., Whiting, B., & Lu, V. N. (2022). Cultural intelligence development during short-term study abroad programmes: The role of cultural distance and prior international experience. *Studies in Higher Education, 47*(8), 1–18. https://doi.org/10.1080/03075079.2021.1957811

Iskhakova, M., & Ott, D. L. (2020). Working in culturally diverse teams. *Journal of International Education in Business, 13*(1), 37–54. https://doi.org/10.1108/jieb-11-2019-0052

Jabeen, Q., Nadeem, M. S., Raziq, M. M., & Sajjad, A. (2022). Linking individuals' resources with (perceived) sustainable employability: Perspectives from conservation of resources and social information processing theory. *International Journal of Management Reviews, 24*(2), 233–254. https://doi.org/10.1111/ijmr.12276

Jaccard, J., & Becker, M. A. (2021). *Statistics for the behavioral sciences.* Cengage Learning.

Jangsiriwattana, T. (2021). Relationship between cultural intelligence and self-adjustment of expatriates in the airline industry. *Journal of Community Development Research.* https://doi.org/10.14456/jcdr-hs.2021.23

Jannesari, M., Zolfagharian, M., & Torkzadeh, S. (2022). Effect of social power, cultural intelligence, and socioeconomic status on students' international entrepreneurial intention. *Psychology Research and Behavior Management, 15,* 1397–1410. https://doi.org/10.2147/prbm.s360901

Javidan, M., & Walker, J. L. (2012). A whole new global mindset for leadership. *People & Strategy, 35*(2), 36–41. https://www.proquest.com/trade-journals/whole-new-global-mindset-leadership/docview/1498386758/se-2

Jose, M. V. (2023). Trends and prospects of human resource management in the twenty-first century. *IJRAR-International Journal of Research and Analytical Reviews, 10*(2), 9–19. https://www.ijrar.org/papers/IJRAR1CYP002.pdf

Kadam, R., & Kareem Abdul, W. (2022). A cultural perspective on knowledge hiding: The role of organisational justice, distrust and cultural intelligence. *Knowledge Management Research and Practice,* 1–14. https://doi.org/10.1080/14778238.2022.2136545

Kamales, N., & Knorr, H. (2019). Leaders with managing cultural diversity and communication. *Asia Pacific Journal of Religions and Cultures, 3*(1), 63–72. https://so06.tci-thaijo.org/index.php/ajrc/article/view/242052

Kelly, L. A., & Chung, W. K. (2013). Organizations in multicultural and international contexts: Insights for the global leader. In R. L. Lowman (Ed.), *Internationalizing multiculturalism: Expanding professional competencies in a globalized world* (pp. 199–225). American Psychological Association. https://doi.org/10.1037/14044-008

Kemmelmeier, M., & Kusano, K. (2018). Intercultural competence: Teaching it is worthwhile. In C. Frisby & W. O'Donohue (Eds.), *Cultural competence in applied psychology* (pp. 621–649). Springer. https://doi.org/10.1007/978-3-319-78997-2_25

Keung, K. E., & Rockinson-Szapkiw, J. A. (2013). The relationship between transformational leadership and cultural intelligence: A study of international school leaders. *Journal of Educational Administration, 51*(6), 836–854. https://doi.org/10.1108/jea-04-2012-0049

Khalilzadeh, S., & Khodi, A. (2021). Teachers' personality traits and students' motivation: A structural equation modeling analysis. *Current Psychology, 40*(4), 1635–1650. https://doi.org/10.1007/s12144-018-0064-8

Kim, Y. J., & Van Dyne, L. (2012). Cultural intelligence and international leadership potential: The importance of contact for members of the majority. *Applied Psychology: An International Review, 61*(2), 272–294. https://doi.org/10.1111/j.1464-0597.2011.00468.x

Krishnaveni, R. R., & Sujatha, R. R. (2012). Communities of practice: An influencing factor for effective knowledge transfer in organizations. *IUP Journal of Knowledge Management, 10*(1), 26–40. https://www.proquest.com/openview/99247a6 5781f5cb7040e4b82663fdf5c/1?pq-origsite=gscholar&cbl=54461

Kristof-Brown, A. L., Zimmerman, R. D., & Johnson, E. C. (2005). Consequences of individuals' fit at work: A meta-analysis of person–job, person–organization, person–group, and person–supervisor fit. *Personnel Psychology, 58*(2), 281–342. https://doi.org/10.1111/j.1744-6570.2005.00672.x

Leiba-O'Sullivan, S. (1999). The distinction between stable and dynamic cross-cultural competencies: Implications for expatriate trainability. *Journal of International Business Studies, 30*(4), 709–725. https://doi.org/10.1057/palgrave.jibs.8490835

Lindholm, Y. (2022). *Cultural awareness for competitiveness in the global market IKEA's Japan adventures as case study.* Dissertation, Linnaeus University, School of Business and Economics. http://urn.kb.se/resolve?urn=urn:nbn:se:lnu: diva-109992

Li, X., Nosheen, S., Haq, N. U., & Gao, X. (2021). Value creation during fourth industrial revolution: Use of intellectual capital by most innovative companies of the world. *Technological Forecasting and Social Change, 163*, 120479. https://doi.org/10.1016/j.techfore.2020.120479

Liu, Z., Liu, J., & Osmani, M. (2021). Integration of digital economy and circular economy: Current status and future directions. *Sustainability, 13*(13), 7217. https://doi.org/10.3390/su13137217

Liu, J., Li, X., Zhang, L., Lu, Q., & Su, X. (2022). Authenticity, psychological ownership and tourist commitment in heritage tourism: The moderating effect of cultural intelligence. *Current Issues in Tourism,* 1–18. https://doi.org/10.1080/13683500.2022.2153650

Livermore, D. A. (2009). *Cultural intelligence: Improving your CQ to engage our multicultural world.* Baker Publishing Group.

Livingston, E. H. (2004). The mean and standard deviation: What does it all mean? *Journal of Surgical Research, 119*(2), 117–123. https://doi.org/10.1016/j.jss.2004.02.008

Lo, M. F., & Tian, F. (2020). How academic leaders facilitate knowledge sharing: A case of universities in Hong Kong. *The Leadership & Organization Development Journal, 41*(6), 777–798. https://doi.org/10.1108/lodj-11-2019-0481

Lovin, D., Capatina, A., & Bernardeau-Moreau, D. (2021). The impact of cultural intelligence on the management of multicultural sports organizations: A comparative analysis between Romania and France. *Revista de Management Comparat International, 22*(3), 301–320. https://www.ceeol.com/search/article-detail?id=1047348

Maker, C. J. (2022). From leading to guiding, facilitating, and inspiring: A needed shift for the 21st century. *Education Sciences, 12*(1), 18. https://doi.org/10.3390/educsci12010018

Manesh, M., Pellegrini, M. M., Marzi, G., & Dabic, M. (2020). Knowledge management in the fourth industrial revolution: Mapping the literature and scoping future avenues. *IEEE Transactions on Engineering Management, 68*(1), 1–12. https://doi.org/10.1109/tem.2019.2963489

Marouf, L., & Al-Attabi, F. (2010). Community of practice in the Kuwaiti medical sector: An exploratory study. *DOMES: Digest of Middle East Studies, 19*(2), 286–300. https://doi.org/10.1111/j.1949-3606.2010.00035.x

Marquez, R. (2022). *Aristotle and his nicomachean ethics: A philosophical analysis.* https://www.researchgate.net/publication/368922243_aristotle_and_his_nicom achean_ethics_a_philosophical_analysis

Martins, V. W. B., Rampasso, I. S., Anholon, R., Quelhas, O. L. G., & Leal Filho, W. (2019). Knowledge management in the context of sustainability: Literature review and opportunities for future research. *Journal of Cleaner Production, 229*(1), 489–500. https://doi.org/10.1016/j.jclepro.2019.04.354

Men, L. R., & Yue, C. A. (2019). Creating a positive emotional culture: Effect of internal communication and impact on employee supportive behaviors. *Public Relations Review, 45*(3), 101764. https://doi.org/10.1016/j.pubrev.2019.03.001

Meyer, J. W. (2007). Globalization: Theory and trends. *International Journal of Comparative Sociology, 48*(4), 261–273. https://doi.org/10.1177/0020715207079529

Mishra, R., Kr Singh, R., & Koles, B. (2020). Consumer decision-making in omnichannel retailing: Literature review and future research agenda. *International Journal of Consumer Studies, 45*(2), 147–174. https://doi.org/ 10.1111/ijcs.12617

Muñoz-Pascual, L., Curado, C., & Galende, J. (2019). The triple bottom line on sustainable product innovation performance in SMEs: A mixed methods approach. *Sustainability, 11*(6), 1689. https://doi.org/10.3390/su11061689

Nocker, M., & Sena, V. (2019). Big data and human resources management: The rise of talent analytics. *Social Sciences, 8*(10), 273. https://doi.org/10.3390/ socsci8100273

Nunnally, J. C., & Bernstein, I. H. (1994). *The assessment of reliability* (3rd ed.). McGraw-Hill.

Osman-Gani, A. A. M., & Hassan, Z. (2018). Impacts of spiritual and cultural intelligence on leadership effectiveness: A conceptual analysis. *Journal of Islamic Management Studies, 1*(2), 12–23. http://publications.waim.my/index.php/jims/ article/view/79

Österlind, J., & Henoch, I. (2021). The 6S-model for person-centred palliative care: A theoretical framework. *Nursing Philosophy, 22*(2), e12334. https://doi.org/10.1111/ nup.12334

Ott, D. L., & Iskhakova, M. (2019). The meaning of international experience for the development of cultural intelligence. *Critical Perspectives on International Business, 15*(4), 390–407. https://doi.org/10.1108/cpoib-05-2019-0036

Oye, N. D., Salleh, M., & Noorminshah (2011). Knowledge sharing in workplace: Motivators and demotivators. *International Journal of Managing Information Technology, 3*(4), 71–84. https://doi.org/10.5121/ijmit.2011.3406

Paiuc, D. (2021a). Cultural intelligence as a core competence of inclusive leadership. *Management Dynamics in the Knowledge Economy, 9*(3), 363–378. https:// www.ceeol.com/search/article-detail?id=1003053

Paiuc, D. (2021b). Cultural intelligence as a main competency for multinational leadership and global management. In C. Bratianu, A. Zbuchea, F. Anghel, & B. Hrib (Eds.), *Proceedings of the 9th International Academic Conference Strategica* (pp. 1079–1089). National University of Political Studies and Public Administration.

Paiuc, D. (2021c). The impact of cultural intelligence on multinational leadership: A semantic review. *Management Dynamics in the Knowledge Economy*, 9(1), 81–93. https://www.ceeol.com/search/article-detail?id=943521

Pandey, J., Gupta, M., Behl, A., Pereira, V., Budhwar, P., Varma, A., Hassan, Y., & Kukreja, P. (2021). Technology-enabled knowledge management for community healthcare workers: The effects of knowledge sharing and knowledge hiding. *Journal of Business Research*, *135*, 787–799. https://doi.org/10.1016/j.j busres.2021.07.001

Pereira, V., & Mohiya, M. (2021). Share or hide? Investigating positive and negative employee intentions and organizational support in the context of knowledge sharing and hiding. *Journal of Business Research*, *129*, 368–381. https://doi.org/ 10.1016/j.jbusres.2021.03.011

Peters, L. H., Greer, C. R., & Youngblood, S. A. (1997). *The Blackwell encyclopedia dictionary of human resource management*. Blackwell Publishers.

Peterson, B. (2018). *Cultural intelligence: A guide to working with people from other cultures*. Independently Published.

Plato (2021). *Theaetetus*. Prabhat Prakashan.

Powers, J. (2023). *The 4 types of organizational culture and their benefits*. BuiltIn. https://builtin.com/company-culture/types-of-organizational-culture

Presbitero, A. (2020). Foreign language skill, anxiety, cultural intelligence and individual task performance in global virtual teams: A cognitive perspective. *Journal of International Management*, *26*(2), 100729. https://doi.org/10.1016/ j.intman.2019.100729

Pretorius, C., Chambers, D., & Coyle, D. (2019). Young people's online help-seeking and mental health difficulties: A Systematic narrative review. *Journal of Medical Internet Research*, *21*(11), e13873. https://doi.org/10.2196/13873

Puzzo, G., Sbaa, M. Y., Zappalà, S., & Pietrantoni, L. (2023). The impact of cultural intelligence on burnout among practitioners working with migrants: An examination of age, gender, training, and language proficiency. *Current Psychology*, 1–15. https://doi.org/10.1007/s12144-023-04641-x

Qi, L., Liu, B., Wei, X., & Hu, Y. (2019). Impact of inclusive leadership on employee innovative behavior: Perceived organizational support as a mediator. *PLoS One*, *14*(2), e0212091. https://doi.org/10.1371/journal.pone.0212091

Qu, Q., Fu, P. P., Kang, F., & Zhao, K. (2017). The development and validation of the cultural leadership scale. *Academy of Management Proceedings*, *2017*(1), 15028. https://doi.org/10.5465/ambpp.2017.15028abstract

Rahman, A. (2019). Leadership for multicultural teams: The challenges in managing cross-cultural conflicts. *Journal of Economics, Business and Management*, *7*(1), 41–44. https://doi.org/10.18178/joebm.2019.7.1.578

Ramalu, S. S., & Subramaniam, C. (2019). Cultural intelligence and work engagement of expatriate academics: The role of psychological needs satisfaction. *International Journal of Cross Cultural Management*, *19*(1), 7–26. https://doi.org/10.1177/ 1470595819827992

Randel, A. E., Galvin, B. M., Shore, L. M., Ehrhart, K. H., Chung, B. G., Dean, M. A., & Kedharnath, U. (2018). Inclusive leadership: Realizing positive outcomes through belongingness and being valued for uniqueness. *Human Resource Management Review, 28*(2), 190–203. https://doi.org/10.1016/j.hrmr.2017.07.002

Rankin, J. (2014, December 22). Kingfisher sells B&Q China stake as DIY fails to take off. *The Guardian*. https://www.theguardian.com/business/2014/dec/22/kingfisher-china-diy-bq

Ratasuk, A., & Charoensukmongkol, P. (2020). Does cultural intelligence promote cross-cultural teams' knowledge sharing and innovation in the restaurant business? *Asia-Pacific Journal of Business Administration, 12*(2), 183–203. https://doi.org/10.1108/apjba-05-2019-0109

Raza, I., & Awang, Z. (2020). Knowledge sharing in multicultural organizations: Evidence from Pakistan. *Higher Education, Skills and Work-based Learning, 10*(3), 497–517. https://doi.org/10.1108/heswbl-09-2019-0114

Richter, N. F., Martin, J., Hansen, S. V., Taras, V., & Alon, I. (2021). Motivational configurations of cultural intelligence, social integration, and performance in global virtual teams. *Journal of Business Research, 129*, 351–367. https://doi.org/10.1016/j.jbusres.2021.03.012

Rickley, M., & Stackhouse, M. (2022). Global leadership effectiveness: A multilevel review and exploration of the construct domain. *Advances in Global Leadership, 14*, 87–123. https://doi.org/10.1108/s1535-120320220000014004

Rigby, D., & Bilodeau, B. (2011, May 11). *Management tools & trends 2011*. Bain & Company. https://www.bain.com/insights/management-tools-trends-2011/

Roberson, Q., & Perry, J. L. (2022). Inclusive leadership in thought and action: A thematic analysis. *Group & Organization Management, 47*(4), 755–778. https://doi.org/10.1177/10596011211013161

Rudd, M. E., & Fowler, J. W. (1989). *Robert Katz: A biographical sketch* (pp. 79). Robert Katz Publications. https://doi.org/10.1016/1359-0189(89)90038-1

Rüth, R., & Netzer, T. (2020). The key elements of cultural intelligence as a driver for digital leadership success. *Leadership, Education, Personality: An Interdisciplinary Journal, 2*(1), 7–26. https://doi.org/10.1365/s42681-019-00005-x

Sandelowski, M. (1995). Qualitative analysis: What it is and how to begin. *Research in Nursing & Health, 18*(4), 371–375. https://doi.org/10.1002/nur.4770180411

Schein, E. (1997). *Empowerment, Coercive Persuasion and Organisational Learning: Do They Connect?* Henley Management College.

Schneider, F., Giger, M., Harari, N., Moser, S., Oberlack, C., Providoli, I., Schmid, L., Tribaldos, T., & Zimmermann, A. (2019). Transdisciplinary co-production of knowledge and sustainability transformations: Three generic mechanisms of impact generation. *Environmental Science & Policy, 102*, 26–35. https://doi.org/10.1016/j.envsci.2019.08.017

Seidu, S., Opoku Mensah, A., Issau, K., & Amoah-Mensah, A. (2021). Does organisational culture determine performance differentials in the hospitality industry? Evidence from the hotel industry. *Journal of Hospitality and Tourism Insights, 5*(3), 535–552. https://doi.org/10.1108/jhti-11-2020-0208

Sharma, R. R. (2019). Cultural intelligence and institutional success: The mediating role of relationship quality. *Journal of International Management, 25*(3), 100665. https://doi.org/10.1016/j.intman.2019.01.002

Shearer, C. B. (2020). Multiple intelligences in gifted and talented education: Lessons learned from neuroscience after 35 years. *Roeper Review, 42*(1), 49–63. https://doi.org/10.1080/02783193.2019.1690079

Shliakhovchuk, E. (2019). After cultural literacy: New models of intercultural competency for life and work in a VUCA world. *Educational Review, 73*(2), 1–22. https://doi.org/10.1080/00131911.2019.1566211

Shmueli, G., Ray, S., Velasquez Estrada, J. M., & Chatla, S. B. (2016). The elephant in the room: Predictive performance of PLS models. *Journal of Business Research, 69*(10), 4552–4564. https://doi.org/10.1016/j.jbusres.2016.03.049

Shmueli, G., Sarstedt, M., Hair, J. F., Cheah, J.-H., Ting, H., Vaithilingam, S., & Ringle, C. M. (2019). Predictive model assessment in PLS-SEM: Guidelines for using PLSpredict. *European Journal of Marketing, 53*(11), 2322–2347. https://doi.org/10.1108/ejm-02-2019-0189

Sima, V., Gheorghe, I. G., Subić, J., & Nancu, D. (2020). Influences of the industry 4.0 revolution on the human capital development and consumer behavior: A systematic review. *Sustainability, 12*(10), 4035. https://doi.org/10.3390/su12104035

Smith, S. M., & Ruiz, J. (2020). Challenges and barriers in virtual teams: A literature review. *SN Applied Sciences, 2*(6), 1–33. https://doi.org/10.1007/s42452-020-2801-5

Stahl, G. K., & Maznevski, M. L. (2021). Unraveling the effects of cultural diversity in teams: A retrospective of research on multicultural work groups and an agenda for future research. *Journal of International Business Studies, 52*(1), 4–22. https://doi.org/10.1057/s41267-020-00389-9

STATISTA. (2021). *Number of employees worldwide from 1991 to 2022 (in billions)*. https://www.statista.com/statistics/1258612/global-employment-figures/

Sternberg, R. J., & Detterman, D. K. (1986). *What is intelligence?: Contemporary viewpoints on its nature and definition*. Ablex Publishing Corporation.

Stoermer, S., Davies, S., & Froese, F. J. (2021). The influence of expatriate cultural intelligence on organizational embeddedness and knowledge sharing: The moderating effects of host country context. *Journal of International Business Studies, 52*(3). https://doi.org/10.1057/s41267-020-00349-3

Sudargini, Y., Raharjo, T. J., Wardani, S., & Sulhadi. (2023). The role of technology to enhance servant leadership in the organisation. *Russian Law Journal, 11*(3). https://doi.org/10.52783/rlj.v11i3.1114

Sun, X., He, Z., & Qian, Y. (2023). Getting organizational adaptability in the context of digital transformation. *Chinese Management Studies*. https://doi.org/10.1108/cms-06-2022-0222

Tama, K. M. (2019). Organizational culture mapping analysis through organizational culture assessment (OCA). *Masyarakat, Kebudayaan Dan Politik, 32*(2), 186. https://doi.org/10.20473/mkp.v32i22019.186-195

Tang, R. (2023). Harnessing insights with NVivo. In J. M. Okoko, S. Tunison, & K. D. Walker (Eds.), *Varieties of qualitative research methods* (pp. 209–215). Springer Texts in Education. https://doi.org/10.1007/978-3-031-04394-9_34

Taras, V. (2020). Conceptualising and measuring cultural intelligence: Important unanswered questions. *European Journal of International Management, 14*(2), 273. https://doi.org/10.1504/ejim.2020.105566

Thomas, D. C., Elron, E., Stahl, G., Ekelund, B. Z., Ravlin, E. C., Cerdin, J.-L., Poelmans, S., Brislin, R., Pekerti, A., Aycan, Z., Maznevski, M., Au, K., & Lazarova, M. B. (2008). Cultural intelligence: Domain and assessment. *International Journal of Cross Cultural Management, 8*(2), 123–143. https://doi.org/10.1177/1470595808091787

Thomas, D. C., & Inkson, K. (2004). *Cultural intelligence: People skills for global business*. Berrett-Koehler.

Thomas, D., & Inkson, K. (2017). *Cultural intelligence: Surviving and thriving in the global village*. Berrett-Koehler Publishers.

Thygesen, J. H., Tomlinson, C., Hollings, S., Mizani, M. A., Handy, A., Akbari, A., Banerjee, A., Cooper, J., Lai, A. G., Li, K., Mateen, B. A., Sattar, N., Sofat, R., Torralbo, A., Wu, H., Wood, A., Sterne, J. A. C., Pagel, C., Whiteley, W. N., & Sudlow, C. (2022). COVID-19 trajectories among 57 million adults in England: A cohort study using electronic health records. *The Lancet Digital Health*, *4*(7), e542–e557. https://doi.org/10.1016/S2589-7500(22)00091-7

Tsoukas, H., & Cummings, S. (1997). Marginalization and recovery: The emergence of Aristotelian themes in organization studies. *Organization Studies*, *18*(4), 655–683. https://doi.org/10.1177/017084069701800405

Vassallo, B. (2021). The role of the school leader in the inclusion of migrant families and students. *Educational Management Administration & Leadership*. https://doi.org/10.1177/17411432211038010

Vinaja, R. (2003). Major challenges in multi-cultural virtual teams. *Proceedings the Conference of the American Institute for Decision Sciences*, *956*, 341–346. https://citeseerx.ist.psu.edu/viewdoc/summary?doi=10.1.1.467.4219

Vlajčić, D., Caputo, A., Marzi, G., & Dabić, M. (2019). Expatriates managers' cultural intelligence as promoter of knowledge transfer in multinational companies. *Journal of Business Research*, *94*, 367–377. https://doi.org/10.1016/j.jbusres.2018.01.033

Walonick, D. S. (2010). *Statistics calculator*. Readkong; StatPac Inc. https://www.readkong.com/page/statistics-calculator-1567936

Whiting, K. (2020). *World economic forum: These are the top 10 job skills of tomorrow – And how long it takes to learn them*. https://www.weforum.org/agenda/2020/10/top-10-work-skills-of-tomorrow-how-long-it-takes-to-learn-them/

Wong, K. K. K. (2013). Partial least squares structural equation modeling (PLS-SEM) techniques using SmartPLS. *Marketing Bulletin*, *24*(1), 1–32. http://marketing-bulletin.massey.ac.nz/

Yang, W. (2021). Designing a CLIL-based cultural training course to enhance learners' cultural quotient (CQ) by introducing internationalisation at home (IaH). *Taiwan Journal of TESOL*, *18*(1), 99–131. https://eric.ed.gov/?id=EJ1288699

Yitmen, I. (2013). Organizational cultural intelligence: A competitive capability for strategic alliances in the international construction industry. *Project Management Journal*, *44*(4), 5–25. https://doi.org/10.1002/pmj.21356

Yuan, L., Kim, H. J., & Min, H. (2023). How cultural intelligence facilitates employee voice in the hospitality industry. *Sustainability*, *15*(11), 8851. https://doi.org/10.3390/su15118851

Zaman, U., Aktan, M., Gohar Qureshi, M., Bayrakdaroglu, F., & Nawaz, S. (2021). Every storm will pass: Examining expat's host country-destination image, cultural intelligence and renewed destination loyalty in COVID-19 tourism. *Cogent Business & Management*, *8*(1), 1–18. https://doi.org/10.1080/23311975.2021.1969631

Zamawe, F. C. (2015). The implication of using NVivo software in qualitative data analysis: Evidence-based reflections. *Malawi Medical Journal: The Journal of Medical Association of Malawi, 27*(1), 13–15. https://doi.org/10.4314/mmj.v27i1.4

Zhang, H., Gupta, S., Sun, W., & Zou, Y. (2020). How social-media-enabled co-creation between customers and the firm drives business value? The perspective of organizational learning and social capital. *Information & Management, 57*(3), 103200. https://doi.org/10.1016/j.im.2019.103200

Zhong, Y., Zhu, J. C., & Zhang, M. M. (2021). Expatriate management of emerging market multinational enterprises: A multiple case study approach. *Journal of Risk and Financial Management, 14*(6), 252. https://doi.org/10.3390/jrfm14060252

Zhou, T., Lu, Y., & Wang, B. (2010). Integrating TTF and UTAUT to explain mobile banking user adoption. *Computers in Human Behavior, 26*(4), 760–767. https://doi.org/10.1016/j.chb.2010.01.013

Zhou, L., Park, J., Kammeyer-Mueller, J. D., Shah, P. P., & Campbell, E. M. (2022). Rookies connected: Interpersonal relationships among newcomers, newcomer adjustment processes, and socialization outcomes. *Journal of Applied Psychology, 107*. https://doi.org/10.1037/apl0000894

Zhu, X., Law, K. S., Sun, C. T., & Yang, D. (2019). Thriving of employees with disabilities: The roles of job self-efficacy, inclusion, and team-learning climate. *Human Resource Management, 58*(1), 21–34. https://doi.org/10.1002/hrm.21920

ZIPPIA. (2022, January 29). *Manager demographics and statistics [2021]: Number of managers in the US.* www.zippia.com. https://www.zippia.com/manager-jobs/demographics/

Printed in the USA
CPSIA information can be obtained
at www.ICGtesting.com
JSHW011457130624
64754JS00004B/64

9 781835 494332